BETWEEN REALISM AND REVOLT

Governing Cities in the Crisis of
Neoliberal Globalism

Jonathan S. Davies

BRISTOL
UNIVERSITY
PRESS

First published in Great Britain in 2021 by

Bristol University Press
University of Bristol
1-9 Old Park Hill
Bristol
BS2 8BB
UK
t: +44 (0)117 954 5940
e: bup-info@bristol.ac.uk

Details of international sales and distribution partners are available at bristoluniversitypress.co.uk

British Library Cataloguing in Publication Data
A catalogue record for this book is available from the British Library

ISBN 978-1-5292-1091-0 hardcover
ISBN 978-1-5292-1092-7 paperback
ISBN 978-1-5292-1094-1 ePub
ISBN 978-1-5292-1093-4 ePdf

Cover design: blu inc, Bristol
Front cover image: Markus Spiske/unsplash
Bristol University Press uses environmentally responsible print partners.
Printed in Great Britain by CMP, Poole

In solidarity with Black Lives Matter
and with love to Natalia

Contents

List of Tables

Contributing Investigators

This volume was developed from an ESRC funded study *Collaborative Governance Under Austerity: An Eight-case Comparative Study* (ES/L012898/1). The author draws on case studies led by co-investigators, citing their published works and unpublished project reports:

Dr Ismael Blanco, Autonomous University of Barcelona
Dr Ioannis Chorianopoulos, University of the Aegean
Dr Niamh Gaynor, Dublin City University
Professor Brendan Gleeson, University of Melbourne
Professor Steven Griggs, De Montfort University
Professor David Howarth, University of Essex
Professor Pierre Hamel, University of Montréal
Professor Roger Keil, York University Toronto
Dr Madeleine Pill, University of Sheffield
Professor Helen Sullivan, Australian National University

Acknowledgements

To lead a major research project was my main ambition, when I joined De Montfort University in 2011. It is thanks to the enabling environment at DMU that I was able to do so. Particular thanks go to colleagues in the *Centre for Urban Research on Austerity*, especially Adrian Bua, Mercè Cortina Oriol, Ed Thompson, Jenni Cauvain, Steven Griggs and Valeria Guarneros Meza for their support over many years. I am also very grateful for support from Leicester Castle Business School and the University's Research Services Directorate. I single out Jan Holland, Suzanne Walker and April Perrie for their immense efforts in getting the administrative side of the project up and running.

Above and beyond colleagues on the project team mentioned in the Preface, I owe a debt of gratitude to many others who encouraged and supported the research. They include David Wilson (formerly of DMU), Crispian Fuller, Mike Geddes, David Imbroscio, Vivien Lowndes and Janet Newman. I am very grateful to Igor Vojnovic, Editor in Chief of the *Journal of Urban Affairs* for giving us the whole of issue 42(1), and to Nik Theodore for writing a fantastic introductory essay (Theodore, 2020). I was honoured to serve on the Governing Board of the Urban Affairs Association as the project developed. The Association, colleagues on the Governing Board and Executive Director, Professor Margaret Wilder, furnished me with a very welcoming, stimulating and collegiate intellectual home. I am extremely grateful for enthusiastic support and patience from publishing and marketing staff at Bristol University Press, especially Caroline Astley and Stephen Wenham, and to anonymous reviewers who wrote invaluable comments on the initial proposal and draft manuscript. Above all, I thank the hundreds of respondents who gave valuable time and invaluable insights to the research. Without them, there would have been no project, and no book.

Preface

This book explores urban governance in the 'age of austerity', focusing on the period between the global economic crisis of 2008–9 and the beginning of the COVID-19 pandemic. It was originally born of a question about how modes of governing have been transforming in the post-war period, particularly the proposition that where hierarchies once ruled, networks now predominate. With this question in the background, the book considers urban governance from the perspective of governability. How did cities navigate the crisis and the aftermath of austerity, with what political ordering and disordering dynamics at the forefront? To attempt an answer, it engages with two influential currents, urban regime theory and Gramscian state theory, with a view to understanding how governance enabled austerity, deflected or intensified localised expressions of crisis, and generated more-or-less resonant political alternatives.

The book follows the critical tradition in exploring mechanisms that produce inequality and weighing struggles for equality. The goal was to locate reasoned, if cautious, grounds for hope, or even optimism, while looking unpalatable realities squarely in the face. This approach is at odds with the managerialist crusade to monetise research through services rendered to 'stakeholders'. It also questions the voluntarist ethos in anarchist and post-Marxist theory, expressed in the proposition that 'we can always just begin by doing things differently' (Biesta, 2008: 176). The reader will judge whether this latest attempt to maintain structure and action in a constructive tension works, or not.

The research was generously funded by the UK Economic and Social Research Council under the title *Collaborative Governance under Austerity: An Eight-case Comparative Study* (ES/L012898/1). An earlier phase of research involving two of the cities discussed in this volume, Barcelona and Leicester, was funded by the Spanish government's Ministry of Economy and Competitiveness under its National Development Plan (Ref: CSO2012-32817) as part of a larger study of austerity governance in Spain and the UK: *Transformations of Urban*

Governance in the Context of the Crisis (TRANSGOB).[1] The research discussed here was inspired by TRANSGOB and the outstanding leadership of its Principal Investigator, Dr Ismael Blanco (Autonomous University of Barcelona).

Research for the ESRC project was conducted over three years by a fantastic team working on eight case studies in the cities of Athens, Baltimore, Barcelona, Greater Dandenong (Melbourne), Dublin, Leicester, Montréal and Nantes. The lead investigators (named as contributors), and research assistants who played a prominent role in the local case studies are due immense thanks: Ioannis Chorianopoulos and Naya Tselepi (Athens), Madeleine Pill (Baltimore), Ismael Blanco, Yuni Salazar and Iolande Bianchi (Barcelona), Helen Sullivan, Brendan Gleeson and Hayley Henderson (Greater Dandenong), Niamh Gaynor (Dublin), Adrian Bua, Mercè Cortina Oriol and Ed Thompson (Leicester), Pierre Hamel, Roger Keil and Grégoire Autin (Montréal) and Steven Griggs, David Howarth and Andrés Feandeiro (Nantes). Our project consultant, Paul O'Brien of the UK Association for Public Service Excellence also played a central role, creating vital channels for communicating the research in the public realm. It was a privilege to work with these colleagues and to be able to draw from their research in the current volume. The author, Principal Investigator on the ESRC project, is entirely responsible for the analytical framework employed and transversal conclusions here drawn, for the secondary analysis of published and unpublished research documents, and for errors of fact and interpretation. A team reading of the project and its practical implications for building alternative urban futures will be published in a collectively authored companion volume (Davies et al, forthcoming).

Until the gravity of the COVID-19 pandemic became clear, I imagined the book to be an up-to-date account of urban politics in the eight cities, and of the emancipatory potentialities in urban struggles. I found the early weeks of the crisis disorienting and the immediate temptation, when it became clear what a game-changer COVID-19 could be, was to try and adapt the text. But the folly of a retrofit quickly became obvious. It would only muddy and obscure the story the book was supposed to be telling about governance and resistance in the age of austerity, while saying little of value about the implications of the virus for urban futures. For this reason, I decided to let the text speak to the period in which it was researched and written, with a few references to the pandemic where they seem prudent and a short Afterword considering early implications for governability and transformation. If the crisis is truly epoch-breaking, and makes the book obsolete, *c'est la vie*. The story of urban austerity governance 2008–20 is, in any case, an important record of the historical and political period preceding the pandemic, the conditions into which it erupted, and for considering the urban worlds that could plausibly emerge from it.

Introduction

In April 2009 soon-to-be British Prime Minister, David Cameron, announced that 'the age of irresponsibility' was 'giving way to the age of austerity'.[2] In his final budget as UK Labour Chancellor in 2010, Alistair Darling warned that repairing the damage to public finances done by the global economic crisis (GEC) would require 'deeper and tougher' cuts than even the Thatcher years (cited in Elliott, 2010). With these soundbites, austerity became the official bipartisan doctrine of the British political establishment, embraced by forces from the centre-left to the Tory right. The national austerity consensus was not seriously challenged in mainstream British politics until the election of democratic socialist, Jeremy Corbyn, to the leadership of the UK Labour Party in 2015. As it was in Britain, so it was across Europe and North America. 'Age of austerity' doctrines became ingrained in the politics of conservatives, liberals and social democratic pragmatists alike. More than a decade after the GEC, cities were still plagued with austerity, even as it lost traction in mainstream political discourse (Jordan, 2019).[3] Its continuing legacies included municipal retrenchment, the evisceration of public welfare, coercive state rescaling and restructuring and pervasive neoliberal groupthink with its complement in corporate handouts and competitive urban growth strategies: the latter often from the realms of fantasy (Dean, 2014).

It is well-established that austerity targeted the worst-off (Meegan et al, 2014; Hastings et al, 2017), while elements of the middle class were also sucked into economic precarity (Blanco et al, 2020; Gaynor, 2020). Cucca and Ranci (2017: 267) diagnosed three common characteristics emerging from neoliberalisation, aggravated by austerity: 'state delegation of further responsibility for local economic development as well as social integration, strong cuts in central funding and tighter constraints on local budgets'. They found that even in cities like Copenhagen and Munich, not commonly associated with austerity urbanism, any balance between social inclusion and competitiveness had tipped so far to the latter that little remained of the so-called 'European City Model'.

This book is about the governance of this seemingly ubiquitous problematic, set against the international backdrop of austerity and the increasing political and economic turbulence arguably constituting what Gramscian thinkers call an 'interregnum' in the hegemony of neoliberal globalism (Stahl, 2019). Neoliberal globalism envisages an open, competitive world market order, under an internationalised regulatory apparatus governed by entities including the IMF, OECD, WTO and the World Bank. In the hegemonic ideal of neoliberal globalism, the primary task of states, always vulnerable to the investment whim of mobile capital, is to residualise public goods through austerity, confect markets and enhance competitiveness throughout the governmental apparatus (Broomhill, 2001). In the neoliberal globalist imaginary, cities and city-regions are particularly important as competing agglomeration magnets. Successful cities equip themselves to attract investors and mobile workers from the financial, informational and 'creative' sectors (Florida, 2003) while unsuccessful ones, unable to rebuild moribund industrial economies, de-populate and go bankrupt, like Detroit (Eisinger, 2014).

Neoliberal globalism constituted a powerful orthodoxy in international political economy. It dominated largely unquestioned by European and American political and economic elites from the fall of the Berlin Wall to the beginning of the GEC, and then provided the ideological warrant for austerity construed as medicine to refit the state, reduce welfare dependency and enhance competitiveness. At times in the intervening decade, it seemed that the orthodoxy had held. As Slobodian put it (in Brandes, 2019: 642), as of early 2016 the 'reproduction of the status quo seemed all but assured'. In the tumultuous period since, it has lost much of its political grip and efficacy, albeit with considerable geographical unevenness. Efforts to restore neoliberal business-as-usual faltered. Recoveries were uneven and often paltry, and global growth stagnated. Recessionary and ecological threats abounded. Public weariness and resentment were mounting, while threats from left and far right were emerging to challenge, and in the latter case try and rescue, the political-economic orders through which austerity was mandated and proselytised. Today, the neoliberal globalist hubris that blossomed with the fall of the Berlin Wall is over (Marquand, 2004). The normalisation of austerity as a governing strategy is over too, and officially declared to be over by leaders of the very parties that were once its greatest enthusiasts. Even before COVID-19, neoliberal globalism confronted a raft of unintended consequences, contradictions and rebellions, whose politics were incubated, enacted and dramatised in cities across the world. The research discussed in this volume was conducted as this portentous historical moment began to crystalise. Gramsci famously wrote (1971: 275–6; Q3, §34),[4]

> If the ruling class has lost its consensus, i.e. is no longer 'leading' but only 'dominant', exercising coercive force alone, this means precisely that the great masses have become detached from their traditional ideologies, and no longer believe what they used to believe previously... The crisis consists precisely in the fact that the old is dying and the new cannot be born; in this interregnum, a great variety of morbid symptoms appear.

Gramsci here alludes to periods of weakening and contested hegemony, stagnant and declining accumulation regimes, fragmenting social orders and sharpening polarisations that can foreshadow sharp, conjuncturally decisive crises of authority, legitimacy and governability. He argued that in periods like this, new political forces take to the stage and begin to contest and re-politicise that which was previously taken for granted or taboo. Outcomes, however, depend on political struggle. Thinking back to the post–First World War period he went on to ask '[w]ill the interregnum, the crisis whose historically normal solution is blocked... necessarily be resolved in favour of a restoration of the old' (1971: 276; Q3, §34)? Stahl (2019: 336) further defines the interregnum as a 'period of uncertainty, confusion, and disagreement among the dominant elite, in which former ideologies, although they still have institutional power, lose traction and become disoriented'. Although there are doubtless many exceptions and qualifications, the notion of the 'interregnum', describing extended periods of turbulence, uncertainty and crisis, is a useful provocation for considering the governance of cities since the GEC. A longstanding premise of urban studies is that the city is no mere agglomeration magnet. It is also the political crucible in which urban, national and international orders are made and unmade (Lefebvre, 2003). Focusing on governance and governability, the aim is to cast light on mechanisms of normalisation, disruption and transformation through the age of austerity, and contribute to theoretical discussions on the provenance and politics of Gramsci's interregnum, as a purportedly defining, if variegated, characteristic of the period in international political economy. Chapter 1 develops this central analytical theme.

Problematising urban austerity governance

The research discussed in subsequent chapters was conducted over three years from April 2015 to July 2018, in eight cities: Athens, Baltimore, Barcelona, Greater Dandenong (Melbourne), Dublin, Leicester, Montréal and Nantes. It sought to explore how the 'age of austerity' was navigated through urban governance, in the wider context of prolonged neoliberalisation, severe economic crises and restructurings, and struggles for alternative political economies. The initial guiding focus was, what happened to 'collaborative governance' in austere conditions? Collaboration, in the generic sense of governmental and non-governmental actors cooperating in pursuit of common or congruent goals, is both as old as government itself and pervasive. Not even the most extreme authoritarian regime can entirely subsume its economy and society to the state (Davies, 2012a: 2700). However, the research was informed by the peculiar ideological significance acquired by the idea of 'partnership' during the 'global capitalist renaissance' of the 1990s and early 2000s (Marquand, 2004) and the neoliberal boom (sometimes called the 'great moderation' in the boom–bust cycle). International organisations and governments sought to construct state–market–civil society partnerships, focusing particularly on the mobilisation of corporate and voluntary and community sector actors. They privileged collaboration variously as a necessity in dealing with 'wicked problems', as a rapidly proliferating phenomenon, and as enacting a new and virtuous form of sociability in de-traditionalising, post-scarcity and knowledge-rich societies (Giddens, 1996; Davies, 2011a; Sørensen and Torfing, 2018). They also privileged locality, neighbourhood and place as promising arenas for 'new' modes of collaborative, participatory and partnership-based governing. This was because of the close proximity of governmental and non-governmental actors in towns and cities and the rehabilitation of cities and city-regions in elite policy discourses, as engines of growth and cultural vitality (Konvitz, 2016). This study took the city as its point of departure for similar reasons, *inter alia* because cities are at the front line of austerity (Peck, 2012), have long been laboratories for governance experiments (Swyngedouw, 2005) constructing socio-spatial proximities and distances between governmental and non-governmental actors

(John, 2009) and are a key locus of resistance to both austerity and neoliberalism (Dikeç and Swyngedouw, 2017).

What made collaborative governance especially attractive to governing elites in this period? Contributory factors included the easing of brute poverty in the Global North in the decades after the Second World War, the emergence of so-called 'post-scarcity' societies (Giddens, 1996), universal education, the apparent moderation in the capitalist boom-bust cycle after the tumult of the 1970s and 1980s and the quelling of organised working-class struggles in stricken industrial heartlands. Another crucial trend was the 'rise and rise' of 'civil society' in liberal-democratic governing ideologies (Edwards, 2009: 11), as the 'working class' lost political and discursive traction (re-emerging in bastardised form when the toxic prefix 'white' became fashionable). These conditions were thought to have unleashed potential for new modes of sociability, complementing much-heralded urban agglomeration dynamos, in which networked relations based on trust could flourish (Davies, 2012a: 2690). Thompson (2003: 40) described the ethos of 'network governance', as being dependent on 'co-existent attributes such as sympathy, customary reciprocity, moral norms, common experience, trust, duty, obligation and similar virtues'. For networks to thrive, 'a generalized trust, honesty, and solidarity must transcend any minor negotiating infringements' and 'a shared common overriding objective' must exist. The presumption that we were entering an epoch of network governance rested on these 'ethical virtues' flourishing in prosperous societies with growing levels of connectivity (Thompson, 2003: 47).

Whereas 'collaboration' in its Fordist or corporatist guise saw worker representatives bargaining with employers over pay, hours and conditions, hailing 'civil society' as a 'partner' gave it a very different valence. The 'new' state–civil society partnership was to be a constructive enterprise, mobilising resources around (at once banal and fantastical) place-based governing objectives articulating what Davies (2010) called the 'contributory principle'. Nor was it confined to the Global North. Although conditions favouring this purportedly new mode of governance never existed in much of the urban world, international organisations and experts nevertheless promoted them through more-or-less coercive policy transfers: from structural adjustment programmes to government grants and assistance from non-governmental organisations (NGOs) (Cooke and Kothari, 2001; Davies and Msengana-Ndlela, 2015). At a meeting in June 2015 to develop parameters for this study, Professor David Howarth (Essex) coined the term 'collaborative moment' to capture the zeitgeist of that period.

Critics quickly tempered the epochal sense of excitement about the transformative potential in networked governance, even as the neoliberal boom continued (Davies, 2002; Marinetto, 2003). Sørensen and Torfing (2018), themselves leading proponents, observed three prominent criticisms: that collaborative governance was a marginal phenomenon within the state apparatus, that even if significant it was nothing new, and that it had 'dangerous implications' for democracy and inclusivity. At the same time, suggestions that the neoliberal boom heralded a 'post-crisis' phase in the development of capitalism, in which old cleavages would dissolve, and trust-based modes of sociability could flourish, were greeted with the warning that nasty surprises lay in store (Callinicos, 2001: 55). The first surprise materialised with the GEC itself, which Giddens wrongly claimed had been 'foreseen by very few if anyone' (2010: 36). In fact, pre-GEC literatures were replete with warnings about mounting contradictions in the neoliberal growth model (for example, Harman, 2007). Žižek (2009: 9) aptly described establishment denials that the GEC was foreseen or foreseeable as a 'sustained effort of wilful ignorance'.

The most intense periods in the GEC occurred in 2008–9 with the international wave of recessions, and again in 2011–13 with the sovereign debt crisis and retrenchment in the Eurozone, and peaks in the international resistance to neoliberal austerity marked respectively by the occupied squares movements and the 'Arab Spring' uprisings against dictatorships in the Middle East and Northern Africa. However, a degree of neoliberal normality was gradually if unevenly restored, even as many countries afflicted by the crisis struggled to recover peak output and trend growth rates (see Chapter 2) and the Arab Spring was defeated by force and attrition. In this period, national and international institutions combined to manage the fallout and re-allocate the costs to working class citizens. Forces seeking to construe the GEC as a crisis of capitalism, financialised capitalism or of neoliberalism did gain traction in public debate (Mason, 2012), but were soon overwhelmed by neoliberal orthodoxy reasserted in the governmental sphere and mainstream media. The faux Keynesianism of the immediate post-crisis period (Evans and McBride, 2017: 3–4) was supplanted by an aggressive neoliberal austerity doctrine, embraced with greater or lesser enthusiasm by mainstream social democrats, liberals and conservatives and which the international wave of rebellions could not overcome (Theodore, 2020). In hindsight, the window of relative normalisation after the 2011 crises and revolts appears to have signalled a brief, tenuous and geographically uneven restoration of neoliberal globalism between phases of tumult. Crouch (2011) labelled this restorationist phase 'the strange non-death of neoliberalism'.

Critical thinkers, however, were sceptical that neoliberal globalism could fully recover its hegemonic position, arguing that the GEC had showed it to be 'dominant but dead', dubbing it 'zombie neoliberalism' (Peck, 2010) or 'zombie capitalism' (Harman, 2009). In the next phase of its crisis, coinciding with the three-year period of this study, neoliberal globalism was de-stabilised by more portentous and dangerous forces. In 2016, neoliberal globalists received a second round of surprises with the UK Brexit referendum and the election of Donald Trump to the US presidency. With the election of Jair Bolsonaro to the presidency of Brazil in 2018, and the coup against Evo Morales in Bolivia in 2019, these were the most dramatic exemplars of a much more extensive international backlash: the rise of conservative nationalist or neo-reactionary forces across a broad spectrum, many tending towards neo-fascism (Brown, 2018). So-called 'populist' and self-anointed 'alt-right' currents pose a serious threat to global peace (such as it was), and to (post-) democracy in its already shrivelled, neoliberalised form (Crouch, 2004). Whether they threaten neoliberalism itself is another matter, for while nativism contradicts the pseudo-cosmopolitan ethos of neoliberal globalism, fascism and other expressions of right-wing authoritarianism have long served as mechanisms of capitalist restoration. Conservative nationalist, or neo-reactionary currents have pursued a variety of measures associated with neoliberalism including tax cuts, corporate subsidies and crony contracts (Peck and Theodore, 2019), while also distancing themselves from the idea of austerity. With the outbreak of COVID-19, austerity has been formally abandoned in the discourse of international organisations, as well as in nation state ideologies and pandemic fiscal policies (Standring and Davies, 2020). The research discussed in subsequent chapters was conceived before the neo-reactionary offensive really gained momentum, and this is not its subject. However, the book does highlight conditions in which such currents have been able to foment.

At the same time, a heterodox array of egalitarian anti-austerity forces re-emerged across Europe and the USA, including 'new municipalist' currents (Russell, 2019; Thompson, 2020). These currents have been strongly influenced by network-theoretical ideas linked to Anarchist, Altermondialiste and libertarian socialist traditions, in which solidarity is anchored by affinity and counter-hegemony is rejected as a strategy

(Day, 2005). Writing in the heady days of 2011, Mason (2012: 84) captured the zeitgeist in his celebration of networked resistance:

> It can achieve those elements of instant community, solidarity, shared space and control that were at the heart of social revolutions in the early industrial age. It can be… a space to form the bonds that would take them through an insurrection… a means absolutely imbued with the nature of ends.

Chapters 5–8 explore the politics of new municipalism and other counter-currents in greater depth, assessing achievements, limitations and potentialities for transforming urban governance.

The study was originally framed as an inquiry into what happened to the 'collaborative moment' after the GEC. Did claims for the transformative potential in collaborative governance stand up, or were they confined – in relative terms – to 'good times' associated with the motherhood and apple pie messaging of the neoliberal boom (Davies and Blanco, 2017: 1532)? Early on, however, it became clear that the question 'What happened to collaborative governance under austerity?' had quite different valences in the eight cities, and so too the extent to which the ideas of the 'collaborative moment' resonated. Nor did the term 'austerity' translate as well across the eight cities as anticipated; either in terms of a state-led effort driving retrenchment and restructuring, or the localised construal of governing dynamics.

These circumstances called for a broader comparative framing, where the 'age of austerity' takes in overlapping but differentiated processes of neoliberalisation, structural crisis and crisis construals, and austerity itself is a concept referencing markedly diverse governing practices. They also called for the reframing of 'collaborative governance'. The book develops a variation on the theme of Stone's (2015) concept of the 'urban political order', through which he revised earlier thinking about urban regimes (Stone, 1989) to take account of the influence of civil society actors in the governing arena. Here, 'urban political (dis)order' denotes the more-or-less durable multi-scalar alliances and conflicts among state, market and civil society actors working in, with or against neoliberalism and austerity. In foregrounding both ordering and disordering dynamics, the concept echoes the Gramscian idea that as an effective governing ensemble, the local state is constituted through alliances of governmental and non-governmental actors whose hegemony is rarely comprehensive, require effort and resources for everyday reproduction, and are generally subject to some degree of political contestation and internal contradictions (Jessop, 1997). The purpose is to problematise governability in a way that discloses mechanisms stabilising and undermining austere neoliberalism, or facilitating resistance and transformation, making them visible as social relations within an encompassing analytical framework. This framework is elaborated in Chapter 1 and applied throughout subsequent chapters. Chapter 8 reflects on what the research reveals about governability in the crisis of neoliberal globalism and the potential for emancipatory politics incubating in the urban sphere. The Afterword reflects briefly on the implications of COVID-19, which erupted just as the first draft of the manuscript was completed.

Eight cities as case studies

The project followed Savitch and Kantor (2002: 15) in studying cities with a degree of similarity, but also variation (also Storper and Scott, 2016). Some similarities and variations were anticipated and designed into the research, while others were disclosed in the study itself or emerged in real-time to disturb prior assumptions. The research derives from a tri-continental sample of one Australian, five European and two North American cities, of different sizes, traditions, populations and positions in urban hierarchies. It was conducted in Athens, Baltimore, Barcelona, Dublin, Greater Dandenong (Melbourne), Leicester, Montréal and Nantes. Chapter 2 provides a brief overview of each city. The selection was intended to capture a spectrum of cities occupying different geo-economic positions, but facing a range of related, if non-identical, socio-economic challenges in the post-crisis period.

All the cities are located in countries which went through Fordist or 'peripheral Fordist' development phases based schematically on (semi)organised capitalism (Lipietz, 1982) and states providing at least some collective consumption goods; what Jessop (1999) called the Keynesian national welfare regimes established across Western Europe, North America, Australia and New Zealand in the post-Second World War period. All have confronted crises and dislocations since the 1970s and pursued a variety of trajectories towards neoliberalisation (see Chapters 4 and 5). For the duration of this study, between 2015 and 2018, the cities were all led by municipal governments gravitating from the nebulous centre towards the left of the political spectrum. Given the international bi-partisan austerity consensus, this alignment was helpful in cataloguing responses and adaptations from the so-called 'progressive' wing.

When site selection was made, austerity was very much an existing or looming problematic for all the cities. However, the combination of urban particularities and changing political circumstances meant that by the time fieldwork commenced, this was not entirely the case. Barcelona had elected an anti-austerity municipal leadership in May 2015, altering its political priorities if not its fiscal situation within the Spanish austerity state, while the city of Nantes saw itself as somewhat insulated from pressures affecting many other French cities and described its response to the increasing squeeze from central government as 'Keynesian' (Griggs and Howarth, 2016). Meanwhile, the threat of an ideologically driven austerity programme in Australia under the brief Premiership of Tony Abbott, had receded by 2015 (see Chapter 2).

According to Mufti (2005), the possibility of having to transform objects of analysis exists in any comparative exercise. With this in mind, and instead of swapping case studies to enhance similarity, the project team decided to work with widening asymmetries between the eight cities. It adopted a de-centred case study approach in place of the anticipated heuristic comparison, and re-problematised the core terms of the project, 'collaborative governance' and 'austerity'. This re-reading of the research, through the framework of governability and urban political (dis)orderings is the author's approach to bringing eight de-centred case studies into comparative dialogue.

Issues in comparative urban studies

Traditional comparative urban research has been subjected to searching critique for its tendency to shrink the urban universe to a small sub-set of cases revolving around Northern 'global' cities and the concepts generated from these studies (for example, MacFarlane, 2010; Robinson, 2011; 2016). Robinson (2016) encourages urbanists to think cities 'through elsewhere', bringing new places and questions into the ambit of urban research. Studying austerity governance through the lens of cities moving away from Fordism pre-supposes that which never existed in much of world: an organised economy and evolved local state apparatus, with its corollary in a relatively mature civil society. Nevertheless, the differential impact of the 2008 crisis on the governance of cities emerging from Keynesian national welfare regimes. Fordist and peripheral Fordist traditions, remains an important endeavour in understanding urban change and merits a defined research programme. This was the premise of the study and it reflects the geographical and analytical positionings of the author.

As a comparative study, this work is anchored in familiar framings of city, city-region and metropolis. So-called 'methodological cityism' (Angelo and Wachsmuth, 2015), the tendency to view urbanity in terms of clearly demarcated settlements defined by administrative and cartographic boundaries, has also been subjected to powerful criticism. In developing the concept of planetary urbanism, Brenner and Schmid (2015) re-read Lefebvre's claim that the world is becoming completely urbanised. In the 21st century, concentrated urbanisation continues, but alongside increasingly extended, elasticated, networked and differentiated forms which tend to erode the distinction between urbanity and its outside (Brenner, 2018). Planetary urbanism has, in turn, been criticised from several standpoints. Post-structuralist thinkers see it as reproducing universalising, masculinist and heteronormative perspectives (Derickson, 2018). Scholars concerned with analytical precision argue that if 'urban' is unmoored from agglomeration, density, centrality, nodality and propinquity, it has no inside, no outside and becomes effectively meaningless (Storper and Scott, 2016). The present work does not directly engage in these debates. Like any analytical lens, the city-regional focus has limitations, but also strengths. It is also reflexive on methodological cityism. All the case studies read urban governance in the context of wider geographies – inside, outside, above and below – and with regard to jurisdictional and territorial complexities associated with governance and resistance.

Robinson (2016) identifies two modalities of comparative analysis. The 'genetic' mode traces interconnected roots of repeated, related but distinctive urban processes: how specific processes or features recur and diverge in different, but inter-linked cities. The comparisons in this study are 'genetic' in that they explore the governance of different cities in and against landscapes of austerity urbanism (itself bounded). In broader terms, the research addresses the question of governance and governability in relation to a problematic articulated in all the cities: rising public need and demand, juxtaposed with diminishing or flat-lining resources (Cucca and Ranci, 2017; Henderson et al, 2020). Robinson observed that in Clarke's (1995) comparative taxonomy of institutional logics arising from urban restructuring and de-industrialisation, we see the postulation of a process affecting many places within the US, in different ways. Similarly, this volume analyses situated case studies through which it discerns ways of governing in and beyond the neoliberalisation–crisis–austerity conjuncture. Chapter 8 draws the threads together in discussing patterns and distinctions.

Robinson's 'generative' mode shifts from interconnected processes to analytical proximity and conceptual insight. Concluding reflections on governability, hegemony and (dis)ordering seek to be generative in this sense.

As explained earlier, tasks of 'complexity reduction' and 'enforced selection' led the project team to construe cities and city-regions as an apt focus for the research (Sum and Jessop, 2014: 151). The locus of comparison within this framing was the governing strategies which cities adopt, and the range of actors involved in producing, executing and resisting them, through more-or-less durable vertical and horizontal coalitions. These strategies and coalitions are exemplified in each city through empirical accounts of policy arenas, programmes, institutions, discourses and practices (Chapters 4 and 5). The objective is to develop an account of the major political-economic currents involved in defining and addressing (or potentially refuting) the austerity problematic in each city. All the case studies are about 'governability' in this strategic sense. The task is to identify prominent themes in the constitution of urban political (dis)orders and develop insights into the characteristics of the period defined by Gramscian thinkers as an 'interregnum' in the hegemony of neoliberal globalism (Chapter 8).

Data and analysis

The following chapters draw on a variety of project resources. Eight case study-based papers, together with an introductory essay by Theodore (2020), were published in issue 42(1) of the *Journal of Urban Affairs* (2020).[5] The team developed a common repository of 26 unpublished (confidential) working papers written in English, constituting a shared data resource. These papers are cited throughout and full details will be found in the References section at the end of the book. The Principal Investigator (current author) coded these sources into a transversal NVivo project, from which the current volume draws. Fieldwork was conducted between autumn 2015 and spring 2018. Each research team applied a common instrument, adapted for locality, snowballing the sample to determine the foci of inquiry. The composition of the dataset varied a little between cities. Teams undertook up to 40 semi-structured interviews, alongside 3–5 observations and focus groups. Respondents included elected politicians, public officials, business leaders, voluntary and community organisations, faith groups, services users, anti-austerity activists and trade unionists. Common themes in the research instrument formed the basis for coding, on NVivo, into major nodes relating to urban governing strategies and resistance in each city. Others were added by investigators to capture localised themes (as described by Henderson et al, 2020: 128).

Over the period of the study, four meetings of the international project team were held in Leicester (June 2015), Dublin (April 2016), Barcelona (January 2017) and Athens (January 2018) to work on emerging research questions, provisional findings and comparative insights. Face-to-face meetings were supplemented with regular online discussions. Local teams organised stakeholder dissemination workshops to inform respondents, validate and extend findings. Original transcripts in English, French, Greek and Spanish are deposited with the UK Data Service (https://ukdataservice.ac.uk) and can be consulted, subject to the consent of local investigators. A stakeholder report, in four languages, can be downloaded from the *Centre for Urban Research on Austerity* website.[6]

Further methodological considerations

One of the difficulties in studying cities in eight countries was obtaining comparable economic data. As a project focused on governance, and unable to measure local economic indicators directly, quantifying retrenchment in one city, let alone attributing it to austerity (of whatever kind) or comparing it with other cities, was fraught with difficulty. Changing patterns in municipal spend, adjusted for inflation provide a rough proxy (Chapter 2) but taken alone, this indicator could be very misleading. For example, baseline statistics suggested that over roughly the same time frame, the municipal budget of Athens was cut by less than that in Leicester, when adjusted for inflation. Yet this could not plausibly be construed as 'less austerity' for Athens, once the impact of the economic crisis itself, the catastrophic collapse of the Greek economy, and the multiplication of human crises is considered. Nor does the proxy take account of population change and its impact on revenues and demands.

At the same time, the multitude of agencies and spatial/scalar/sectoral complexities involved with determining funding and spending patterns makes it impossible to obtain a complete picture of austerity at urban, metropolitan and municipal scales without dedicated, granular research. The question of jurisdiction (Skelcher, 2005), which authority/agency funds and runs which services, was an important factor in all the cities, particularly the three tier systems of Australia, Canada, Spain and the USA where competing political parties, each with different responsibilities and sometimes different priorities, often occupy the tiers making inter-scalar political relations difficult (see Chapter 3). It was further complicated by the territorial organisation of functions at the municipal, metropolitan and city-regional levels.

Over and above these complexities, austerity data is also politically contentious. For example, the Irish government closed the national Combat Poverty Agency (CPA) shortly before the GEC, a move perceived to have been politically motivated. According to one respondent, it 'was to take out this particular body, to disperse it, and to disperse its staff. To make sure the kind of work that it had been doing – it had been documenting poverty, and issue-based poverty – didn't happen anymore' (Gaynor, 2020: 79). Closure left the city bereft of data on the impact of austerity in Dublin's neighbourhoods. This move was not a one-off. Government funded state–civil society partnerships were instructed not to hire researchers, and community development projects warned not to employ social policy officers. As Gaynor (2020: 79) observed, the squeeze on budget and remit, limiting activities to service provision alone, eliminated research capabilities in many civil society organisations. Consequently, Dublin lacked socio-economic data on trends in poverty and inequality arising from austerity. The inability of city councillors and officials to detail the extent of cuts or provide documentation, when asked, was also noteworthy. Dublin reinforced the message, also heard in Athens (Chorianopoulos, 2016), that the collection and control of data is political and that eviscerating public knowledge is a potent weapon in the armouries of austere neoliberal and other right-wing regimes.

Structure

Chapter 1 explains the analytical framework through which urban political (dis)orderings are read in subsequent chapters. It begins by engaging ongoing debates about vantage-point: whether it is better, from an anti-austerity perspective, to focus on diagnosing the workings of power through critical political economy, the disruptive potentialities in everyday and organised resistance or to hold the two positions in constructive tension. Second, it develops a framework for Gramscian regime analysis, through which it aims to avoid unhelpful (dominance vs resistance) dualisms (Las Heras, 2019). Third, it navigates overlaps and distinctions between concepts often used inter-changeably, but which diverge empirically: crisis, neoliberalism and austerity. The discussion is framed by Gramscian approaches to the periodisation of capitalist development, highlighted in urban studies by Peck's two-part conjunctural analysis of late entrepreneurialism (2017a,b) and the positing of an interregnum in the hegemony of neoliberal globalism (Stahl, 2019). The research problem arising from this framing is how diverse experiences of crisis–neoliberalism–austerity interact and contribute to shaping urban political (dis)orders. The remaining chapters employ the analytical lens to discuss research undertaken in Athens, Baltimore, Barcelona, Greater Dandenong, Dublin, Leicester, Montréal and Nantes.

Chapter 2 introduces the eight cities and sets out data to provide a very rough indication of how each has been affected (or not) by the GEC and subsequent fiscal squeeze. It proceeds to dis-aggregate and re-capitulate local configurations of neoliberalism–crisis–austerity. The main finding is that urban histories and traditions mediate the variable economic impact of the GEC, in sometimes unexpected ways. Second, variants of economic rationalism dominate governance thinking, even in Barcelona, the beacon of anti-austerity struggles. Third, however, while crises occur in cities as part of the tempo of capitalist boom–slump cycles, they are also weaponised to justify, oppose, or downplay austerity. Diverging construals are significant determinants of urban governance, although (neoliberal) logics of scarcity and growth remain prevalent. Fourth, it is important to consider temporalities of neoliberalisation as well as its forms and hybridisations: fast, slow and static, forwards, sideways and also reverse. Finally, the chapter suggests caution in diagnosing an emerging late neoliberal or late entrepreneurial conjuncture (Peck, 2017a), a question revisited in Chapter 8.

Chapters 3, 4 and 5 explore different facets of urban regime politics – the political coalitions and alliances that accrete and deplete governing capacity in each city. Chapter 3 focuses on state rescaling and territorialisation from the perspective of how fiscal and jurisdictional reforms since the GEC affected local political autonomy. One of the most important dimensions of regime politics is the relationship between tiers of the state and the jurisdictions of public authorities. Accordingly, the chapter considers structural changes in local government finance, fiscal disempowerment mechanisms, changes in functional and spatial jurisdiction, including developments in and barriers to city-regionalism. It concludes that whether or not directly implicated in austerity, municipalities have been subjected to further upward and downward constraints on effective political autonomy, either narrowing the scope of legal and legitimate political action or exposing cities to market forces and lending urgency to the search for alternative sources of revenue through place-marketing and business partnerships.

Chapters 4 and 5 explore lateral relations between state, market and civil society actors and the regime configurations through which the eight cities are (un)governed, together with evidence of change since the GEC. Chapter 4 explores Athens, Baltimore, Dublin and Leicester, where harshly austere and authoritarian modes of neoliberal governance were entrenched. Chapter 5 focuses on the cities that diverged from this pattern. It first discusses Montréal and Nantes, cities where regime capacities appear weak or diminishing, and then turns to Greater Dandenong and Barcelona. The latter cities were in a period of regime construction, respectively at a distance from, and against, austere neoliberalism. These chapters follow a similar structure, explaining local state strategies and tactics, restructuring in civil society, patterns in collaborative governance including coalition–building and maintenance, and regime continuity and change.

Chapters 6 and 7 explore resistance to austerity and its impact on urban regime politics. The chapters consider how resistance is effective, or not, limiting and containing the activities of multi-scalar neoliberal austerity regimes, blurring or hybridising agendas or leading towards more thoroughgoing transformations within the local state in its inclusive sense. Chapter 6 is concerned with how resistance politicises spheres of civil society, its generative capacity in producing durable forms of organisation, and rolling resistance forward beyond inaugurating events. It explores the resources for contentious politics and other progressive forms of activism within civil society itself, where this depletes the co-optive power of the governing regime but without necessarily altering its trajectory. Where Chapter 6 focuses on how resistance multiplies contradictions and forges new solidarities, Chapter 7 returns to the ever-present problem of containment, de-mobilisation and defeat. This endeavour casts light on a number of issues: the means by which urban regimes manage resistance, and insulate themselves from it, the chilling effects of social partnership traditions on anti-austerity struggles, and the limits of regime transition at the city scale disclosed by the study of Barcelona.

Chapter 8 considers insights and lessons drawn from conjunctural comparative analysis. It identifies five more-or-less prominent and widespread characteristics, which recombine to explain each city's position in and against the conjuncture of austere neoliberalism. These are the prevalence of economic rationalism(s) (Chapter 2), weakening hegemony (Chapters 4 and 5), the retreat to dominance (Chapters 3–5), weak counter-hegemony and radically contagious politicisations (Chapters 6 and 7). Here, discussion returns to the question of what happened to the 'collaborative moment' as a moving spirit of governance in the pre-austerity period and reflects on Gramsci's notion of an 'interregnum' in the hegemony of neoliberal globalism, further mooted in urban concepts like 'late neoliberalism' (Enright and Rossi, 2018) and 'late entrepreneurialism' (Peck, 2017b). It suggests four plausible trajectories from the standpoint of Peck's conjecture, including the possibility that entrepreneurialism might function, if not flourish, in conditions of weak hegemony. The chapter concludes with reflections on governability and its limits in the continuing crisis of neoliberal globalism, now in arguably its most intense phase with the eruption of COVID-19. The Afterword offers brief considerations on the implications of COVID-19 for the analysis developed in Chapters 1–8.

1

Studying Urban Political (Dis)Orders

Introduction

Chapter 1 develops the framework through which urban political (dis)orders are explored in subsequent chapters. It begins by engaging debates about critical vantage-point: diagnosing the workings of capitalist power through critical political economy, privileging disruptive potentialities in acts of resistance, or considering power-resistance relationally. It advances a Gramscian approach to urban regime analysis, through which it pivots between perspectives, and explores the encounter between power and resistance in struggles over the normalisation, disruption and transformation of austere neoliberalism (Las Heras, 2019). The discussion is further framed by neo-Gramscian conjunctural analysis (Hall et al, 1978), which derives from Marxist thinking about the history and periodisation of capitalist development and phases of struggle. Conjunctural analysis was brought to renewed prominence in the urban field by Peck's two-part essay positing an incipient phase of late entrepreneurialism (2017a, 2017b), which is allied to the broader thesis of an interregnum in the hegemony of neoliberal globalism (Stahl, 2019). The problem arising from this framing is how the dynamics of crisis, neoliberalisation, austerity and resistance play out in cities and constitute urban political (dis)orders, and what these in turn reveal about conjunctural continuity and change. The remaining chapters employ this perspective to explore empirical research in the eight cities.

Studying urban political (dis)orders: between pessimism of the intellect and optimism of the will?

The concept of urban political (dis)orders is positioned as a contribution to recent debates about the most fruitful way to approach critique and transformation. Means and ends blur, but two broad perspectives can be discerned, each drawing on a multiplicity of theoretical traditions. Those influenced by Marxism and modern socialist theory focus on the critique of capitalist political economy and see the quest to replace it in terms of project-based systemic struggles, which occur through revolutionary or reformist means (for example, Luxemburg, 1900; Miliband, 1961; Callinicos, 2006). Anarchist, autonomist, open Marxist and libertarian socialist currents, are more concerned with negating power, interstitial struggles for autonomy and pre-figurative practices unbound from, uncontained by and overflowing capitalism and the state. Though divided on theoretical questions about dialectics, periodisation and structure and action (see Söderberg and Netzén, 2010 for a review), these traditions see counter-hegemony as impractical and debilitating, as totalising and undesirable or as obsolete (for example, Day, 2005; Dinerstein, 2015; Hardt and Negri, 2004; Holloway, 2005; Olin-Wright, 2019).

At stake in these debates are very different understandings of reality, and principles of organising, which means that they are prone to taking a polarised form. The Anarchist thinker Richard Day (2005), for example, announced Gramsci to be 'dead'. Gramsci is manifestly not dead as an influence on contemporary political struggles and debates (Purcell, 2012), but if Day's provocation is understood as a judgement on prevailing anti-capitalist practices in the 21st century it resonates much more strongly. Day argued that the Deleuzian–Guattarian commitment to 'becoming minor', through political acts that affirm difference and seek to dissipate all power and domination is fundamentally at odds with the 'majoritarian' (in fact, universalising) Gramscian–Marxist objective of transcending capitalism through revolutionary counter-hegemony (Day, 2012). In anarchist thought, the expression of affinity constitutes both means and ends. Gramscian currents, even post-Marxist derivations, seek to harness solidarity-in-struggle to build alternative hegemonic discourses and apparatuses (Thomas, 2009).

'Minor Marxist' currents begin with Deleuze and Guattari (Holland, 2011), but seek to overcome what they see as binary perspectives on autonomy and structure (Dinerstein, 2015). For example, Bailey et al (2017) begin by acknowledging the analytical power of diagnostic research in critical political economy but call for a change of perspective taking issue with what they see as domination-focused accounts. For Bailey et al, Minor Marxism positions itself against a pessimistic, 'capitalism always wins' mode of theorising and 'macro-analyses that depict forebodingly powerful structures of inequality and domination' (Bailey et al, 2017: 2). Gibson-Graham (2006) memorably dubbed this the epistemology of 'capitalocentrism'. For them, 'capitalism' becomes an intellectual and political yoke of our own making. Minor Marxism contends, similarly, that critical political economy accounts of the post-GEC period have fallen into what Brown (1999) earlier termed 'left melancholy'. They blame epistemological error, and while distancing themselves from voluntarism, pivot the quest for knowledge towards 'disruptive agency' (Bailey et al, 2017), or 'the art of organising hope' (Dinerstein, 2015). Dinerstein discloses four elements of autonomy from capitalism: negating, creating, contradicting and exceeding, through which she seeks to overcome structure–action binaries. All four elements, she argues, are played in the 'key of hope', a concept she draws from Ernst Bloch, where hope is a wilful act of subversion that conjures utopias. Hope motivates and is made concrete through the praxis of the four autonomies (Dinerstein, 2015: 61–80).

The critique of 'major Marxism' is that while its systemic analyses of capital accumulation might be broadly correct, it induces 'left melancholy'. The counter-hegemonic gaze, preoccupied with large-scale transcendent and ruptural struggles is, if not totalising, then debilitating if only because history shows that they occur so infrequently. Counter-hegemony tends to overlook the vitality of political agency and resistance in the fissures and cracks of everyday life (Holloway, 2005), making neoliberal domination appear ubiquitous and seamless. The purpose of disruption-focused critical political economy, and minor Marxism in general, is to make visible myriad practices of and potentialities for radical change that purportedly cannot be seen from the vantage point of counter-hegemony. Cleaver (1979) (cited in Las Heras, 2019: 228) captured the rationale for this shift:

> If one's attention is focused uniquely on the enemy's activities on the battlefield, the battle will assuredly be lost. In the class war, as in conventional military encounters, one must begin with the close study of one's own forces, that is, the structure of working-class power. Without an understanding of one's own power, the ebb and flow of the battle lines can appear as an endless process driven only by the enemy's unilateral self-activity.

The case for strategic pessimism

Should the 'key of hope', important as it surely is, negate other keys? In Gramsci's famous formulation, the revolutionary needs to maintain a constructive relationship between pessimism and optimism: 'the challenge of modernity is to live without illusions and without becoming disillusioned'. He continued, 'I'm a pessimist because of intelligence, but an optimist because of will' (1994: 300). Intelligence and will might be much more closely related in human cognition than this binary suggests, while as Yanis Varoufakis recently commented, 'hope' does not require 'optimism' (cited in Eaton, 2020). Beyond this conceptual muddle, however, Gramsci's point was that it is necessary to undertake a hard-headed assessment of forces, including the strengths of the enemy, while seeing in the key of 'hope' that courage, determination and political imagination do confer political agency. Minor Marxist, anarchist, autonomist and libertarian socialist currents shun pessimism in the Gramscian sense. In doing so, they arguably overlook ways in which strategic pessimism, as distinct from emotional pessimism, is also a source of agency.

The existence of left melancholy is scarcely deniable, and some wear it as a badge of honour. 'Bleak is the new red' announced Salvage, an online magazine of Marxist intellectuals attempting to retrieve a 'desolate left' from the ashes.[1] 'Optimism is cowardice' declared Olusoga (2019), targeting the asinine and mendacious cheeriness of Brexit fundamentalists on the British right. Elaborating the case for pessimism in an essay provocatively titled *For A Left with No Future*, Clark (2012: 57) argued that socialists should reject utopianism and transpose politics not into 'the key of hope', but rather 'a tragic key'; a 'tragic sense of the life possible for the left'. The left should begin with the 'bitter moment' of its defeat and embrace present-centred politics, while 'mocking its own presage' (2012: 73), in which caricature the next big crisis always looms, and the revival of a revolutionary proletariat is just around the corner. In diagnosing the epochal defeat of the proletariat, the tragic key shares one common premise with Anarchist voluntarism, expressed in Day's assertion (2005: 126) that 'the masses of the First World have chosen quiescence, and nothing we can do will change their behavior for the better'. The purview of hope is thereby strictly limited to micropolitical experimentation and occasional eruptions in public space (Carroll, 2006: 31–2).

In another defence of 'uncompromising pessimism', Burawoy (2011: 75) took critics to task for erasing the distinction between research and politics. The former, he insisted, must speak unpalatable truths to inform the latter:

> sociology is of little use if it cannot give some guidance to labor as to the tendencies of capitalism, a theorization that pays attention to history and geography, it is of little use to labor if it fixes the data so that labor appears stronger than it is, or if it ignores the data and declares an imminent upsurge on the grounds that we can never know when the next upsurge will arrive. It is the responsibility of professional and public sociologists alike to combat arguments and claims that have neither concrete nor theoretical foundation.

Burawoy concluded, invoking the spirit of Gramsci, that 'in times of defeat and retreat as intellectuals we should be all the more ready to rethink our assumptions, redirect our studies, and entertain alternative theoretical frameworks'. Cogitating on defeat might be distasteful, but it is necessary medicine.

Anchoring these perspectives is a purposeful and strategic 'pessimism of the intellect'; bound up, in other words, with the recognition that people can and do 'make history', a reality that defines and gives concrete grounds to both 'hope' and 'optimism', rendering them politically meaningful. There is a qualitative distinction, then, between active, strategic pessimism and lachrymose despondency. The latter abnegates not only 'hope' but also the very premise of critique: that disclosing injustice is what makes justice intelligible as a concept, and conceivable as a goal (Fraser, 2012). As Roitman (2013) observed in her critique of the concept, inhering in Marxist theories of crisis (and all critical theory) is precisely a wager on contingency. From a Gramscian point of view, strategic pessimism authors not passivity or despair, but rather a more acute understanding of the ever-shifting grounds on which political agency is constituted. The retort to Cleaver in the spirit of strategic pessimism might therefore be that 'unless one also knows the strengths and weaknesses of the enemy, we cannot know our own'. Minor Marxist scholarship recognises that it means little to consider autonomy without also considering its enmeshment in structure. However, it arguably misconstrues the strategic and agentic locus of 'major' Marxist pessimism. Partly for this reason, it also neglects how changes in capital accumulation – of kind, tempo and the very possibility of realising surplus value – impinge on the conditions of possibility for autonomy, and the variable configurations of Dinerstein's autonomies that emerge over time and always in a relationship with constraints.

The duality of 'power' and 'resistance'

The contention here is that the study of hegemony makes little sense, either methodologically or politically, without the study of disruptive agency. Conversely, the study of disruptive agency makes little sense without understanding its positioning in and against hegemony. Instead of privileging either 'domination' or 'disruption', Gramscian perspectives provoke a productive tension between power-centric and resistance-centric accounts, positioning research at the point of encounter and pivoting between them. The encounter is readily observed in the urban environment, where urbanity constitutes a 'mediating' sphere between struggles in everyday life to negate the power of capital, and putative counter-hegemonic apparatuses (Kipfer et al, 2012: 117). The Gramscian proposition is that transcending austere neoliberalism and developing new political economies rooted in democracy, common ownership, equality and solidarity requires repeated shifts between and syntheses of these perspectives. Las Heras (2019) saw, for example, that labour occupies a contradictory position. Workers simultaneously challenge and legitimise the social order, something that can only be seen by looking both ways. Gramsci's methodology of the subaltern demonstrates that worker struggles pull in contradictory directions (as Enright and Rossi's (2018) concept of 'ambivalence' also recognises). Gramsci 'theorised both working class and state formation as a process of *shaping* and *being shaped* by the space in which social classes and the capitalist state exert their ideological and coercive powers' (Las Heras, 2019: 235, original emphases). The methodology of the subaltern requires the researcher to grasp hegemony, domination, subalternity and resistance as relations, which play out in different configurations over time and produce more or less defined and durable socio-spatial (dis)orders.

The conceptual framing of 'urban political (dis)orders' establishes a range of overlapping dualities through which to consider the problem of governability relationally and temporally: governance and resistance, realism and revolt, revolution and restoration, stability and flux, as well as normalised and exceptional and recuperative and disruptive politics. Concrete configurations might be situated near one polarity, in conflictual and ambivalent positions, and move between them (Enright and Rossi, 2018). As Newman (2014a: 139) put it, anti-austerity activism is 'both implicated in, and stands in opposition to, transformative governing projects'. The starting point in exploring collaborative governance under austerity was the proliferation of institutionalised participatory governance mechanisms during the neoliberal boom and how they evolved or retreated in the age of austerity (Davies and Blanco, 2017). Yet, making sense of these processes also required attention to state power and resistance. From this perspective, it is difficult to understand disruptive agency without considering who or what is, or is not, disrupted through which actions, the efforts those vulnerable to disruption undertake to prevent it, the efficacy of different modes of disruption through history, and the lessons that can be drawn from prior experiences of disrupting more or less successfully. Conversely, research into capitalist domination must recognise in practice, as well as theory, that there are always cracks and fissures in a contradictory hegemonic apparatus, including small-scale disruptive actions that sometimes alter the subjectivities and practices of the actors involved in significant and durable ways (Bailey et al, 2017).

Ultimately, the point is to learn from the balance of continuity and change arising from any act of domination or resistance. As Dikeç and Swyngedouw (2017) ask, what happens after the 'rupturing event' of an urban uprising, in which an ostensibly novel political subjectivity is inaugurated? Very often, the newly inaugurated politics is quickly 'exaugurated' whether through defeat, repression, recuperation or simply de-mobilisation. Intensity dissipates, lessons are forgotten, the movement vacates or is compelled to vacate the squares, or it ossifies (Deaton, 2015; Hearne et al, 2020). The political challenge, say Dikeç and Swyngedouw, is 'to move from outbursts of indignation to the slower process of sustained transformative strategies through which a new socio-political spatialization becomes imagined, practiced and universalized' (2017: 14).

The never-ending mystery is how, through what kind of apparatuses, practices, institutions and ensembles? Taking up this theme, Deaton (2015) argued that to endure, urban revolutions must colonise secondary spaces to provide leadership, physical protection and resources for activists – an apparatus. His research on uprisings in Tehran, Prague and Paris, found secondary spaces in theatres, mosques, churches, factories, shops and civic organisations. For good or ill, many of the great international mobilisations against neoliberal austerity answered the question of how to move from insurgency to transformation, by looking once again (albeit with trepidation) to the local state. This occurred most notably with the anti-austerity platforms in Spain, making the leap from street to City Hall in 2015. The institutional turn foregrounds the question of what organisational resources are required, if episodes of disruption are to transform a 'consolidated order' (Dikeç and Swyngedouw, 2017: 13).

Sources of socialist agency

Davis (2018: 18) identifies three sources of socialist agency in Marx: 'organizational capacity, structural power, and hegemonic politics', through which transformational capacities are assembled and executed. For Thomas (2009: 226), the ensemble constitutes an alternative hegemonic apparatus. A hegemonic apparatus 'is the wide-ranging series of articulated institutions (understood in the broadest sense) and practices—from newspapers to educational organisations to political parties—by means of which a class and its allies engage their opponents in a struggle for political power', throughout state, economy and civil society. In an extraordinary diatribe, the distinguished Open Marxist Werner Bonefeld (2016: 29) made the untenable claim that 'hegemony is not a critical concept'. He asserted that it ignores the capital relation and that it 'smacks of capitulation to the capitalist economic interests'. Moreover, he asserted, counter-hegemony 'posits the people as righteous, demands government in the interest of the nation, requires the investment of money into productive activity to secure the employment and welfare of the dispossessed' (2016: 30). In short, Gramsci's entire conceptual framework is conflated, without any textual engagement (Thomas, 2020), with meagre social-democratic programmes for colonising the state and managing capitalism (also Day, 2005). The far more serious reconstruction of Gramsci's thought by Peter Thomas (2009, 2020) contends that anti-hegemony scholars falsely conflate the concept of hegemony with state sovereignty, because they read not through Gramsci, but through 'conjuncturally overdetermined interpretations' by others (2020: 15).

Thomas argues that in Gramsci, the potential for subalterns to assume political power depends, in equal measure, on 'the elaboration of an alternative hegemonic project and its concretisation in a hegemonic apparatus adequate to it' (Thomas, 2009: 227). Far from merely forming a government, and seeking to retrofit the state counter-hegemony entails the rejection of 'sovereignty' and the construction of democratic institutions throughout all spheres of society. In the Bolshevik period, the hegemonic apparatus consisted in a revolutionary party, a bespoke repressive apparatus, the communist press, unions and worker, peasant and soldier councils constituting – initially – an alternative source of political authority to both the old Tsarist regime and the Duma. The Third International was founded to cultivate international solidarity and (in its pre-Stalinist phase) globalise the revolution. This apparatus was sufficient for the initial revolutionary period in which it arose in Russia, but insufficient to internationalise the revolution. The importance of Thomas's reading is that it posits the alternative hegemonic apparatus as something that arises independently of the bourgeois integral state, purposefully articulating the goals, desires, practices and organising mechanisms that evolve through a cycle of contention (Barker et al, 2013: 2).

The Battle of Seattle in 1999 is often seen as a watershed in the re-constitution of the radical left in the West after the collapse of Stalinism, the crises of Fordism and setbacks for organised labour. Themes that converged in Seattle – anti-capitalism, feminism, environmentalism and anti-racism – drew inspiration from earlier waves of struggle in the Global South and united around the slogan purportedly coined by Subcommandante Marcos, 'another world is possible' (George, 2004: 250). These themes have continued to influence struggles for the past 20 years, including anti-austerity movements and new municipalisms in which anarchist and libertarian socialist traditions ally uneasily with institutionalist and state-friendly variants of democratic socialism (Taylor, 2013; Barcelona en Comú, 2019). Any counter-hegemonic apparatus emerging from 21st-century cycles of contention will undoubtedly be imbued with contemporary experiences of building democracy, solidarity and equality through overlapping feminist, anti-racist, ecological and class struggles. It is likely to have a very different complexion than the apparatuses of October 1917, while building on innovations from the early 20th century, such as workers' councils, and having to find ways of disarming the capitalist states system.

At its most radical, new municipalist thinking begins to grapple, somewhat indirectly, with the question of alternative apparatuses – if not their potentially hegemonic character. Bookchin (2019: 16), for example, suggests that 'municipal assemblies' could comprise countervailing powers to the nation state. Alt-governance institutions, such as worker councils, and worker-occupied factories, have come and gone throughout the 20th and 21st centuries, usually as social crises and waves of struggle peak and recede. The experiences of Solidarnosc, and the occupied factory movements in Latin America are but two examples (Atzeni and Ghigliani, 2007). Chapter 8 reflects on the potential for alternative hegemonic apparatuses to emerge from anti-austerity struggles. The central point is that Gramscian theory problematises the question of what kinds of apparatuses are necessary and sufficient to overcome capitalism and seeks to evaluate and influence the efficacy of the struggles from which they emerge.

Despite many appropriations of Gramsci, the notion that the concept of hegemony necessarily induces passivity, excessive abstraction or involves subsumption into the capitalist state apparatus, is ill conceived. In practical terms, the struggles discussed in subsequent chapters are considered at a granular level to establish what powers and liabilities accrue to which actors and institutions (Ward, 2010), through what ordering and disordering mechanisms. This framing brings the tools of urban regime analysis to the fore.

Gramscian regime analysis

The following paragraphs borrow from Davies and Blanco (2017), Davies (2017a) and Davies et al (2020) in developing a framework to explore how urban political (dis)orders assemble around particular (austerity) governance strategies and the powers and liabilities they amass. Urban regime theory is about the dynamics of building and maintaining governing coalitions among governmental and non-governmental actors. In developing regime theory, Stone (1989) argued against structural Marxism that the spheres of state, economy and civil society are contingently and loosely coupled (following Tilly, 1984). At the urban scale, profit-seeking corporations control production, development and real estate, while in representative democracies citizens exercise electoral oversight. The prevalent coupling of state and corporate spheres materialises in US cities because neither can accomplish its goals without the resources of the other: local government needs the confidence of investors to raise revenues while business requires support from city hall to extract higher rents and profits. The capture of economic and municipal power, respectively by business and city leaders, creates a structuring environment in which resource interdependent actors attempt to constitute governing agendas and coalitions capable of delivering them. Regime theory therefore downplays 'power over' for a social production model, 'power to', where pragmatic actors build alliances to 'get things done' (Davies et al, 2020). Durable alliances of governmental and non-governmental actors capable of setting and executing governing agendas for a city are what Stone called 'urban regimes'.

Nevertheless, regime theory sees the local state and profit sectors as better able to pre-empt the governing agenda than other actors. Stone's (1980) theory of systemic power, distinguishes public democratic and private business power constituted at the national and international scales, and enacted in cities through regime politics. Urban regimes are founded on the dilemmas this context imposes on city leaders: the need for business to secure political support for development, and for political leaders to obtain investment from the private sector, while satisfying an electorate. These structuring factors create an urban environment where business and city leaders are more likely to find congruent interests and construct governing alliances around them than others, although the discussion of Baltimore in Chapter 4 shows that universities, hospitals and non-profits can be powerful regime actors too (Pill, 2020). On the other hand, lower class opportunity regimes are rare because resource mobilisation and sustenance are much harder to achieve. Stone saw greater potential in policy areas like education not (historically at least) tied directly to the mobilisation of business resources, pointing the possibility of multiple, perhaps competing, circuits of regime power in a given city – an idea elaborated further by Blanco (2015a). In theory, neoliberalisation blurs or eliminates these distinctions by subordinating all domains of public life to the rules of competition and utilising them as mechanisms to instil economic rationalities among policymakers, educators (particularly managers) and students.

Regime theory has elective affinities with the neo-pluralist proposition that in market economies, elected governments are likely to indulge the preferences of business leaders, especially in economic development policy, but that coalition dynamics vary across policy domains. Within these structuring parameters, urban regimes emerge contingently from the concrete objectives and coalition building endeavours of resource-privileged urban political actors. Stone's central point was that whatever the structural parameters, and whatever the implications of increased capital mobility might be in altering the balance of power, governability arises from constructive political action to create durable alliances: regime building of any kind takes effort (Davies and Msengana-Ndlela, 2015).

Regime theory has generated much debate in the past 30 years; notably over its purported neglect of capitalist political economy on the one hand (Imbroscio, 2003) and the interpenetration of state and civil society on the other (Jessop, 1997). Marxists saw it as over-privileging the political, because it set aside the crisis-prone dynamics of capital accumulation, the impact of class struggles and financialisation, the role of education and media in ideology-production, and the tendency (with support from higher tiers of government) for corporate interests to encroach and make ever-greater demands on municipalities. In the neoliberal period, they must become ever-more competitive and responsive if they are to appeal to footloose capital and thereby sustain governing capacity. In contrast with Marxist critics, Stone himself suggested that regime theory had focused too much on the state–corporate nexus and neglected civil society as a repository of governing demands and resources. He accordingly elaborated the concept of the *urban political order* (Stone, 2009) which inspires the question of governability addressed in this volume, and reformulated the core principles of regime analysis (Stone, 2015: 103):

> The guiding tenet in inner-core regime analysis (its 'iron law') is that for any governing arrangement to sustain itself, resources must be commensurate with the agenda being pursued... A companion proposition is that for any substantial and sustained agenda, a stable coalition is needed to provide the necessary resources.

Stone here re-affirms the theoretical core of regime theory as being about the collaborative effort involved in creating and sustaining governability, but in a helpful way that opens it to dialogue with other theoretical approaches. Nevertheless, Davies and Blanco (2017) argued that regime analysis required further adaptation, refining the parameters of the iron rule. They suggested, first, that while governing depends on coalition building through persuasion, negotiation and bargaining around congruent goals (power to), it also rests on hierarchy, coercion and administrative diktat (power over). In other words, studying governability requires a more expansive and relational perspective on power than is typical of regime approaches, recognising the interpenetration of coercion and consent as well as structured and emergent inequalities (Jessop, 1997).

Second, Davies and Blanco (2017) argued that regime theory, even with the extended concept of the urban political order, tends to focus on a limited terrain of urban politics around city government, local business elites and, latterly, non-profits. They argue that austerity governance necessitates consideration of how multi-scalar politics – international, national, regional and municipal, as well as 'scaling from below' (Nielsen and Simonsen, 2003) – concatenate in the city and metropolis, and delimit its powers. They also point to the need for an enlarged conception of the 'local state' encompassing all governmental and quasi-governmental agencies situated within the city/metropolis and having the city/metropolis as their primary concern (a formulation developed by Magnusson, 1985).

Stone's latest work (2018) lends further weight to the case for bringing inter-governmental relations into the study of urban political (dis)orders. This point speaks to the two-sided question of jurisdiction addressed in Chapter 3. Local government may be situated in subordinate or competitive relationships with other governmental actors and agencies responsible for critical functions, such as welfare, infrastructure, social services, education or housing. Moreover, municipal and other local state administrative jurisdictions are often poorly aligned with the economic, demographic and infrastructural characteristics of an extended urban area, its agglomeration dynamics and metropolitan, suburban and city-regional governance mechanisms (Scott, 2019). Finally, scale and jurisdiction are central to the stakes of the struggle for and against austerity. The local state is a 'landscape of antagonism' (Newman, 2014b) constituted through provisional, partial and contested ensembles of governmental and non-governmental actors that might only rarely be fully concerted across an entire urban area, if ever.

Third, and critically for the concept of urban political (dis)orders, Davies and Blanco (2017) suggested that privileging the study of governing coalition insiders led regime theorists to overlook the disruptive effects of occasional eruptions and episodes of urban rage, but also the efficacy of resistance as a durable facet of urban political life, capable of throwing grit into the machine and altering its focus as well as constituting new autonomies. Just as neoliberalism shapes the character of urban resistance (Mayer, 2016), so resistance, like the fly in the ointment, might influence the character or deplete the capacities of austere neoliberal regimes. This brings us back to the question of disruptive agency. Everyday struggles can produce new solidarities and transform the subjectivities of activists. Davies and Blanco suggest that they can also denude neoliberal coalitions of governing capacity, or alter the nature of those capacities, and in this sense should be seen as co-constitutive of regime outcomes that open and shut down the space in which autonomies flourish. In other words, before and after the inaugural staging of an 'equalibertarian' event (Dikeç and Swyngedouw, 2017), everyday resistance, including organised labour, can deflect, divert, impede or deplete urban regimes of their capacity to govern without necessarily challenging them directly, or gaining access to decision-making processes. Disruption can also occur without disruptive intent. The attempt to impose neoliberal reforms has always encountered 'difficulties, problems and obstructions' (Bailey et al, 2017: 5), attesting to both the durability of resistance, and the faltering development of neoliberalism in some cities and parts of the world. Bringing resistance inside the regime analytical space addresses the need to consider molecular disruptions in the study of urban political (dis)orders, without according them epistemological privilege.

These adaptations are consistent with Stone's iron law, and they also point regime analysis towards a renewed dialogue with Gramscian state theory, concerned with the nexus of 'power to', 'power over' and 'counter-power'. Early Marxian critics of regime theory developed a body of scholarship on how to work with and adapt the concept (for example, Lauria, 1997). Jessop (1997), suggesting that the regime perspective on coalition building was useful, when situated in a dynamic account of international transformations linked to crises of Fordism and the fading international Keynesian national welfare regime system. To this end, he brought Gramsci's concept of the Integral State to urban studies. This strand of dialogue with regime theory quickly died out but is worth reviving in light of later theoretical developments in both fields.

The Gramscian approach begins from a very different position, rooted in Marxism and conceiving bourgeois society as an emergent-emerging provisional totality, animated by accumulation dynamics and riven by structural contradictions – what Gramsci called the 'historical bloc' (1971: 137; Q13, §10). Crisis-tendencies inscribed in the historical bloc (Gramsci, 1995: 428–435; Q10II, §33, §36, §41vii) foment instability and periods of radicalised political contingency; the power to enact transformations pursuant to communism. Accordingly, sustaining a hegemonic political order requires persistent work, continuous ideological and political effort against crosscurrents from within and without. Every social order encounters structural limits and contradictions, as well as everyday agential disruptions within the sphere of 'normal' politics.

The theory of the integral state is Gramsci's conception of the political order, within the parameters of this propulsive, contradictory historical bloc (Davies, 2011b; 2012a). It connotes the provisional unity of 'political society + civil society' (Gramsci, 1971: 262–3; Q6, §88), where political society is the ruling class in its state form, with attendant coercive, ideological, cultural and administrative machineries. Civil society is the terrain of 'so-called private organisations, like the church, trade unions, schools and so on' (Gramsci, 1971: 56 fn; Q19, §24). These organisations today include countless varieties of non-profit, NGO, transnational organisation and charitable foundation, as the research discussed in Chapter 4 particularly highlights (Chorianopoulos and Tselepi, 2020; Pill, 2020). For Gramsci, civil society is the terrain of the struggle to constitute a hegemonic apparatus. In trying to make sense of the durability of modernising capitalist states after the revolutionary period of the early 20th century, he observed that when the state 'trembled, a sturdy structure of civil society was at once revealed... a powerful system of fortresses and earthworks' (1971: 238; Q6, §138). This suggests that civil society is ultimately the grounds of state power. Without robust civil society institutions to resource political leadership and nurture consent, bourgeois regimes would depend on direct coercion. Governability is rooted in the capacity of governmental and non-governmental actors to secure hegemony through interpenetrating repertoires of coercion and consent operating throughout state, economy and civil society.

A schematically Gramscian hegemony occurs when a durable alliance of class forces wins control of economic, political, cultural, ideational and bio-political levers of power and exercises leadership across the governmental and societal realms, signifying the 'cathartic', or 'ethico-political moment' of the state (Gramsci, 1971: 208; Q10II, §15). Or, as Arrighi put it (2005: 32), hegemony refers to the 'additional power that accrues to a dominant group in virtue of its capacity to lead society in a direction that not only serves the dominant group's interests but is also perceived by subordinate groups as serving a more general interest'. The theory of hegemony explains why, as discussed later, economic crises rarely trigger immediate political crises, but also why hegemonies in this elevated sense are generally incomplete, if not fleeting in historical terms. Rather, the familial concepts of passive revolution and interregnum imply that periods of true hegemony, where the ideas of the ruling class are widely held by subalterns to represent their interests, are unusual and perhaps increasingly so as the bourgeois epoch ages (Arrighi, 2005; Stahl, 2019).

Despite foundational differences between the Stonean and Gramscian perspectives, there are helpful affinities. Like regime politics, the reproduction of hegemony requires continuous effort (Thomas, 2009: 255). Moreover, like regime theorists, Gramscians see that hegemonies are never closed, and rarely comprehensive and encompassing (Jessop, 2007: 241). Stone, relatedly, conceived the power of pre-emption (1988: 83) as the 'capacity to occupy, hold and make use of a strategic position'. He argued that powers of pre-emption can be exercised without hegemony in Gramsci's sense of ethico-political catharsis occuring in a revolutionary transformation. The concept of pre-emption lends support to the Gramscian distinction between leadership and domination, illustrating how a governing regime can subsist from a narrow social base, without mass consent, and at the same time how domination itself requires effort and resources. It is distinguished analytically from co-optive power (Guarneros-Meza et al, 2018), through which a governing bloc interpolates an extended social base to its ideas and agendas, secures legitimacy and proactive assent.

Just as hegemony is bound up with coercion and consent, regime power derives from combinations of pre-emptive and co-optive power.

In short, Gramscian and regime analyses converge at the point of studying how broader or narrower combinations of actors mobilise material and ideational resources to produce and contest more-or-less durable urban governing arrangements. They are concerned with coercive and consensual means through which governing capacity accretes – but also how it is undermined, depleted and transformed. With the third adaptation suggested by Davies and Blanco (2017), the study of Ward's (2010) 'liabilities' becomes central to regime analysis: what does disruptive agency accomplish, but also how do internal contradictions and urban struggles burden governing coalitions and contribute to the accretion of contradictions and pathologies? Are liabilities absorbed by re-allocating costs or do they accumulate and mature into more-or-less acute and extensive political crises (Hay, 1999)?

Crises, neoliberalism and austerity

Urban regime and Gramscian theories part company in the latter's understanding of the structural interpenetration of state, economic and civil society domains, and the tendencies to crisis inhering in the capitalist system. Gramscian scholarship has sought to extend Marxist theory by grasping crises as political phenomena, discerning phases and tempos of development in which periods of relative stability are interrupted, respectively, by impasse between contending forces and sharper moments of political upheaval and transformation. Such periods have resulted historically in significant changes in the organisation of capitalism, through second-order passive-revolutionary transformations that reconstitute bourgeois power, while de-mobilising or recuperating subaltern classes (Morton, 2011). Gramsci-influenced analysis of crises is concerned with the spatio-temporal dynamics of normalisation, upheaval and transformation.

Crisis, interregnum and conjuncture

The language of 'crisis' is ubiquitous, but often poorly specified (Hay, 1999). Roitman's (2013) provocative intervention *Anti-Crisis* sought to deconstruct the concept and displace it from what she called its position in modernist theory as a 'transcendental place-holder', substituting God and religious redemption with a secular philosophy of contingency. The concept of 'crisis' has been hugely influential in urban studies, perhaps even more so since the GEC (Weaver, 2017). Few would disagree that this was a 'crisis' of some kind, perhaps a plurality of multi-causal crises, but like neoliberalism and austerity, discussed later, it is a slippery concept (Bayırbağ et al, 2017).

In Marxist theory, 'crisis' refers simultaneously to the capitalist slump dynamic that invests social class with its material animus, and to the radicalisation of political contingency in periods of structural turbulence: the capacity of forces competing for hegemony decisively to shift the course of historical development. At the heart of the concept are ideas about contradiction and upheaval (May, 2017). The Greek term 'krisis' denotes a decisive and unexpected turning-point (Haus and Kuhlmann, 2013: 7). Then British Prime Minister Tony Blair invoked this meaning after 9/11, when he stated: 'This is a moment to seize. The kaleidoscope has been shaken, the pieces are in flux, soon they will settle again. Before they do let us reorder this world around us and use modern science to provide prosperity for all.'[2] A useful reminder that the meaning of crisis is always the subject of struggle (Weaver, 2017), Blair's soundbite also identified crisis as a tipping point at which decisive political interventions can change the course of history.

In accentuating the political dimensions of crisis, Gramsci sought to understand the often-extended lag between structural economic crises, and political expressions through conflicts and uprisings. He distinguished crisis in this acute and transformative sense from 'organic crisis', understood as a breakdown in hegemony and signifying a 'radical rupture in the links between representatives and the represented' (Kouvelakis, 2019: 78), characteristics pervading international political economy today. For example, Jessop (2016: 2) explained how the conjunctural events of the UK Brexit referendum articulated and further aggravated 'a long-running split in the establishment, a worsening representational crisis in the party system, a growing crisis of authority for political elites, a legitimacy crisis of the state, and a crisis of national-popular hegemony over the population'. These are characteristics of a Gramscian interregnum, conceived as an extended breakdown of hegemony, itself punctuated by disruptions and upheavals of greater or lesser significance.

Stahl (2019: 355) observed in his analysis of hegemony in the 20th century that turbulence and instability are 'natural' states within capitalism, and an interregnum between stronger hegemonies can drag on for decades, with more or less frequent and critical punctuation points. Only rarely (perhaps only once so far) does organic crisis result in a decisive systemic rupture of the kind marked by October 1917, and as the Bolshevik experience also showed, even sharp ruptures are vulnerable to reversal, recuperation and defeat. Nevertheless, in the post-GEC period, economic pathologies and political conflicts have conjoined to begin unravelling the dominant politics of the post-Thatcher, post-Soviet global capitalist renaissance (Marquand, 2004). According to Streeck (2016), the interregnum is characterised by generalised social entropy and increasingly ungovernable societies, but with no plausible alternative world order on the horizon.

If weak hegemony is unremarkable in the history of capitalism, passive revolutionary dynamics are an important part of the explanation and also (arguably) one of the main mechanisms by which capitalism reconstitutes itself. Gramsci further distinguished the rupturing revolutions in France in 1789 and Russia in 1917 from passive revolutions, where revolutionary impetus was recuperated and the transition to bourgeois society enacted through a conservative 'revolution-restoration'. For Gramsci, passive revolution became the dominant trait in capitalist state formation after the European uprisings of 1848. With bourgeois forces losing revolutionary zeal and impetus, partly in fear of the rising working class, they enacted 'revolution from above', to neutralise bottom-up revolutionary ferment. Gramsci saw passive revolutions leading to a weaker form of capitalist state, characterised by 'dictatorship without hegemony' (1971: 106; Q15, §59), and exemplified by the Italian Risorgimento through which the North subordinated the South without ever truly absorbing it into a national project.

The revolutionary period in Europe after the First World War, which achieved its zenith in the October revolution, marked a short break from the passive revolutionary phase of bourgeois development. In Gramsci's and later re-readings, passive revolution is also associated with major transitions occurring within capitalism through 'revolution from above' (for example, Morton, 2011): the concepts of Fascism, Fordism, Keynesianism and neoliberalism exemplify phases or modes of capitalist development enacted through passive revolutionary means. Hay (1999), for example, employed conjunctural analysis to explore the intense period of political crisis through which Britain reached a tipping point, moving beyond its moribund Keynesian national welfare regime into early Thatcherite neoliberalisation (also Hall et al, 1978 and Clarke, 2010). For Gramsci, imprisoned by Mussolini, fascism was the 'current or actual' form of passive revolution (Thomas, 2009: 154 fn). It rears its head again today, as neo-reactionary elements within the capitalist class look for ways to resolve growing crises of authority and revitalise faltering accumulation regimes, now cratering because of COVID-19 (Thomas, 2009: 154–5, Peck and Theodore, 2019).

A central premise of Marxist analysis is that no political–economic order can be sustained indefinitely because of the tendency towards exhaustion in capitalist accumulation regimes (Rosenberg, 2005). In what conditions an interregnum matures into a sharp crisis and whether any resulting change is 'conjunctural' in the sense of preserving an existing social form like neoliberalism, or 'fundamental' in the sense of rupture (or decline and collapse), depends on politics. What are the competing visions and apparatuses? Who can be made to bear which costs? How high a price can be extracted from subalterns across the spheres of production and reproduction, and in which parts of the world, in order to sustain austere neoliberalism in, perhaps, neo-fascist, post-fascist or some other authoritarian guise? What transformations might be possible? Through what means? The task of conjunctural analysis is to parse and intervene in the struggles that answer these questions.

Conjunctural analysis

Excavating the roots of the concept, Koivisto and Lahtinen (2012) trace the origins of 'conjuncture' to Machiavelli's revolutionary break with the mediaeval notion that fate was pre-ordained by the astronomical/ astrological conjunction of heavenly bodies. They see Machiavelli's claim that even when 'fortuna acts like an enraged river' people can 'prepare for the flood', as the first step to secularising the concept and deeming humans capable of acting upon fate. Gramsci referred to this trait as Machiavelli's 'neo-humanism' (1971: 248–9; Q5, §127; Thomas, 2009: 425-6).

Like critical theory in general, the raison d'être of conjunctural analysis is emancipation from capital and oppression. What aligns it to Marxism, argued Rosenberg, 'is the central explanatory role accorded to the organic tendencies of capitalist development'. Marxist analysis takes on a conjunctural form through the double-historicisation of organic tendencies: first disclosing their 'character at a given stage of their historical development' (diachronic analysis), and second by revealing how they operate 'in the historically given circumstances of the time' (synchronic analysis) (Rosenberg, 2005: 29–30). Minor Marxist thinkers, like Holloway (2005), are sceptical of Marxist periodisation on the grounds that it draws overly rigid distinctions between continuity and change, where change is confined to rare moments of upheaval and granular ever-present struggles are passed over or trivialised. The account of hegemony elaborated earlier is sensitive to both everyday and exceptional forms of resistance, but 'major' Marxism nevertheless rests on the argument that human development is usefully classified into dominant modes of production, extended historical periods of which (late) capitalism is the latest. Conjunctural analysis seeks to disclose political-economic rhythms of development and disruption within capitalism, and its points of crisis and punctuation.

Stuart Hall played a founding role in bringing Gramscian conjunctural thinking into political, social and cultural theory, particularly through his work on the emergence of Thatcherism and neoliberalisation in the UK (Hall et al, 1978; Hall, 1979). *Policing the Crisis*, the seminal analysis of proto-Thatcherite crisis-making, was read through the rising moral panic around mugging. Reflecting on the project 30 years later, one of its co-authors, John Clarke (2010: 342), defined a conjunctural crisis as the point 'where different temporalities – and more specifically, the tensions, antagonisms and contradictions which they carry – begin to come together'. Conjunctural crises usually have structural characteristics but are constituted and politicised through struggles over 'construal' (Jessop, 2015) and 'narration' (Hay, 1999). An 'organic crisis' with structural roots only becomes 'fully articulated' as a political crisis, when captured, construed and, in the vernacular of Bayırbağ, Davies and Münch (2017), 'owned' by a class fraction and hegemonic bloc. The politicisation of a structural crisis depends, as Lenin put it, on whether a ruling class can discover the means of continuing in its old way, and whether the working and subaltern classes can be entreated or coerced into doing so. 'There is no such thing as an absolutely hopeless situation' for the bourgeoisie, he warned.[3]

In the Marxist tradition, the objective of conjunctural analysis is to 'expand the capacity to act politically by helping to examine the conditions of a political intervention in their complexity' (Koivisto and Lahtenen, 2012: 267). Whether conjunctural crises brewing within the arc of a prolonged interregnum turn out to be decisive, and whether they are resolved through revolution from above or below, is a political question resolved through praxis. The series of conjunctural crises provoked and won by Thatcherism in the UK (moral panic, struggles with the trade unions, the collapse of the Eastern bloc) are instances of punctuations through which the interregnum of the 1970s was resolved in favour of neoliberal globalism at multiple tipping points (Jessop, 2016).

In reflections on 'urban crisis', May (2017: 2191) suggests that in the post-GEC period, the world has moved from political 'slow time' to a quickening tempo. In the wave of urban revolts since 2008, he observes an 'increase in the intensity of oscillations between continuity and discontinuity'. May's analysis suggests that as with hegemony, Gramscian conceptualisations of crisis, conjuncture, and interregnum can fruitfully be read across scale, place and territory (Davies, 2012a). Taking up this theme, Peck's conjunctural urbanism (2017a,b) diagnoses 'late entrepreneurialism' as the urbanised expression of the interregnum in neoliberal globalism.

Peck proposes that the age of the entrepreneurial city announced famously by Harvey (1989) is increasingly subject to diminishing returns, disclosed through his paradigmatic case study of Atlantic City (Peck, 2017b). Late entrepreneurialism draws attention to distinctively urban contradictions and pathologies co-constituting the larger crisis of neoliberal globalism, marked by a neoliberal hegemonic project that 'seems increasingly to have given up on its own future, as the horizons of even nominally free market action and imagination seem to be collapsing' (Peck and Theodore, 2019: 263). The study of Atlantic City reveals a concatenation of pathologies emerging, to a greater or lesser extent across the international urban landscape well before COVID-19.

The logic of late entrepreneurialism is that the more cities copy entrepreneurial blueprints to attract investors (such as the casinos of Atlantic City, or the obligatory 'smart-city', museum, cultural, sporting and tourism projects of urban revitalisation), the harder it becomes to achieve competitive gains, particularly in the context of prolonged economic stagnation marked by the failure of the world economy to recover trend growth rates after the GEC (Roberts, 2016). Competitive advantage accruing to early adaptors quickly mutated into fiscal liability as the urban landscape became saturated, returns on investment failed to materialise, demand was exhausted, speculative debt accrued without supporting revenue streams, and cities proclaiming unique characteristics were revealed to be imitative, aesthetically monotone and culturally banal, if not fiscally bankrupt. Like any other market product, an abundance of entrepreneurial cities creates an excess of supply over demand. In the post-GEC climate of growth stagnation, this tendency has been augmented. In a shrunken investment pool, the law of diminishing returns asserts itself, and losers in the entrepreneurial game multiply.

Yet, Harvey noticed many of these pathologies early in the entrepreneurial conjuncture (Merrifield, 2002: 150–1), as did others observing the 'monochrome monism' of neoliberal consumerism (Marquand, 2004: 127). The pathologies and contradictions we see today arguably appeared early in the entrepreneurial phase, posing the question of how we recognise what is 'late' and how 'late' it might be, especially in relation to concepts like 'late neoliberalism' (Enright and Rossi, 2018) and the larger and equally problematic concept of 'late capitalism' (Jameson, 1991).

Peck's conjunctural urbanism is motivated, in part, by his critique of 'flat ontologies' animating post-structuralist comparative urban studies (Robinson, 2011). It entails 'spiralling up and down through cases and contexts as a different (but arguably complementary) strategy to that of working laterally, "between" cases'. This mode of analysis is inherently comparative, place and scale-sensitive, seeking to establish 'dialogic interconnections between (situated) case studies, (pliable) midlevel concepts and (revisable) theory claims' – that is to say both genetic and generative comparisons. Most importantly, it (tacitly) re-iterates the Marxist principle that studying social phenomena requires movement between levels of abstraction and concreteness, distance and proximity. This is to recognise, for example, that the appearance of mess and disorder at the molecular level does not preclude the existence of 'real' orders and patterns at other scales, or indeed vice-versa if the appearance of molecular normality was to obscure exploding contradictions at a systemic level.

What makes urbanity a fruitful terrain for conjunctural analysis? Gramsci noted (as had Engels nearly 100 years before) that national hegemonies were 'complicated by the existence within every State of several structurally diverse territorial sectors, with diverse relations of forces at all levels' (Gramsci, 1971: 182; Q13, §17). He classified Italian urban political economies according to revolutionary potential: industrial Turin was favourably contrasted with bourgeois reformist Milan, Rome the city of parasitic bureaucrats and Florence and Naples as cities dominated by landowners and the agricultural bourgeoisie (Kipfer, 2012: 87). Gramsci's urban political (dis)orders differed markedly within post-Risorgimento Italy, viewed from the standpoint of economic, social and political development, and revolutionary potential.

From a Gramscian perspective, then, urban political (dis)orders are fruitfully read as co-determinants – and potentially antagonists – of national, international and global (dis)orders. Tendencies towards late entrepreneurialism, and repeated waves of urban revolt against austerity, maybe constituent and perhaps even decisive elements in the interregnum of neoliberal globalism. Accordingly, subsequent chapters explore dynamics of continuity and change, crisis and upheaval, propinquity and distancing as they play out through eight cities grappling with different facets of the neoliberalism–crisis–austerity problematic. The final chapter then reflects on the character of the interregnum and the concepts of 'late entrepreneurialism' and 'late neoliberalism' (Enright and Rossi, 2018).

Neoliberalism

Like 'crisis', the messy concept of neoliberalism has often generated more heat than light. However, in essence 'the ascendency of the neoliberal paradigm entailed the wholesale discrediting of Keynesian-era managerial urban policies and the concomitant valorization of market-oriented forms of urban governance' (Theodore, 2020: 1). Neoliberalism differs from classical liberalism by construing alternatives as enemies and far from retreating, aggressively confecting market mechanisms through state action in civil society, and within the state itself (Le Gales, 2016: 161–2). It is possible retrospectively to detect a cluster of conjunctural tipping points in its evolution, such as Augusto Pinochet's coup, James Callaghan's declaration that Britain could not spend its way out of a crisis or Ronald Reagan's defeat of the Air Traffic Controllers union in 1981, but like all phases of capitalist development neoliberalism is iterative. Cities are 'strategic targets and proving grounds for an increasingly broad range of neoliberal policy experiments, institutional innovations, and political projects' (Theodore et al, 2011: 24). Theodore (2020: 1) continues, 'in large part, it has been through the politico-institutional reorganization of urban economies that the ideological hegemony of neoliberalism has been achieved'. Within the compass of this definition few if any cities, north or south, have escaped some form of neoliberalisation. One common denominator is the spread of market rationalities (Henderson et al, 2020). These make 'economics the model of everything' (Peck and Theodore, 2019: 251), and lead to the 'disenchantment of politics by economics' (Davies, 2017).

Yet, the literature discloses enormous complexity in varieties and hybrids of urban neoliberalism, and the recuperative capacities of neoliberalising agents as they re-purpose ostensibly antagonistic concepts like community, empowerment, equality, inclusivity, innovation and good governance. The concepts of 'rollback' and 'rollout' describe different modalities of neoliberalism. They can be read as phases, but also as intersecting currents. Rollback refers to 'the active destruction or discreditation of Keynesian-welfarist and social-collectivist institutions' (Peck and Tickell, 2002: 37), and the concomitant employment of force characteristic of what Bruff (2014) called 'authoritarian neoliberalism'. Rollout neoliberalism refers to the construction of institutions to enrol citizens into the dispositions, cultures and practices of a marketised and responsibilised way of life. It is a term often used in discussing urban revitalisation and social inclusion programmes during the neoliberal boom (such as Head Start or Sure Start). The related term 'social neoliberalism' (Cerny, 2008) further captures the rollout idea of an investment state superseding Keynesian institutions, seeking to instil entrepreneurialism in citizen consumers, particularly working-class communities previously schooled in Fordist labour practices that required little in the way of personal entrepreneurship.

Neoliberal policy regimes are closely associated with the tactics and strategies of austerity, but are not inherently austerian. Rollback has more immediate affinity with austerity than rollout, because the latter is investment dependent. Callinicos (2012) observed that neoliberal policy regimes oscillate between episodes of austerity and fiscal stimulus, encouraging asset price bubbles to underwrite consumption financed through personal and household debt; the policy regime of 'privatized Keynesianism' (Crouch, 2009). Like rollout and rollback neoliberalism, austerity and stimulus can overlap, with austerity occurring in one sphere, such as wage suppression, welfare or social care, and investment in another, like big infrastructure.

Beyond variations within neoliberalism itself, hybridisation occurs when neoliberalisation conjoins with other traditions, like welfarism or clientelism (Ferguson, 2010; Davies and Blanco, 2017). Hybridity poses boundary questions explored by Le Gales (2016), for whom 'variegated neoliberalism' stretches the concept too far. This critique might also apply to the notion of 'ambivalence' developed by Enright and Rossi (2018) to capture periods of uncertainty in which re-emerging and reconstituting urban solidarities become enmeshed with and implicated in radicalising neoliberalism (also Taylor, 2013).

For clarity, neoliberalism here references an initially potent hegemonic project, described by Perry Anderson (2000) as the most successful in world history. 'Neoliberalisation' better captures the diversity, processual character and forward-momentum of combined rollback–rollout approaches, whose unity lies in Theodore's state-driven 'valorization of market-oriented forms of urban governance' (also Whitham, 2018). Variegated neoliberalisation captures the interplay of rollback and rollout or 'authoritarian neoliberal' and 'social neoliberal' approaches and cycles of austerity–stimulus that follow pro-market principles. Hybridised neoliberalisation is about the sometimes-conflictual entanglements of neoliberalisation with non- or anti-neoliberal traditions (Davies and Blanco, 2017). It also encompasses the encounter between neoliberalisation dynamics and forces seeking to resist them. These forces sometimes halt or reverse it, fall before it, or become enmeshed with it, as Enright and Rossi's concept of 'ambivalence' implies, and as the research revealed in liminal practices of urban governance at the cusp of assistance and resistance, discussed in Chapters 6 and 7.

Ogman (2020: 838) defined 'progressive post-neoliberalisation' as calling for 'market-constraint and potentially transcendence' involving 'neo-Keynesianism, a Green New Deal, expanded social protections, the increased employee share of profits, and the de-commodification of social goods'. This concept, as baggy as neoliberalism itself, can be extended to include the array of more-or-less insurgent political economies espousing decommodification, de-growth or slow-growth, socialism, solidarity, democracy and equality. These too may be hybridised in the double sense of deriving from radically different but overlapping political traditions and also operating in, with and against neoliberalism. They include ostensibly non-adversarial everyday urban governance encounters, cooperative endeavours and community wealth building programmes (Guinan and O'Neill, 2020) to counter the impact of austere neoliberalism without direct conflict, as well as uprisings and insurgencies.

Conjunctural thinking about neoliberalism may be explicit as it is in the work of Hall, Hay, Clarke, Jessop or Peck, or implicit as it is in the looser diagnosis of 'late neoliberalism' by Enright and Rossi (2018: 7). They define 'late neoliberalism' as

> the critical period leading up to and following from the financial crisis, in which the political economic underpinnings of late capitalism are in upheaval. While this era most obviously features a deepening of financial capital's institutional architecture and intensified forms of austerity and retrenchment, the late neoliberal condition also entails the strengthening of countermobilizations and power struggles pursuing alternative non-market agendas and politics.

They argue that diagnosing 'late neoliberalism' is not 'a definitive statement of regime consolidation but a heuristic device to signal the distinctive reformations in rule regimes governing urbanisation as well as the shifts in political discourses, institutional formations, subjectivities and organisational dynamics that have been occurring in diverse urban contexts' (2018: 8). Whereas Peck's 'late entrepreneurialism' focuses on the tendential exhaustion of entrepreneurialism as a vehicle for neoliberalised urban development, Enright and Rossi relate 'late neoliberalism' in terms of politicisations and contradictions between deepening neoliberalism and rising opposition. Both approaches are useful foils for investigating urban political (dis)orders and reflecting on how we might know 'lateness' when we see it. The discussion returns to this issue, particularly in Chapters 2 and 8. The problematic addressed in this volume is that of 'governability' in a Gramscian sense; how durable urban political (dis)orders turn out to be in post-GEC conditions? How resonant are concepts that diagnose 'lateness' in the austere neoliberal conjuncture? Under what conditions do alternatives incubate and fail? The focus on crisis construals in Chapter 2, casts further light on these issues.

Austerity

Like crisis and neoliberalism, finally, the concept of austerity is also multivalent and contested. It has become indelibly associated with the intensification and radicalisation of neoliberalism since the GEC. However, David Cameron was not the first British politician to talk about an 'age of austerity'. It was also common parlance for the privations endured in the post-war period (Sissons and French, 1963). Kynaston (2007: 298) quoted a British schoolteacher speaking in 1948. Capturing the oppressive spirit of austerity three years after the Second World War she observed, 'Dreariness is everywhere. Streets are deserted, lighting is dim, people's clothes are shabby and their tables bare.' Yet, this post-war age of austerity coincided with the construction of the welfare state, channelling the Second World War ethos of collective sacrifice into the creation of public goods (Hill, 2015: 51), a fundamentally different *dispotif* than the post GEC preoccupation with balanced budgets, marketisation, individual responsibility and entrepreneurship of the self.

A further distinction between modes of austerity occurs in Keynesian economics. Where neoliberal economists argue for pro-cyclical austerity to reduce the tax burden on business, Keynesians argue for austerity 'at the top of the business cycle, to prevent the economy from over-heating and causing inflation' and to fill the state's coffers for difficult times. 'From this perspective, austerity is the counterpart to stimulus, which is the preferred strategy during the slump, when the problem is unemployment' (Konzelmann, 2014: 723). Even the newly fashionable Modern Monetary Theory has its putative phase of austerity, exercised through tax-raising to control inflationary effects of money created by the state. As a government policy for public spending restraint, austerity can – in principle – be implemented in pursuit of competing individualist or collectivist goals and at the opposite ends of economic boom–bust cycles. As an ethos, austerity is yet more widespread, found also in the secular idea of the 'revolutionary ascetic' (Mazlish, 2017), who repudiates lavish consumption, favours frugality and employs the latter as a weapon against the gluttony and ostentation of the ruling classes in the manner of Spanish Communist leader, Julio Anguita (2008) who described austerity as 'a revolutionary lever'. Virtually all political traditions see episodic belt-tightening as a necessity if not as morally and politically righteous, motivated by virtues of sacrifice and self-mastery also familiar in religious traditions like Lent and Ramadan.

Like other key terms in this discussion, 'neoliberalism' and 'crisis', 'austerity' is contested, but it too has a common analytical core. Whereas neoliberalism is anchored by the proselytisation of market-based economic competition, and crisis by notions of upheaval and amplified contingency, austerity is anchored by the politics of enforced or purposeful frugality, justified by politically wide-ranging ideas about the nature of scarcity and the necessity or virtue of restraint.

Conclusion

The chapter proposes a Gramscian-regime analytical framework, in order to pivot between the perspectives of normalisation, resistance and transformation in exploring the question of governability through the age of austerity and contribute to understanding urban characteristics of the putative interregnum. Furthermore, distinguishing three key terms in the analytical lexicon, crisis, neoliberalism and austerity, sensitises the research to historical continuity and change, and to significant nuances within and between the eight cities. Subsequent chapters discuss key themes emerging from the study. Chapter 2 explores the inter-relationships between neoliberalisation, crisis and austerity, before considering collaborative governance through the Gramscian-regime theoretical lens in several steps. Chapter 3 explores spatial, scalar and jurisdictional relations of austerity governance from the perspective of the state, while Chapters 4 and 5 look at the character of the governing coalitions co-constituting the urban political (dis)orders constituted within each city. Chapters 6 and 7 explore the constitution and impact of resistance to austerity, both on regime dynamics and co-optive power, and the incubation of alternative political economies and potential hegemonic apparatuses. Chapter 8 reflects on the nature and extent of the interregnum of neoliberal globalism and key mechanisms of stabilisation and disruption constituting today's urban political (dis)orders.

Dynamics of Crisis, Neoliberalisation and Austerity

Introduction

Theodore (2020: 2) argued that since the GEC, 'austerity has become the primary means for the further neoliberalisation of inherited arrangements': neoliberalisation upon earlier waves of neoliberalism. Chapter 2 delves into this proposition. It begins by exploring the impact of the GEC, and its aftermath, in the eight countries and cities studied. It proceeds to examine the interplay of key terms introduced in Chapter 1: crisis, austerity and neoliberalisation. The chapter allocates the cities to three groups: those in which austerity is recognised as a central concept or challenge and a warrant for neoliberalisation (Athens, Dublin and Leicester), those in which it is concealed or re-signified within an otherwise vigorous neoliberalisation agenda (Baltimore and Montréal), and those positioning themselves critically, at a distance or outside it (Barcelona, Dandenong and Nantes). The chapter concludes by discussing theoretical implications of convergence and divergence in the cross-cutting relationships between crisis, austerity and neoliberalisation.

Eight cities in and beyond the global economic crisis

Table 2.1 characterises the eight cities in relation to population, economic performance and political control in the 2015–18 period. As explained in the Introductory chapter, the statistics are imprecise and drawn from a range of sources, some more up to date than others. Athens is the capital of Greece, and the epicentre of European austerity. Baltimore is at the southern end of the mega-region stretching several hundred miles

Table 2.1: Urban populations, economies and municipalities

	City population (2019)	Metropolitan population (2020)[a]	Metropolitan per capita GDP (2015) $[b]	National per capita GDP (2015) $[c]	Political leadership (2015–18)
Athens	664,000	3.153 million	32,167	22,615	Centre-left platform. Mayor Georgis Kaminis.
Baltimore	619,500	2.325 million	69,590	52,099	Democrat. Mayors: Stephanie Rawlings Blake (to 2016) Catherine Pugh (2016–).
Barcelona	1.61 million	5.586 million	45,752	30,595	Barcelona en Comú. Mayor Ada Colau.
Greater Dandenong	169,000[d]	4.968 million[e]	41,062	55,183	Labor. Non-executive Mayor elected annually.
Dublin	554,000	1.228 million	55,909 (2011)	50,304 (2011)	Centre-left coalition. Non-executive Lord Mayor.
Leicester	348,000	0.552 million	33,355	41,756	Labour. Mayor Sir Peter Soulsby.
Montréal	1.78 million	4.221 million	35,498	50,255	Centre-left platform. Équipe Denis Coderre pour Montréal. Projet Montréal (2017–). Mayor Valérie Plante.
Nantes	306,000	0.678 million.	38,736	41,765	Socialist Party. Mayor Johanna Rolland.

[a] Data from Macrotrends at www.macrotrends.net. All metropolitan areas, bar Athens (99.3 per cent) saw significant population increases between 2008 and 2020.

[b] Data drawn from the Regions and Cities section of OECD.Stat, https://stats.oecd.org.

[c] Data drawn from Trading Economics website at https://tradingeconomics.com.

[d] The figure for Greater Dandenong is from www.planning.vic.gov.au/__data/assets/pdf_file/0009/11106/Greater_Dandenong_VIF_2016_One_Page_Profile_Output.pdf.

[e] This figure is for the urban area of metropolitan Melbourne.

Table 2.2: Growth and recession in and after the global economic crisis

	% National peak-to-trough GDP in/after GEC[5]	% Metro peak-to-trough GDP in/after GEC[a,b]	% Municipal budget real terms growth/fall 2008–18[6]	% Metro GDP growth relative to pre-GEC peak[7]
Australia/ Melbourne	+4.2 (2008–9)	-0.96 (2007–8)	+15.4	+24.2
Canada/ Montréal	-4.6 (2008–9)	-1.23 (2007–8)	+20.5 (2019)	+15.6
France/ Nantes	-4.0 (2008–9)	-2.4 (2008–10)	-7.5	+13.0 (2015)
Greece/ Athens	-29.5 (2008–13)	-26.3 (2008–15)[8]	-28.4	-26.3 (2015)
Ireland/ Dublin	-13.6 (2008–13)	-7.2 (2007–9)	-20–25 (no data)	+24.1 (2014)
Spain/ Barcelona	-10.3 (2008–13)	-9.0 (2008–13)	+0.25	-3.4 (2015)
UK/Leicester	-6.4 (2008–9)	-5.3 (2007–9)	-39.9 (2020)	+16.4
USA/ Baltimore	-5.1 (2008–9)	+7.3 (2007–10)	-2.2	+12.24

[a] Data drawn from the Regions and Cities section of OECD.Stat, at https://stats.oecd.org.

[b] Data for Baltimore from US Bureau of Economic Analysis (BEA), at www.bea.gov/data/gdp/gdp-metropolitan-area.

from Boston to Washington, DC in the USA. Barcelona is the capital of Catalonia and, in terms of size and stature, Spain's second city. Greater Dandenong is a relatively small city within the South Eastern part of the Melbourne metropolis. Melbourne itself is the major city-region in the Australian state of Victoria, comprising over 75 per cent of the state's population. Dublin is Ireland's capital and, like Athens, looms large in the political economy of its host country. Leicester is a medium-sized city in the East Midlands region of England and on some measures the poorest in the UK. Montréal comprises a large metropolitan area in the largely Francophone province of Québec, in the Eastern part of Canada. Nantes is situated near the eastern coast of France in the Pays de la Loire region and is of similar size to Leicester.

Table 2.2 estimates four economic outcomes of crisis, recession and austerity in the eight cities: national GDP trends, metropolitan GDP trends, real-terms municipal budget growth and metropolitan GDP growth relative to the pre-GEC peak. As explained in the

Introduction, these are weak proxies for 'urban austerity', because figures for municipal budgets represent only a fraction of urban governmental spend, particularly in federalised systems, and the size of a budget may be less important in terms of austerity than how it is, or is allowed to be, spent. Austerity can be introduced in ways that do not directly erode municipal service budgets, such as by reducing pension benefits for public sector workers (Baltimore), channelling revenues into debt/deficit reduction (Barcelona, Québec) or a rise in local taxes, as executed in Montréal between 2017 and 2019 under the new left-leaning Mayoralty of Valérie Plante. Around half the significant budget growth in that city since the GEC occurred in 2018 (5.2 per cent) and 2019 (4.3 per cent). Moreover, budget growth may be slower than population growth, or fail to reflect other significant demographic changes, and disguise declining spending power.

The Eurozone recessions

The Greek economic collapse between the GEC and COVID-19 was unprecedented in post-war Europe. Only part of the collapse is attributable to proximate factors that triggered the GEC. Greek finances were dominated by the three EU–IMF economic adjustment programmes; 'memoranda' signed in 2010, 2012 and 2015 (Chorianopoulos and Tselepi, 2019; 2020). The memoranda mandated not only drastic austerity, with a primary budget surplus of 3.5 per cent required until 2022, but also fundamental restructuring of the state system and substantial downloading from central to local governments: additional municipal responsibilities with fewer resources and caps on municipal borrowing, alongside the enormously increased need for social assistance.

Greece's recession was, accordingly, more severe than any other by a factor of more than two. Its GDP decline began in 2007 and continued with greater or lesser intensity until the first quarter of 2013, by which time it had plummeted by an aggregate 29.3 per cent. Thereafter, quarterly GDP growth moved up and down, but effectively the economy flat-lined in this period, with a further aggregate decline of 0.2 per cent between Q2 in 2013 and Q2 in 2016 (a total aggregate decline of 29.5 per cent over nine years). Weak growth resumed from Q3 in 2016, such that by the beginning of 2019, Greek output was 25.3 per cent lower than it was at the beginning of the crisis in 2007. Figures for Metropolitan Athens are broadly consistent with the national picture, showing a decline of 26.3 per cent in metropolitan GDP by 2015.

Throughout this period, Greece was also subjected to mandatory austerity designed (ostensibly) to reduce its government debt to GDP ratio. In real terms, the municipal budget in Athens shrank by 28.4 per cent between 2008 and 2018 – with a reduction of 60 per cent in central government funding (Chorianopoulos and Tselepi, 2019: 87). After 30 years running budget deficits vastly in excess of the putative Eurozone limit of 3 per cent, Greece finally brought its annual borrowing below the threshold in 2016–18. Yet, the government debt to GDP ratio was higher than ever before in 2018, at 181.1 per cent compared with the Eurozone limit of 60 per cent. The human impact of this combined structural crisis and neoliberal policy disaster is well known (for example, Arapoglou and Gounis, 2015) and although not the main focus of this inquiry, it is necessarily touched upon in subsequent chapters.

Ireland's recession was also unique in its post-war history. GDP decline began in the second quarter of 2007, plummeting by an aggregate 11.3 per cent by the end of 2009. Between January 2010 and December 2013, there was a further aggregate decline of 2.3 per cent – a recessionary impact of 13.6 per cent over seven years. Despite its weight as a proportion of the national economy (51.9 per cent of GDP in 2014), OECD data shows that the metropolitan economy of Dublin shrank by 7.2 per cent over a much shorter period, suggesting that the worst recessionary effects were concentrated in the rest of the country. In the period to 2014 (the last available data), Dublin's economy grew by 24.1 per cent from its recessionary trough while its municipal budget was cut by 20–25 per cent according to informal estimates (Gaynor, 2020: 78). National growth in the post-2013 period was steady, including two extraordinary quarters of 22.6 per cent (Q1, 2015) and 10.3 per cent (Q4, 2016) and one sharp slump, of 5 per cent Q1, 2017. The exceptional growth figures arise from what economists call an 'inversion', where companies switch base from one country to another, bolstering the beneficiary state's balance sheet. From the standpoint of capturing real dynamics in the economy and human wellbeing, this practice exposes one of many limits of the GDP measure.

Spain experienced the third most severe recession among the eight countries. Output began to fall in the second quarter of 2008, continuing until the end of 2013. It suffered an aggregate peak-to-trough GDP decline of 10.3 per cent, before growth resumed in 2014, averaging around 2.8 per cent until the end of 2018. The recession in Barcelona was slightly shallower, aggregating at 9.0 per cent peak-to-trough. In 2015, metropolitan output had yet to recover to 2008 levels, falling short by 3.4 per cent despite heating effects from development and tourism booms in the heart of the city.

In Athens, Barcelona and Dublin, Eurozone discipline exacerbated the depth and duration of the recessionary period. Nantes was in a stronger position. The French recession was again severe by historical standards, but the shallowest among the eight countries. Peak-to-trough decline totalled 4.0 per cent across five successive quarters in 2008 and 2009. Between the country's exit from recession at the beginning of 2010, and the end of 2018, annual growth averaged 1.3 per cent – feeble by comparison with all other countries bar Greece. Per capita income only recovered to pre-crisis levels in 2016. A similar picture emerges in Nantes, where output declined by a relatively mild 2.4 per cent during the GEC; but it too saw sluggish post-crisis growth on a par with that nationally.

Then President Sarkozy introduced austerity reforms in 2010, freezing public employment and limiting the capacity of local authorities to raise taxes (see further in Chapter 3). However, in 2012, France elected socialist François Hollande to the Presidency on a platform rejecting austerity and pledging higher taxes on wealth. Yet, two years later, Hollande performed a U-turn, announcing government spending cuts and corporate tax cuts (McDaniel, 2017). With the formulation of the *pacte de responsabilité et de solidarité* in 2014, a shift sometimes compared with the 1982 policy reversal by François Mitterrand, the French government planned €50 billion reductions in public spending from 2015 to 2017, €11billion of which were to come from local government (Griggs et al, 2018).

Hollande's austerity took time to percolate into Nantes. Its overall budget was reported to have fallen by 7.5 per cent in real terms. Mayor Rolland, elected in 2014, committed to 8 per cent budget savings during her mandate, with projected falls in running costs of the authority of 3.5 per cent in 2016. Transfers from the centre declined by 10.7 per cent in 2016, while as part of the partnership agreement within Nantes Métropole, grants from the intercommunal organisation fell by 20 per cent. As the research concluded, cuts 'of an amplitude and speed not experienced before' were beginning to bite (Griggs et al, 2020: 97).

Recession beyond the Eurozone

The GDP recession in the UK was also unprecedented by post-war standards, though nowhere near as severe as in Greece, Ireland or Spain. GDP declined for five successive quarters commencing in the second quarter of 2008, a peak-to-trough fall of 6.4 per cent. Metropolitan Leicester declined by 5.3 per cent, achieving growth of 16.4 per cent by 2016, relative to the pre-recessionary peak. Like France, the UK as a whole failed to regain pre-GEC trend growth rates in the following decade, averaging a mere 1.8 per cent by the end of 2018. The UK had one 'good' year in 2017, when growth reached 2.8 per cent. Cuts to the municipal budget have been out of any proportion to growth and recession. Leicester City Council saw a real-terms budget cut of 39.9 per cent between 2008 and 2020. Discretionary spend on non-statutory services was projected to have been cut by 63 per cent by 2020 (Davies et al, 2020: 60). Statistically, this was the most severe case of austerity encountered in the eight cities, among which Leicester was also the second poorest on per capita GDP measures.

Canada experienced three quarters of GDP decline amounting to a sharp peak-to-trough fall of 4.6 per cent in 2008–9, with a much shallower decline of 1.23 per cent recorded in Montréal. Canadian growth recovered quickly, and continued at an average of some 2.2 per cent per annum. Respondents in Montréal suggested that the city was more vulnerable to contagion effects from the USA than its own direct exposure to the financial crisis, and by 2015 the economy had grown by 15.6 per cent compared with the pre-crisis peak. By 2019, the city's budget had increased by 20.6 per cent, though this figure occludes the impact of cuts to budgets controlled by the provincial government of Québec.[1]

The recession in the USA, finally, was relatively short but very sharp, occurring between the first quarter of 2008 and the second quarter of 2009, and a peak-to-trough drop of 5.1 per cent. Growth resumed thereafter and was sustained at an annual average of some 2.4 per cent in the period until the end of 2018. In July 2019, the US economy surpassed the record for its longest unbroken growth streak since the 1850s. Despite its duration, post-GEC growth was shallow, surpassing the pre-GEC peak by only 20 per cent compared with the 41 per cent increase achieved after recession in the 1990s (Wigglesworth, 2019). Notably, however, the Bureau of Economic Analysis figures for metropolitan Baltimore show sustained growth throughout the crisis-period amounting to 7.3 per cent (the OECD's growth estimate of 5.66 per cent for Greater Washington from 2007 to 2010 includes Baltimore). Growth data for Baltimore and Dublin in particular highlight unevenness in the experience of recessions at national and urban scales, and the need for more granular comparative urban economic data than OECD or Eurostat are currently able to provide.

Australia: the exception

Australia was an outrider among the eight countries, avoiding recession and growing for perhaps the longest continuous period of any OECD economy prior to COVID-19. Metropolitan Melbourne experienced a short and shallow decline in GDP (0.96 per cent), but sharp growth thereafter. Greater Dandenong saw the biggest increase in municipal budgets among all eight cities in the post-GEC period, but also significant population growth. The Australian economy survived the GEC without a recession for two main reasons. It was greatly helped by geo-economic distance from the crisis-heartlands in the North, and its proximity to the immense Chinese boom of the past three decades. The Australian government also employed counter-cyclical stimulus measures in the 2008–10 period (Armingeon, 2012: 549). Annual GDP growth in Australia continued at a rate of 2.75–3 per cent, though with uncertainty growing due to pre-COVID turbulence in the Chinese economy and Donald Trump's on–off trade war. As the following discussion of austerity construals explains, this relatively benign economic context had significant implications for the political economy of Greater Dandenong and the geographical and political reach of austere neoliberalism.

Radicalising neoliberalism through austerity

Athens sat at the epicentre of the 2008 crisis and austere neoliberalism. Until the shock of the GEC, and subsequent austerity mandates, neoliberal 'good governance' in that city was stymied by weak reform efforts and the persistence of established governing traditions. In a poor country, the local state apparatus emerging after the military dictatorship of the 1970s proved weak and incapable of driving through reforms. Clientelism was (and arguably remains) a significant cultural and institutional practice, reinforcing vertical dependencies, distorting and impeding reforms oriented to creating an efficient, rationalised and joined-up local government system (Chorianopoulos and Tselepi, 2020). Clientelism was also invoked by political elites trying to summon collective guilt for the crisis, articulated by a former minister who said, 'we ate them [the money] together' (Koutrolikou, 2016: 185). Athens is a reminder that aspects of neoliberalisation require a strong and competent state apparatus (Gamble, 1994).

In July 2015, the newly elected Syriza government signed Greece's third austerity memorandum with the Troika. It did so in the face of the 61 per cent '*Oxi*' vote in a national referendum on whether to accept the terms, a vote for which it had campaigned. The question of how, in a matter of a few days Greece could decisively reject austerity in a plebiscite, only for its government, until that point the elected voice of the anti-austerity movement, to perform a volte face and accept austerity in full has fomented much debate about Greek cultural political economy and its relations with Europe.

One aspect of the explanation is that the leading Tsipras faction was not serious about fighting to deliver the Syriza manifesto, and naively saw the referendum as a lever to extract concessions from the EU on the debt-burden (Kouvelakis, 2016). Another is that the question posed in the referendum failed to capture a pivotal dilemma in Greek society: the juxtaposition of national anti-austerity sentiment with an equally potent sense of European identity (Della Porta et al, 2017). Syriza was able to resolve this dilemma in favour of the EU project, the Euro and austerity, despite *Oxi*, because the decision connected with a widely shared desire to remain part of the EU, and because Grexit appeared to threaten an even greater collapse. Forces committed to Grexit were always a small minority and unable to counter-mobilise against the capitulation (Kouvelakis, 2016).

Consequently, July 2015 can be seen as a conjunctural tipping point (Hay, 1999). The grand moment of recuperation, absorption or Gramscian *trasformismo* signified by the political collapse of Syriza, marked a clear victory for pro-austerity forces (Gramsci, 1971: 58–9, 108–9; Q19, §24, Q15, §11). If the concept of passive revolution has any resonance in considering the consolidation of austere neoliberalism after the GEC, it is in the Greek case. At stake was not simply incremental radicalisation, but the resolution of a proximate conjunctural struggle over the identity and politics of Greece through the political representatives of one side being absorbed into the other (*trasformismo*). This cultural–political leap did not bring anti-austerity struggles to an end, far from it. However, it settled a clear course for the Greek state, and the city of Athens, which anti-austerity forces were unable to reverse. The politics of austere neoliberalism became dominant (if not hegemonic) in Greek society.

Between 2010 and 2019, Athens was led by Mayor Giorgos Kaminis, an 'independent' candidate supported by the centre-left and formerly of the discredited Greek social democrat party, PASOK. Kaminis embraced the letter and the spirit of austerity. He boasted in his 2012 budget statement that 'in the first year of our administration [2011], we didn't borrow a single euro. Instead, we reduced our debt to creditors from 47 million euros to 26' (cited in Chorianopoulos, 2016).[2] The attainment of administrative and fiscal self-reliance was a central goal of Kaminis's leadership (Chorianopoulos and Tselepi, 2020: 45). In the 2015 referendum, he captured the national dilemma highlighted earlier by playing a leading role in the '*Nai*' campaign, and stating 'we want to stay in Europe, and let's not be ridiculous: this is what the referendum is about' (cited in Hope, 2015).

Although this should not be exaggerated, the period after July 2015 saw the relative normalisation of austerity in the Athenian local state apparatus, reflected in processes of urban regime formation and the changing contours of resistance discussed in subsequent chapters. This process was reflected in the pragmatic discourse of municipal politicians. Said one: 'We made a choice. The municipality of Athens is taking care of 20,000 people. You can't just ignore that, or let it go by. ... If someone says I won't do it because that's not the right way forward, well he/she is taking a risk: we don't' (Chorianopoulos and Tselepi, 2019: 89). Chapter 4 elaborates further on this ethos.

Though not as severe, or prolonged, the experience of Dublin echoes Athens to some extent. On 29 September 2008, stocks of the three main Irish banks fell between 20 per cent and 50 per cent in a single day. The Irish government immediately guaranteed not only public deposits, but also €80 billion in bank bonds owned by international investors. Liabilities were transferred directly to Ireland's citizens, a sum equivalent to 40 per cent of the country's GDP (Gaynor, 2020: 78). As the costs of servicing bonds escalated, the Irish government signed an €85 billion bailout with the Troika, marking the onset of mandatory austerity. Austerity comprised large-scale spending cuts over a prolonged period, and a portfolio of extractive measures: increases in indirect taxes and hikes in fees and charges, a universal social charge (2011), property tax (2014) and water charges (2015). The latter triggered a major rebellion forcing the Irish government into retreat, discussed in Chapter 6.

In transferring responsibility for the crisis from the banks to its citizens, the Irish government also sought to impose collective moral responsibility (like Greece) in construing the GEC as one of zealous over-consumption: 'we all partied' said then Taoiseach, Brian Lenihan. At the same time, the de-politicising invocation 'we are where we are' permeated throughout state and media (Gaynor, 2020: 79). This strategy worked insofar as the local state became a pliable vehicle for the national austerity project, made possible by the combination of authoritarian Irish state traditions, the weak, managerialised system of local government (Spotlight, 2013) and, more contingently, the fragmentary politics of Dublin City Council. It was abetted by the political evisceration of data on austerity and poverty discussed in the introductory chapter, drastic cuts to voluntary and community sectors, and the resulting curtailment of participatory governance discussed in Chapter 4.

Throughout most of the 20th century, Leicester's economy was underpinned by food, apparel and engineering industries (Gunn and Hyde, 2013). Like other cities, much of its large-scale industrial base was destroyed in the 1970s and 1980s. For city leaders, this period marked a loss of shared identity in a city considered to have developed a 'collective inferiority complex' (Councillor, cited in Davies et al, 2020: 63). Though severely exposed to the wave of Thatcherite and post-Thatcherite marketisation and modernisation programmes, Leicester embraced entrepreneurialism and place-marketing as a positive governance strategy relatively recently. As an example of a 'super-diverse' city (Vertovec, 2019), its development strategy is inter-woven with the celebration of multicultural entrepreneurship, especially among elements of the Commonwealth Asian population that migrated to Leicester over the past 50 years (see Chapter 4).

After the GEC, the UK government proselytised and administered a programme of austerity with the partially fulfilled, now abandoned goal of eliminating the country's annual deficit. The successful re-narration of economic crisis as a crisis of an over-extended state opened the door to a prolonged and radicalised wave of neoliberalisation, through austerity measures warranted by the homespun economic wisdom proselytised by the Conservative Party: like a responsible household, a responsible state should pay its debts and not live beyond its means. Local government and welfare spending were notable targets. Austerity severely aggravated urban poverty, while welfare claimants were subjected to a harshly authoritarian workfare regime, causing a massive increase in foodbank dependency (Davies et al, 2020: 64). This regime aggravated already existing deep poverty and multiple deprivations within Leicester. In addition, like other UK cities, Leicester was undergoing a fiscal restructuring, towards a 'localist' and 'privatist' model of local governance (see Chapter 3), increasingly resembling US cities. The 39.9 per cent real terms cut to the city council's budget between 2010 and 2020 emphasises the severity of the Leicester case.

Most respondents in Leicester opposed austerity at the level of ideas. However, in the face of growing fiscal stress, government downloading and institutional churn, Leicester City Council (LCC), an overwhelmingly Labour authority, employed a crisis-muting 'austerian realist' discourse. This emphasises in different combinations and guises, that normal life continued for most, the futility of resistance, dangers in provoking conflict with central government, the opportunity to experiment with service reorganisations and make efficiency gains that would not otherwise have arisen, and the need to develop an attractive city centre, or 'shop window' to enhance Leicester's job market and revenue base. Whereas the UK government proved very effective as a crisis-maker in the aftermath of the GEC, Leicester, in contrast, muted crisis-talk because 'drama and conflict are not in the best interests of the city' (Councillor). This meant cutting 'without fuss' (Davies and Blanco, 2017: 1522), attempting to mitigate and manage the fallout from austerity, and employing discourses that recall the defeat of municipal rebels at the hands of Mrs Thatcher in the 1980s, as a warning that compliance was the only sensible approach (Davies et al, 2020; see also Chapter 7).

The case of the garment industry exemplifies the power of austerian realism as a governing logic. The Leicester urban area hosts some 28 per cent of the national garment manufacturing industry in terms of gross value added (Hammer et al, 2015: 9). Many thousands of workers labour in sweatshop conditions, earning half the national minimum wage. This level is achieved by employers under-declaring working hours and getting away with it in the weak regulatory climate of austere neoliberalism and the collusion of major brand retailers purchasing goods upstream. This production ecology was made possible by 'a flexible labour market based on permissive regulatory and enforcement structures' (Hammer et al, 2015: 43). However, the prevalent 'austerian realist' governing disposition meant that the local politics of garment production were muted rather than amplified, so as not to deter investors (Davies et al, 2020: 62). Chapter 4 discusses austerian realism in more depth.

In short, the GEC, austerity and the distinct crisis-construals pursued by national and local governments delivered a step-change in the neoliberalisation of Leicester. The forces of national state discipline and control combined with the multi-tonal politics of austerian realism to keep the question of whether to cut, or whether to focus on attractiveness, a long way from the political agenda. As Marcuse (2015: 156) wrote in his reflections on neoliberal governing power, contentious discourses did not have to be repressed. They were 'simply not generated anywhere near the arena of policy discourse or power'.

Neoliberalisation without 'austerity'?

Athens, Dublin and Leicester have in common that local state actors remain locked into politics of crisis and austerity that borrow heavily from repertoires of rollback and authoritarian neoliberalism, and warrant austerity respectively as something over which the city has no control (Leicester), as a necessary (even welcome) discipline in making a globally competitive city (Athens) or as a necessary form of public penance (Athens and Dublin). Baltimore and Montréal face many of the same fiscal stresses and socio-economic polarisations, but without narrating 'austerity' as a central problematic.

Baltimore diverged from Athens, Dublin and Leicester in one notable way, which is revealing both of urban political economy in the USA and the dimensions in which it is distinct among the eight cities. It is a city in which, for the past 30 years, has lived with continuous fiscal retrenchment following more than half a century of economic and population decline, itself layered upon a century of planned racial segregation. Most of Baltimore's majority population (64 per cent) of African American citizens live in dispossessed neighbourhoods, while the gentrified, and highly subsidised city centre investment magnet thrives. The city's polarising model of economic and spatial governance engenders enormous violence, among citizens trapped in the drug economy pervading poor neighbourhoods and by the Baltimore Police, seen by some respondents as a greater threat than gangsters (Pill, 2020, see also Chapter 4). The official murder rate in Baltimore is vastly greater than the rest of the cities combined. Baltimore is the epitome of racial capitalism (Robinson, 1983). Its authoritarian, austere neoliberal governing regime seeks to manage a highly racialised form of dispossession in a manner that continually facilitates gentrification and down-down development.

The neoliberalisation of Baltimore, however, has been so intense over such a prolonged period that most of the respondents did not see the period since the GEC as significant. Nor did they discern any notable shift towards austerity policies. The explanation was partly that, as noted earlier, the economy of Baltimore grew through the recession and partly that recurring episodes of fiscal retrenchment have long been normalised, with much more pronounced falls in municipal revenue occurring in the early 2000s. Here, respondents suggested that Baltimore was 'used to austerity and functions like that all the time'. They described a long-standing 'culture of scarcity', dating back to the Reagan presidency (Pill, 2020: 146).

To the extent that urban governing elites employed crisis vocabularies, it was to support retrenchment. The trailing of a 'doomsday budget' by the then Democrat Mayor Stephanie Rawlings Blake (2010–2016) was represented as a means of restoring confidence after the previous Mayor was ousted, and softening up city councillors to the urgent need for further retrenchment (Pill, 2020: 146). While criticising 'mindless austerity', Rawlings Blake spoke of 'harsh realities' and asserted that Baltimore should 'stop kicking the can down the road'. Referring to borrowing and pension liabilities (discussed further in Chapter 3), she continued: 'You can put these things off. But at some point the bill comes due' (cited in Klepper, 2013). Budget-balancing since the 'doomsday budget' includes measures that echo severe austerity in Europe: a hiring freeze, employee furloughs, agency rationalisation, cutting 'duplicative and underperforming' services, reducing agency administrative costs, charging retirees a proportion of prescription drug premiums, cutting 1000 jobs, and scaling back services such as after-school programmes. What was called 'an immediate pension crisis' in 2013 was averted by reducing benefits for fire and police personnel. Elites present the relentless squeeze as the only means of dealing with the fiscal crisis, 'the bill' always looming. Hence, whereas austere neoliberalism in Athens was cemented through *trasformismo*, Baltimore's authoritarian neoliberalisation dynamic was so routine for so long that the vocabulary of 'austerity', understood as a set of intense post-GEC interventions, was redundant.

Like European and US counterparts, commercial and industrial activity in Montréal formed the base of its 20th-century economic and demographic growth and development. In the 1970s and after, it suffered an exodus of industries to peripheral areas, as well as relative decline vis-à-vis Toronto in the aftermath of the 'Quiet Revolution'. The Quiet Revolution refers to a period of transformation in Québec during the 1960s, leading to the secularisation of a governmental apparatus previously steeped in Catholicism (Sait, 1913), the development of social welfare and the rise of Québécois nationalism. These processes hastened Québec's shift to becoming a Francophone province. Political leaders accepted that this project would incur costs in terms of slower economic growth and development (Hamel and Autin, 2017; Hamel and Keil, 2020). The city's urban regime actors have struggled with this legacy since (see Chapter 5). Savage (2003: 237) encapsulated Montréal's economic predicament, observing that 'the deindustrialized landscape, like a ruined battlefield that heals over, is ripe for commemoration'.[3]

In Canada, as explained earlier, the post-GEC recession came later than in the US, mainly as a side-effect of secondary disruption. It was notably shorter and shallower and recovered faster. Moreover, the economy of Montréal experienced a shallower recession than Canada as a whole and the municipal budget has risen – sharply so since the election of Valérie Plante. Hence, the GEC was viewed by respondents as a relatively minor perturbation in the context of a much more prolonged crisis of urban development (Hamel and Autin, 2017). In April 2014, the newly elected Liberal government of Québec led by Philippe Couillard decided to try and eliminate provincial debt. Couillard insisted that his policy should be called *rigueur* and not *austérité*, an attempt to confer legitimacy on the former and link it with virtues like 'truth' and 'reality' (Radio Canada, 2017), while avoiding the political toxicity of the latter. Couillard imposed new fiscal constraints and cut budgets to health and education, the two most important items of provincial governmental expenditure, as well as welfare programmes and government salaries. He insisted, however, in the face of stiff resistance that austerity was a 'figment of the imagination' (cited in Marier and Béland, 2018: 10).

Rigueur in Couillard's register echoes the harsh, disciplinary neoliberalism dominating Athens, Baltimore, Dublin and Leicester. However, it was not linked to the GEC but rather the political struggle over the future of Montréal, the role of the state and the meaning of social solidarity. Respondents argued, 'it is a choice. It's wrong to say it is objective. It's a political choice. Fundamentally, it's a conservative political choice' (urban planner, cited in Hamel and Autin, 2017: 168). The Couillard government depicted the state as oversized and excessively indebted, with overtaxed citizens at risk of being attracted to harsh 'populist' discourses (Hamel and Autin, 2017). For critics, Couillard was undoubtedly implementing austerity (Marier and Béland, 2018).

Municipal actors were more ambivalent towards this multivalent discourse of *rigueur*, sometimes seeking subtly to impede provincial cuts, mitigate the effects (like Leicester) or re-appropriate Couillard's vocabulary. A voluntary sector respondent observed,

> this puts us in a weird situation because we end up working with civil servants to maybe mitigate what's happening, the decisions taken by their own government. And they're stuck in a sandwich, trying to do their job, to not lose their job. So, they manage those changes that happened and

then try to bypass them because they have their own social consciousness. To say: this doesn't make any sense, but we'll try to find ways to bypass things. (Hamel and Keil, 2018)

Several respondents distinguished *rigueur* as prudence from *rigueur* as retrenchment. For a city official, 'if it means a good public budgets management, I'm in. If it means cutting public action as a… as a pretext so that the State has less of a role in society and that it serves an ideology, then I have more problems' (Hamel and Keil, 2018). None of the public sector respondents challenged logics of prudence and restraint. Even those strongly opposing Couillard's ideological conception of *rigueur*, saw restraint as legitimate. That is to say, opposition to retrenchment was threaded with a pragmatic expression of economic rationalism together with the exercise of discretion in mitigating the impact of cuts imposed by upper tier authorities. In municipal hands, the *rigueur* of Montréal echoed the 'fiscal conservatism' of Dandenong (discussed later), or the austerity realism of Leicester, more than it did the zealous austerity of Québec, Athens or Dublin.

To reiterate, the reference point for these debates was not the GEC as such, but long-term strategic dilemmas about Montréal's political economy. This situation was not typically construed in the language of crisis, but as Chapter 5 explains, it created a political interregnum, in the sense of governing impasse or non-hegemony (Loopmans, 2008) amid the search for a new governing regime after decades of developmental inertia (Hamel and Keil, 2015). Forces organising against austerity had a critical role in this search, discussed in Chapters 6 and 7.

Austerity? Not here!

Barcelona suffered a period of contraction lasting, with the occasional quarterly interruption, for five years between 2008 and 2013, and of similar intensity and duration to that of Spain as a whole. Like Greece and Ireland, Spain institutionalised austerity in return for an EU bailout in 2012, an arrangement it exited promptly in 2013. Although a wealthier city than Athens, citizens of Barcelona were also severely exposed to the social impacts of the GEC. The crisis there reflected the character of the preceding property boom. Barcelona hosted the 1992 Olympics, the beginning of an intense and very successful branding of the city as a tourist and investment centre. Unlike Montréal in 1976, or Athens in 2004, the Barcelona Olympics triggered a boom. Property prices and rents spiralled, particularly in the city centre, leading to an exodus of local people. Barcelona's property bubble collapsed in the GEC, creating a major foreclosure and homelessness crisis. Unemployment spiralled, aggravating the mounting crisis of subsistence in the city (Blanco et al, 2020).

Like France (discussed later) and Greece, part of the story of austerity in Barcelona is the implosion of the social democratic Partit dels Socialistes de Catalunya (PSC) which had dominated the politics of the city for more than 30 years after democratisation. In 2011, conservative politician Xavier Trias was elected to the Mayoralty. Between 2011 and 2015, the three tiers of the Spanish state, the Federal, Catalan and City of Barcelona governments, aligned behind the austere neoliberal agenda. As in Greece, the Spanish state introduced fiscal centralisation measures to limit the ability of municipalities to introduce countervailing policies (discussed in Chapter 3). Interestingly, and in contrast with the overt radicalisation of workfare in the UK and Leicester, Mayor Trias argued that the City Council had increased social welfare budgets under his tenure. However, the housing and unemployment crises caused an overwhelming upsurge in demand. This meant that though technically not subject to 'austerity' in the form of budget cuts, the service was residualised through underfunding and the parallel shift from an ethos of welfare as solidarity to a neoliberal ethos of welfare as safety net (local politician, cited in Blanco, 2016).

From 2011 to 2015, Barcelona followed a relatively orthodox path through austerity. However, the politics of the city are famously contentious and the election of a radical left anti-austerity platform in 2015, after a decade or more of sustained mobilisation against neoliberalism and austerity, shifted them dramatically. The year 2015 was as significant for Barcelona and other municipalist platform cities in Spain as it was for Athens, but in the opposite way. Whereas Athens embraced austerity, Barcelona sought to oppose it by building a 'new municipalist' politics around the Barcelona en Comú electoral platform, rooted in aspirations for economic justice, participatory democracy, feminisation, racial equality and radicalised co-production (Barcelona en Comú, 2019). At the same time, as Chapters 3, 5 and 7 explain, the functional, fiscal and spatial jurisdictions of the City Council are limited and have been curtailed. Its grip on municipal power is precarious and forces aligned against it on the conservative right and pro-independence groups unaffiliated with the municipalist agenda are significant (Blanco et al, 2020).

Barcelona, however, is one of the leading, most cited and inspiring international exemplars of 'new municipalism' in office. As part of its governing strategy, crisis-construals shifted towards foregrounding the experience of dispossession and enhancing social protection. Barcelona en Comú also sought to turn 'austerity' against the right, by emphasising its governing competence and prudence against the fecklessness of the conservatives (Blanco, 2017). This sensibility contributes to justifying strategies for re-municipalisation, progressive procurement policies, a new partnership with grass-roots organisations and subduing the tourism and property bubbles. In Barcelona, therefore, the concepts of crisis and austerity shifted out of alignment with neoliberalism, with the second and third elements now employed against the first. The resignification of austerity in Barcelona, with echoes of the socialist asceticism articulated by Julio Anguita (2008), was unique among the eight cities.

In the context of Europe, Nantes is something of an outrider. As a port city, it experienced a severe industrial crisis with the closure of its shipyards in the late 1980s. However, it adapted and became a successful entrepreneurial city. The Mayor of Nantes between 1989 and 2012 (and thereafter PM), Jean-Marc Ayrault, was able to convene a powerful urban and metropolitan growth coalition, around three inter-related and enduring policy objectives: attractiveness, participation and sustainability. The coalition became known as 'system Ayrault', with the governing agenda and participatory apparatus around it as the Jeu à la Nantaise (the Nantes Game explored in Chapter 5). As an entrepreneurial city, the governing strategy pursued in Nantes falls partly – but not exclusively – within the compass of the rollout and social neoliberal traditions, particularly in its emphasis on sustainability, greening and participation. However, it is also imbued with Keynesian and Republican values affecting its stance towards both austerity and broader governing principles (Griggs et al, 2020).

Respondents saw austerity imposed from the national level as a challenge for Nantes, but also pointed to significant positional advantages including its fiscal base and borrowing powers. As Table 2.1 indicates, this combination helped offset the impact of both the GEC and later austerity. Respondents explained that local fiscal policy was governed not by the doctrines of austere neoliberalism, but Keynesian commitments exemplified by the decision to loosen cyclical rules for borrowing (discussed further in Chapter 3). Despite national budget cuts to local government and slow growth, the vocabulary of austerity did not resonate with the prevailing growth mentality of a governing regime also able to employ some counter-cyclical measures.

If the economy of Nantes was relatively resilient to the GEC and the political upheavals that followed, it was nevertheless embroiled in struggles to define ongoing socio-economic and political crises. The most intense effects of the GEC fell on disadvantaged black and minority ethnic neighbourhoods, like Bellevue, where household incomes fell and employment opportunities were sparse (Griggs and Howarth, 2015). The word décrochage has multiple contextual meanings linked to stalling or falling off. In Nantes, it was employed as a metaphor for the uncoupling of neighbourhoods from the urban growth machine. It warranted the idea that re-coupling could be accomplished through targeted cohesion/inclusion policies, rather than having to change the rules of the game itself (Griggs and Howarth, 2016).

Respondents pointed to a variety of dislocations in French society, interpreted as the multi-dimensional crises of politics, prevalent models of service delivery, and social exclusion, amounting to a looming crisis of the Republic (Griggs et al, 2020). This sensibility was validated by the explosion of the Gilets Jaunes in 2018, the durability of this phenomenon, and national strike waves of late 2019 and early 2020. As in Leicester, 'crisis' was not vocalised in the dominant governing strategies at the city or metropolitan levels. It was rather deflected downwards to neighbourhoods and upwards to the state, the latter reflected in the abysmal poll ratings of outgoing President Hollande in 2016, plunging support for the French Socialist Party, the electoral threat of the far right (not prominent in Nantes), and the almost immediate nose-dive in support for the avowed centrist President Emanuel Macron, elected in May 2017 and subsequently engulfed in multiple conflicts.

At the same time, the struggle against a proposed international airport development to serve the Nantes city-region, at Notre-Dame-des-Landes, became an ideological battle, challenging the growth model and further calling into question the legitimacy of the French state. Chapter 6 discusses this notably successful struggle. Prominent crisis-construals in Nantes thus faced two ways: downwards towards pockets of multiple deprivation and upwards towards maladies afflicting the Republic, away from a city insulated by governance strategies linked to economic resilience, the system Ayrault and the Nantes game. Subsequent chapters discuss tensions in this strategy to compartmentalise and externalise crises orthogonal to neoliberal austerity, and suggestions that the Nantes Game was becoming vulnerable to re-politicisation (Griggs and Howarth, 2020).

The vocabularies of austerity had still less resonance in Greater Dandenong. Like other cities, it experienced longer-term economic turbulence including the loss of blue-collar jobs, labour market deregulation and wage stagnation (Hutchens and Jericho, 2018). According to the Development Victoria agency (n.d.), 'Dandenong was once the social and economic centre of Melbourne's south-east.

However, during the 1990s and early 2000s, competition from neighbouring areas resulted in reduced investment in retail, entertainment, and amenity infrastructure'.[4]

Henderson, Sullivan and Gleeson (2020) argue that a form of 'economic rationalism' is pervasive in mainstream Australian politics, and Greater Dandenong. This term refers to an ethos of 'fiscal conservatism', consensus around a logic of restraint but with tonal variations among the two main political parties. Whereas Liberals are more inclined to restrain public spending and promote market-based approaches, Labor governments tend to be more interventionist. Municipalities in Australia are weak, and significant funding decisions affecting cities are made by the federal government and states, in much the same way as they are in Canada and the US.

Australian business leaders were unsettled by the GEC, leading to a slow-down in investment. Rather than austerity, however, the federal government embarked on a substantial stimulus (Armingeon, 2012), including helicopter money distributed directly to citizens. Australia's positioning in the South Pacific region and economic relations with Asia, particularly China, provided additional insulation from the GEC. Exceptionally, until COVID-19, it had not suffered a technical recession since the early 1980s (Fenna, 2013).

Shortly before the research commenced, then Liberal PM Tony Abbott attempted to introduce a full-blooded austerity programme to Australia. However, many of the measures were blocked, and Abbott was ousted in an internal coup in September 2015 (a frequent occurrence in Australian politics). Hence, Greater Dandenong was not exposed to the austerity envisioned by Abbott. Though market-friendly and underpinned by a private sector-led growth model, the politics of 'fiscal conservatism' were imbued with the ethos of prudence rather than a radical ethos of retrenchment and restructuring. A state official commented (Henderson et al, 2020: 128),

> austerity is a term that is talked about by people in Europe, we think about it more as a heavily constrained fiscal outlook where there is largely a flat line or negative growth in discretionary spending because revenue isn't growing. This combines with increasing service delivery pressures (for example, with ageing population) to create the constrained fiscal environment.

This quote captures a prominent narrative to the effect that there is a growing structural imbalance between public service capacity and public service need (Cucca and Ranci, 2017). A central focus of the Greater Dandenong study was the long-term urban revitalisation project launched in 2006 by the then, and now once again, Labor-led state of Victoria. From the standpoint of post-GEC politics in the other cities, its very existence presents a striking contrast with austere neoliberalism. As Chapter 5 highlights, neither fiscal conservatism nor neoliberalisation fully captures the governance story of Greater Dandenong. Moreover, the combination of sustained growth and revitalisation meant that the crisis construals operating in other cities made little sense there. Most respondents were optimistic about the future, but at the same time anticipated threats. Popular memes including 'debt crisis', 'migration crisis' or 'budget crisis' (Henderson et al, 2016), echoed the notion that needs and demands were rising in a context of revenue stagnation and population growth, partly engendered by the state of Victoria's decision in 2016 to impose a rate cap on local authorities (see Chapter 3). These crisis construals tended to be future-oriented, however, and, despite closures in the automotive industry, unemployment rates in the area were falling in 2018–19. Consequently, Greater Dandenong was positioned very differently than the other seven cities in relation to the neoliberalisation–crisis–austerity problematic. It was not immune to fiscal pressures, but the need for restraint was construed in terms of prudence rather than ideological austerity.

Conclusion

The political histories and traditions incubated in cities over decades, or longer, shape the economic impact of the GEC as a local and global phenomenon, its construals and the contemporary politics of austerian idealism, austerian realism, *rigueur*, prudence and fiscal conservatism. In Athens, Dublin and Leicester, the confluence between the GEC, crisis-construals, austerity and the qualitative radicalisation of harsh disciplinary forms of neoliberalisation were very clear. In all three cities, be it with enthusiasm or pragmatic regret, governmental institutions were committed to delivering austerity and regressive local state restructuring and rescaling. Whereas austerity was a huge challenge in the governance of Leicester, it sought to mitigate crisis-talk in favour of the managed transition to an entrepreneurial city model, warranted by the widespread dispositions of 'austerian realism', a counterpart to the (now formally abandoned) 'austerian idealism' of the UK government. In Dublin, construals of excess and guilt were employed to depoliticise the crisis and justify Ireland's austerity programme. Athens never fully exited the GEC, and in that city the crisis construal that settled the course after 2015 was the perceived choice between a breach with Europe, or austerity with all its implications for the local state. Baltimore is where the most elementally brutal forms of racialised neoliberalism were found. However, neither the GEC nor austerity as a specific policy regime affected a trajectory the city had been on for decades. Crisis-construals in City Hall were employed to drive it further down this path.

Barcelona deviates from this pattern since 2015, primarily because years of anti-austerity mobilisation propelled a movement-based coalition into office in 2015, with a weaker coalition regaining office in 2019. Barcelona en Comú initiated a struggle to transform the political economy of the city, discussed in Chapters 5–7. The City Council employed notions of crisis and austerity against neoliberalism, valorising efficiency, prudence and restraint. It was notable that in none of the eight cities did respondents cite the abundance of wealth in capitalist societies as an argument against austerity.

Montréal was not severely impacted by the fallout from the GEC. The challenge it faces has more to do with the limits of its development model over a much longer period. It has been subjected by the government of Québec to a radicalised form of disciplinary neoliberalisation. This is warranted by the discourse of *rigueur*, a concept moderated by governance actors in Montréal, who accepted the case for restraint and efficiency but viewed the Québec approach as ideologically motivated. Yet both the radicalised and moderated versions of *rigueur* rest on variants of economic rationalism. The moderated version was also found in Dandenong, the city least impacted by the GEC and its aftermath. Australia privileged 'fiscal conservatism', but this did not have the radical and disciplinary connotations of Québecer *rigueur* or European austerity. In Dandenong, it operated alongside a market-focused strategy for urban revitalisation, where crisis-threats were recognised, but not of immediate concern.

It was only in Nantes, finally, that scarcity logics were challenged. The city and Metropole proved relatively resilient to the GEC, and national austerity measures were only beginning to cause problems at the city level as the research concluded. Though Nantes was exposed to austerity and experienced slow growth, respondents within the local state depicted it as economically vibrant. As an entrepreneurial city competing with other cities, the political economy of Nantes was hybridised, employing Keynesian ideas alongside a longstanding strategy for (sustainable) market-led growth and participatory governance. Prominent figures sought to deflect any sense that national austerity signified a crisis for Nantes, perhaps with diminishing success (Chapter 5).

Four further points conclude the chapter. First, despite the uneven grip of austerity and the distinctiveness of crisis-construals, variations on neoliberal economic rationalism were pervasive, brought into relief particularly by the partial outlier discourses in Barcelona and Nantes. It took four main forms: overt ideological commitment to austerity or neoliberal retrenchment (Athens, Baltimore, Dublin and Québec), regretful but diligent compliance with austerity ('austerian realism' in Leicester), the validation of restraint (Barcelona, Dandenong and Montréal) and boosterish confidence in the urban growth machine (Nantes).

Second, if crisis is something that happens to cities as part of the tempo of capitalist boom–slump cycles, it is also a weapon employed by political actors in and above the city to justify, oppose, or downplay austere neoliberalism. Effective construal is as important in making, owning, muting and deflecting urban crises as the intra- and extra-urban pathologies of neoliberal capitalism that gave rise to GEC (Jessop, 2015). How adeptly cities construe crisis, and take ownership of its politics, is one determinant of governability.

Third, the concepts of variegated, hybridised, social and disciplinary neoliberalisation explored in Chapter 1, continue to capture a great deal of the urban experience in the post-GEC period. In addition, the research points to dynamic temporalities of neoliberalisation: fast, slow and static, forwards, sideways and reverse. Within cities, by extension, spheres of public action do not always move in parallel, but at different speeds and sometimes in pursuit of different political and economic principles as we note particularly in Barcelona and Montréal where political control was fragmented by tier and function. Furthermore, even within a global political economy long dominated by neoliberalism, political and institutional impediments and oppositions mean that there are vast terrains of urban political and economic space yet to be subsumed to it (Gibson-Graham, 2006). Although all the cities passed through the GEC with some pre-existing inheritance of crisis, neoliberalisation and associated restructurings, subsequent change has not everywhere been merely incremental. In Athens and Leicester, for example, the research pointed to qualitative radicalisation: a step-change bringing these two European cities closer to the localist and privatist characteristics of US cities, like Baltimore (Davies and Pill, 2012; Davies et al, 2020; Pill, 2020).

This conclusion suggests that disclosing where cities sit in relation to prominent concepts in the urban lexicon is useful, while the de-centred case study method shows that it is possible to capture significant inter- and intra-urban nuances and tonalities in doing so. It also, finally, introduces an initial note of caution to conjunctural analyses positing that we are entering a global phase of late neoliberalism or late entrepreneurialism, augurs of Gramsci's interregnum. This notion might be problematic because although many of us have lived with neoliberalism our entire adult lives, it is still relatively new within the arc of capitalist development. As the research shows, neoliberalism is less highly evolved in some cities than others, others, like Baltimore, where rounds of disciplinary neoliberalisation occur in endless increments: more and more of the same thing. This was not so in Athens or Leicester, where the GEC and austerity policies were ushering in qualitative transformations, or in Barcelona, Dandenong and Nantes where neoliberal austerity has been contained, moderated and hybridised.

One question, then, is whether the theoretical scope, in many cities, for further radicalised and qualitative transformations can be actualised through national and urban political strategies – including crisis-making – that lend new impetus to entrepreneurialism, and by extension to neoliberalism. A tentative suggestion is that it might be possible, particularly outside the USA, which provided Peck (2017a, 2017b) with his primary analytical compass and empirical exemplars; or rather that the answer will be found as much in politics as in structurally determined economic trends. The cautionary tone and many qualifications in Peck's own analysis further point to this possibility. Chapter 8 revisits these issues. Chapter 3 turns to the politics of state rescaling.

3

Austerity and State Rescaling

Introduction

One of the most important, perhaps neglected facets of urban regime analysis is the relationship between tiers of government and the functional and territorial jurisdictions of public and quasi-governmental authorities. These facets overlap in that relations between tiers of the state intersect with the territorial jurisdictions of municipalities, city-regions and other public agencies operating in urban areas. These, in turn, are more or less densely consolidated, concentrated, dispersed, poly-nucleated or splintered – not only in terms of physical agglomeration, density and infrastructure, but also administration, jurisdiction and politics (Skelcher, 2005; Graham and Marvin, 2001; Keil, 2017). Moreover, the capacity of local authorities to govern, limit or control market economies has long pre-occupied urbanists concerned with the dynamics of capital mobility and place-dependency (Cox and Mair, 1988). The perceived limits on urban political power is why few conventional city leaders dare eschew the quest for attractiveness, even when a propitious mix of high wage, labour intensive, environmentally friendly and spatially equitable employment is a pipedream. These issues cut across the eight cities in ways that impinge upon the character of urban political (dis)orders, governability and the parameters of collaborative governance.

The story of austerity is entwined with experiments in city-regionalism, authoritarianism, fiscal and political centralisation and downloading or scalar dumping from upper tiers (Peck, 2012). Interpenetrating institutional, territorial and scalar restructurings have significant implications for politics and governing cultures, and relations between local states and citizens. This chapter therefore focuses on the evolving powers and liabilities accruing to sub-national

Table 3.1: National local government spending as a percentage of general government spending

	National LG spending as % of general govt 2016 (OECD)
Australia	6.5
Canada	20.8
France	19.8
Greece	7.1
Ireland	7.6
Spain	13.7
UK	24.2
USA	No data

governments in the period since the GEC (Ward, 2010), read through revenue streams, fiscal rules and changes to spatial and jurisdictional capacities. Chapters 4 and 5 bring corporate and civil society actors into the discussion together with the horizontal and cross-sectoral dimensions of urban regime politics. The politics of 'rescaling from below' is discussed in Chapters 6 and 7 (Smart and Lin, 2007).

The analysis of state rescaling draws from OECD[1] and Eurostat data[2] to highlight rule changes impacting, mostly negatively, on the effective political autonomy of local governments. The OECD highlights four distinct elements of local government finance, which affect the ability of municipalities to mitigate or counter measures from other tiers of government. The first is the relative strength of local government within its national system. Table 3.1 shows how dramatically this varies across the eight cities, with some countries channelling a relatively high percentage of general government spending through local government, others a very low percentage. The second element is what the OECD calls 'revenue autonomy'. This refers to the proportion of revenues raised, respectively, through local taxation versus transfers from other tiers, for example fiscal equalisation schemes and grants. High revenue equalisation is defined as low revenue autonomy. The 'autonomy' depends on the taxable wealth and income in a given area, and the formal and informal rule regimes governing revenue collection and expenditure. Third, for the OECD, 'fiscal autonomy' is the extent to which a local authority can devise its own tax regimes, which partly determine its revenue autonomy. Again, the 'autonomy' accruing from fiscal powers depends on urban economic vitality and taxability, and the extent to which higher tiers of government determine spending patterns through transfers, ring-fencing and delineating statutory and non-statutory functions.

A fourth element is the rules governing sub-national and municipal borrowing: the extent to which, and in which domains, local authorities can incur debts or deficits. The so-called 'golden rule' for local government spending, coined by Musgrave (1959), is that authorities can borrow for investment in capital projects but not for recurrent spending. As explained later, most cities were already observing this rule, but austerity brought local governments in Greece and Spain further into line with it. Equally, as the bankruptcy of Detroit famously attests (Schindler, 2016), freedom to take on liabilities is no freedom at all if a lender cannot be found, credit ratings agencies are hostile and interest rates high, and there are insufficient revenues to service debts without detriment to other functions; such as where revenue autonomy is high, but fiscal autonomy is low. On the other hand, where fiscal autonomy is high, the local fiscal base is healthy and wealthy, credit ratings are favourable and interest rates low, recurring deficits might theoretically be employed sustainably to mitigate other downward pressures on spend. Such options are not open to the cities afflicted by economic decline, disinvestment and austerity, low growth, poor credit ratings and high interest rates, corporate flight and rising debt. The combinations of these elements can differ significantly within countries and regions as well as between them. Together, they determine the effective political autonomy or political capacity of local governments, understood as the discretion they can exercise in deciding how much to spend, from what sources, on what, and when, thereby having the option to deviate from the political priorities of upper tier authorities. From an institutional point of view, in other words, effective political autonomy depends in part on powers and liabilities deriving from fiscal and revenue autonomy, partly on the functional and spatial jurisdictions of elected authorities and partly on the extent to which actionable decisions can be made by elected local governments about priorities for spending within and across statutory and non-statutory functions in their purview.

The financial and juridical squeeze on local government

Greece has a weak local government system (Chorianopoulos, 2012) and according to the OECD, it remains (with Ireland) among the most centralised fiscal systems in the world. All subnational government accounts for a mere 3.5 per cent of GDP, or 7.1 per cent of general government spending. In addition to national austerity measures increasing 'revenue autonomy' by reducing central government grants, the so-called 'Kallikratis Reform' of 2010 launched a major round of fiscal and territorial restructuring, linked to the Greek austerity drive (Chorianopoulos and Tselepi, 2020). Kallikratis dealt primarily with territorial rationalisation (see later), but also rolled out tax reforms, including caps on municipal borrowing. The borrowing cap led Athens City Council to suspend all investment in physical infrastructures between 2011 and 2013 (Chorianopoulos, 2016). Greece also established the Observatory for Financial Autonomy of the Local Government Organizations 'to ensure realistic and balanced budgeting in local authorities' and curtail debt. According to the OECD, outstanding sub-national governmental debt as a proportion of GDP was very low, at 1.3 per cent. For Athens, this regime squeezed political capacity by increasing revenue autonomy, and reducing the fiscal and borrowing autonomies that might be employed to compensate; measures that were supported by Mayor Kaminis (Chapter 2).

A similar nationally mandated squeeze occurred in Barcelona. Spain is a decentralised unitary state, with a system of autonomous regional communities. These decide the organisation of local governments, within the framework of national law. OECD figures for Spain highlight the proportions of expenditure going directly to local government: 5.8 per cent of GDP and 13.7 per cent of total government expenditure, compared with 21.2 per cent of GDP and 48 per cent of total government expenditure allocated to all sub-national governments. This balance arises from the devolved government settlement after the death of Dictator Franco and the establishment of democracy.

Barcelona City Council was considered to be in relatively good financial health (Blanco et al, 2020: 32). However, over and above other austerity measures the most significant attack on fiscal autonomy came under the Troika's austerity mandate. A constitutional reform was adopted in 2011 to underpin fiscal consolidation targets for all Spanish administrations. Moreover, the Organic Law on Budgetary Stability and Financial Sustainability enacted in 2012 introduced a structural balanced budget rule and debt ceilings for all levels of governments, as well as tighter rules governing expenditure. The infamous 'Montoro laws' for the Rationalisation and Sustainability of Local Administration compelled local authorities to use any financial surplus for debt repayment and prohibited them from re-employing private sector workers in re-municipalisation projects, creating an incentive for workers to oppose them (Miró, 2019).

Echoing Greece, an 'independent' authority for fiscal responsibility was set up to monitor and report on compliance. Debt to GDP ratios in Spain are relatively high, mostly accruing to the autonomous communities (regions) at 29.3 per cent, compared with 5.7 per cent for local government. In the context of the new rules, squeezing regional debt further intensified the impact of austerity in Spanish cities (Davies and Blanco, 2017). According to Eurostat, 'revenue autonomy' has also increased, likely due to declining transfers from central government, pointing to a further erosion in effective political capacity. For Barcelona, like Athens, the financial and legal squeeze was a harsh, disciplinary facet of austere neoliberalism and one of the major constraints on 'new municipalism' discussed in later chapters.

UK municipalities face a very different but perhaps even more challenging reform. There is no regional tier in the UK, and according to OECD, 11.3 per cent of UK GDP is spent through local government, 24.2 per cent of general government spending. UK local government is renowned for its 'culture of dependency' (Davies and Blanco, 2017: 1533) following a succession of centralising national governments. UK local authorities have been subject to central rate capping since the mid-1980s, significantly limiting fiscal autonomy. They have been compelled to balance recurrent spending budgets since the 1960s. Central government decides by how much local authorities can increase residential property taxes in any given year and determines the 'rateable value' of businesses across the country. Some limited devolution of tax-raising powers has occurred. In 2015, the UK government introduced the 'Adult Social Care Precept', allowing authorities to add a ring-fenced 2 per cent levy to Council Tax bills (Cromarty, 2019). In addition, it removed the long-standing cap on borrowing against local authority housing revenue accounts for home-building, though it immediately introduced compensatory constraints by raising interest rates on loans for public works (Curry, 2020). Austerity imposed by central government cannot be compensated by additional borrowing or greatly increasing local taxes (municipalities can incur debt to finance capital investments). Some UK local authorities faced threats of bankruptcy as a result, further exacerbated by COVID-19.

During the second half of the 2010s, moreover, a major restructuring of local government revenues was rolled out, qualitatively changing the character of municipal government in England (Crewe, 2016). The national fiscal equalisation scheme, the Revenue Support Grant, was being phased out and municipalities were becoming ever-more dependent on local business and residential property taxes, as well as user fees and charges. Local business taxes were also moving away, at a slower rate, from equalisation towards localisation. The restructuring leaves local government heavily reliant on local revenues, but with very limited fiscal autonomy and, for poor cities like Leicester, a meagre tax base. Without a substantial, durable and taxable boom in the 'real' economy or a radical change in national and local governing priorities, Leicester, with its weak labour market and harsh deprivation, is vulnerable to a US-style race to the bottom. The new regime may spawn a handful of self-confident urban growth machines, but many towns and cities will lose, becoming public service and growth deserts. A recognisable form of traditional full-service municipalism survived Thatcherism and New Labour. However, the signs were that it would not survive 'the age of austerity' (Association for Public Service Excellence, 2016; Crewe, 2016).

Montréal is under different kinds of financial stress. Like the USA and Spain, Canada is a federal system where constitutionally enshrined provinces determine the organisation of local governments. Like Baltimore and Greater Dandenong (discussed later), Montréal subsists 'within the realm of provincial omnipotence' (Lightbody, 2006: 39, cited in Hamel and Autin, 2017: 165). Municipal powers thus vary between provinces. Government expenditure is highly devolved in Canada, amounting to 31.1 per cent of GDP, and 76.5 per cent of general government spending. Figures for local government are 8.4 per cent and 20.8 per cent respectively.

Prior to the election of federal 'anti-austerity' President Phillipe Trudeau in 2014, the Liberal government introduced balanced budget legislation, reflecting the high levels of debt accruing, in particular to the provinces (61 per cent of GDP in 2013). Subnational government debt ratios were the highest of all OECD members, 85 per cent of it in the form of provincial debt incurred, for example, through servicing bond issues which are the bane of any public institution having to supplement tax revenues and grants with private investment. Municipal debt, it said, was moderate by international standards. Following the Golden Rule, municipalities are prohibited from incurring deficits in recurrent spend. The debt figures provide some context for Couillard's *rigueur* policy discussed in Chapter 2. The division of powers between federal, provincial and municipal tiers leave the latter in a weak position. Chapter 5 discusses centralising forces within the provincial administration, but we saw no direct changes in the structures of local government finance in Montréal, however, urban public services under the jurisdiction of city and province were squeezed, partly on account of ideology, partly debt servicing obligations on upper tier authorities, and partly the increased pressure on municipal and voluntary services arising from the former. At least the debt from the 1976 Olympics, the so-called 'big owe', was finally paid off in 2006 (Moser et al, 2019: 127).

Like Canada, the United States is founded on a constitution sharing sovereignty between the federal and state tiers. Powers not explicitly reserved to the federal level are devolved to states. Federal taxes do not devolve either to states or municipalities, so there is no national equalisation mechanism that could be abolished. As in Australia and Canada, the structure and fiscal rules for local government are determined by states under home rule provisions, again making local authorities 'creatures' of their states (Bliss, 2018: 72). The rules vary from state to state, including the ceilings, prohibitions and conditions on deficits and debt, enacted most dramatically in the post-GEC period by the bankruptcy of Detroit (Eisinger, 2014). In most states, local government must maintain a balanced operating budget. In addition, long-term debt is usually permitted for capital projects, another familiar theme among the eight cities in keeping with the 'golden rule'. Subnational government expenditure accounted for 18.6 per cent of annual GDP, and 48.1 per cent of general government revenues in 2013, though OECD data is not available for local government. Subnational debt is high at 29.4 per cent of GDP, predominantly incurred through bond issues (60 per cent) and pension liabilities (25 per cent).

Debt-servicing lies at the heart of continuous public service retrenchment in Baltimore (Chapter 2). The state of Maryland has a variety of laws de-limiting debt and deficits, with specific ordinances for the city of Baltimore (Department of Legislative Services, 2016). The City Charter requires it to run a balanced budget, and prioritise funding the payment of principal and interest on municipal debt.[3] The city was burdened with a per-capita debt estimated at $5172 in Baltimore City and counties, levels which by 2013 had increased by nearly 30 per cent since the GEC (Department of Legislative Services, 2017). It held an unfunded pension liability of $2546 per capita that year (explaining the pensions 'crisis' described in Chapter 2). Despite the continuous squeeze, however, the post-GEC period did not see any radical reconfiguration of fiscal rules. The neoliberal orthodoxy of the city's leadership, which had maintained a 'conservative approach to all aspects of debt management' since 1990 (City of Baltimore, Maryland, 2018: ix), damps down the potential for inter-jurisdictional conflicts over the trajectory of continuous retrenchment. The main impact of the GEC on municipal finance was rather the increased debt liabilities translating into further downward pressures on other spend, curtailing the notional political capacity of the city, should an anti-austerity Mayor ever be elected.

Ireland is one of the most centralised countries among OECD members. Local authorities have very limited spending responsibilities amounting to 4 per cent of national GDP or 7.6 per cent of national government spend. They can borrow for capital expenditure, but only with the approval of central government. In 2004, Ireland introduced a limit of €200 million for new annual borrowing across the whole local government sector, a mere 0.1 per cent of annual GDP. As a result, local government debt is well below the OECD average. There was no significant change in fiscal rules linked to post-GEC austerity. However, Ireland introduced a range of extractive charges as part of its bailout agreement with the Troika, including a local property tax in 2013. This is a banded tax resulting in much higher payments for most households. Some of the revenue goes into city budgets, the rest into the national equalisation scheme. The water charge proved to be the most politically contentious of these measures, provoking the rebellion discussed in Chapter 6.

In France, subnational government spending amounted to 11.9 per cent of GDP, or 19.8 per cent of general government expenditure. Sub-national government debt was 9.4 per cent of general government debt, and of this only 4.9 per cent was incurred through bond financing. Although revenue spending must balance year-on-year under the 'golden rule', capital borrowing is more flexible than some other countries. According to the OECD, subnational governments were able to borrow without approval. In 2015, due to the national spending squeeze, revenue transfers from the centre accounted for 25 per cent of Nantes Métropole's funding, down from 30 per cent in 2012 (Griggs and Howarth, 2015). Moreover, Sarkozy's 2010 reform abolished the local business tax (taxe professionelle), replacing it with the 'contribution économique territoriale' (CET). The new tax was capped at a lower level than the taxe professionale and also exempted productive investments such as machines and equipment. According to Béal and Pinson (2015: 416 fn), the reform put local government finances under further pressure, while manipulating 'the parameters of local governments' fiscal revenues for political consideration or to reduce the public debt'.

In response to financial pressures, Nantes introduced performance and efficiency contracts between service units, seeking €7 million savings in 2016, as well as increases to local taxation, including the first rises to housing tax (taxe d'habitation) since 2011 and property tax (taxe foncière bâti) since 2012. To further counter fiscal pressures, Nantes

Métropole made use of borrowing autonomy to raise its debt allowance from four to seven years, measured in terms of the time required to clear liabilities if all savings were allocated to the task (Griggs and Howarth, 2015). Hence, while the language of austerity was eschewed, and the city had greater capacity to moderate the squeeze than others, Nantes was by no means exempt from downloading or the mandatory rebalancing of local tax burdens away from business towards citizens.

Under the Australian constitution, the Commonwealth government is the central governing body within a three-tier federal system. All other constitutional powers accrue to the state or provincial level, responsible for health, education, transport, urban planning and agriculture. Australian local governments are, like their US and Canadian counterparts, 'creatures' of the provincial tier (Stilwell and Troy, 2000: 926). The OECD indicates that 16.9 per cent of GDP was channelled through sub-national governments, 6.5 per cent at the metropolitan level (Table 2.2). The only local government tax was the land property tax (shared with states). This accounted for some 37 per cent of national local government revenue in 2013.

In this context, the decision by the Labor government of Victoria to impose rate-capping from 2016, the so-called 'Fair Go', signified a further squeeze on Greater Dandenong's limited political autonomy. In preceding years, Dandenong City Council had been raising the tax by around 5.5 per cent, anticipating that the cap would come in at this level. However, it was imposed at 2.25 per cent in 2018–19. According to the city, the harshness of the cap created a shortfall of $45 million in anticipated revenues over the next five-year period. The City Council expected the shortfall to slow infrastructure investments, because they generate recurrent operating costs that can no longer be offset by raising property taxes (City of Greater Dandenong, 2018: 1). Although transfers from higher tiers of government remained stable, and the municipal budget had risen in previous years (Chapter 2), the cap signified a loss of effective political capacity for an already restricted local government tier.

Austerity and functional jurisdiction

Evidence gathered across the eight cities was patchy in relation to jurisdictional issues, but nevertheless sufficient to suggest that with more-or-less draconian financial constraints come devolved responsibilities. In Athens, under the Kallikratis reform, sub-national governments were delegated new roles in the governance of environment, life quality, social protection, education, culture and sports, agriculture, breeding and fisheries. In a fiscally neutral transfer, these responsibilities would increase jurisdictional autonomy for local government. However, in the context of austerity and statutory ring-fencing, they created further financial strains. For example, new municipal responsibility for social protection was not accompanied by additional powers of taxation, the removal of ring-fencing on grant transfers, or flexibility with debt-obligations. Devolved responsibilities for statutory services simply added to pressure on other functions, particularly in the discretionary sphere. According to a politician in the city of Athens, however, 'clearly the crisis offered a window of opportunity to the national authorities to transfer responsibilities to lower tiers of government. It's a "now you take it 'cause I can't do it any more" logic... but it's also an opportunity for the municipalities to get stronger' (Chorianopoulos, 2016). Those optimistic about the city's future, in the mode of Mayor Kaminis, interpreted responsibilisation as a challenge, but potentially empowering in better times.

A similar reform took place in Ireland, with Dublin given new responsibilities in planning, local and community development and support for economic development and enterprise. However, respondents were sceptical that these measures were much more than cosmetic – for example arguing that 'reform means cuts' or 'austerity was actually done under the heading of reform' (politicians, cited in Gaynor, 2017). Moreover, respondents suggested that reforms had done nothing to empower or revitalise the moribund City Council. Chapter 6 explains how the city's housing crisis became a lightning rod for further mobilisations, in the afterglow of the water wars. Part of the reason for the crisis was the failure of public–private partnerships to deliver new stock, and the inability of the City Council to respond to market failure, because it was not allowed to build houses itself. In a different resource configuration devolved responsibilities could empower local government, but not under Ireland's disciplinary mode of austere neoliberalism.

In addition to squeezing the resources and powers of local governments, and downloading responsibilities, higher tiers of government reorganised themselves in ways that further concentrate power in authorities upscale. Respondents in Montréal highlighted power grabs by provincial government, pointing to the Ministry of Finance as the centralising force behind *rigueur*. According to one public official, 'I think that what we see more of is the omnipresence of the Treasury in the decisions, the Ministry of Finance: less freedom of action for ministers in specific sectors of intervention.' A voluntary sector respondent explained some of the devices employed in controlling payments to contractors (Hamel and Keil, 2018):

> it's the State within the State. It's always been like this: The Ministry of Finance always had an impact on how the payments are paid. Except that there was still some respect between the Ministry of Finance and the Council of the Ministers. ... Well the Ministry of Finance would set rules and the ministries would apply those rules. But the ministers had some freedom of action. Now, we're told... sectoral ministers tell us: 'Here, I have no choice. It's the Ministry of Finance which validates the payment.'

Accordingly, the Québec Ministry of Finance exercised significant control over where and what to cut. Most of the respondents saw these mechanisms as authoritarian, implemented without meaningful consultation or collaboration with affected parties. New laws implemented by the Couillard administration ripped up localised accountability and established governance mechanisms in healthcare, while further concentrating authority upscale. Said a trade unionist, 'we're in front of a government which is austere but also has an authoritarian attitude. When we look at it, the way certain laws are drafted, like the project Law 10 that creates new powers, that transforms Barrette [Minister of Health and Social Services] into a super-minister, damn, this is stunning' (Hamel and Keil, 2018). At the same time, municipalities were exposed to direct and indirect increases in responsibility for welfare, through having to manage the local impacts of *rigueur*. Given the centrality of provincial power in the political life of the city, these measures were blamed for undermining collaborative traditions, discussed in Chapter 5.

Respondents in Barcelona said the City Council had greater room for manoeuvre than other Catalan and Spanish municipalities, because of the city's economic wealth and special powers conferred (also on Madrid) under the 1999 municipal charter in relation to welfare, education, housing and health. However, in addition to the financial and legal squeeze on municipal competence discussed earlier, Barcelona City Council faced significant jurisdictional constraints, with limited competence in relation to tourism, employment, housing, refugees, energy and public procurement (EU single market rules played a role here). Jurisdictional constraints obviously matter more for authorities whose politics are out of line with those of higher tier authorities, than for those which are compliant (Blanco et al, 2020: 29–31).

Starting in 2006, the Revitalise Central Dandenong programme received funding of $290 million, mostly from the state of Victoria. As part of the programme rollout, Victoria transferred planning powers from Greater Dandenong upwards, to counter perceived parochialism, decision-making bias and development obstacles (Henderson et al, 2017). However, Chapter 5 explains how despite the loss of formal planning powers, the city exerted softer forms of influence over the politics and delivery of the revitalisation programme (Henderson et al, 2020).

Austerity and territorial jurisdiction

City-regionalism has become a major policy priority in many parts of the world, as well as a rich subject of research (for example, Jonas and Moisio, 2018). A key insight emerging from this study was that although city-regionalism is fashionable with global and local elites, collaborations and combines remain difficult to assemble, whatever the national government incentives or perceived benefits in terms of agglomeration, consolidation, efficiency, enhanced competitiveness or indeed equality. When compared with the other cities, Nantes provides a useful contrast, because it was the most strongly consolidated metropolitan region emerging from considerable experience and decades of inter-communal cooperation, supported by local actors and legislated by national government.

France is classified as a centralised political system by OECD, but local government is famously multi-tiered and organised into nearly 36,000 small municipalities, constituting some 41 per cent of all municipalities in the EU. To bring some coordination to this diffuse system, the French state gives strong support to inter-municipal cooperation. OECD recorded 2145 inter-municipal arrangements generating their own tax revenues, forming what it called a 'quasi-fourth subnational level'. In 2014, national government created a newly rationalised system of 13 regions, and conferred new powers on the 15 largest métropoles, including Nantes. Comprising the city and 23 other communes, the Nantes Métropole is governed by a council of 97 directly elected councillors, with an executive of 24 comprising the communal Mayors as vice-presidents, the City Mayor, Johanna Rolland as President (Griggs and Howarth, 2015).

In the context of a system encouraging inter-communal cooperation, the creation of Nantes Métropole did not come out of the blue. Griggs,

Howarth and Feandeiro (2020: 96–97) record how the City Council under Ayrault pursued metropolitan ambitions through the 1990s, and progressively coordinated policies and shared services with other communes to create a de-facto métropole. Consolidating this process in the national restructuring of 2015 reinforced city-regional powers in economic growth and competitiveness, research and innovation, urban development, physical infrastructure including transport, and environment and sustainability. The Métropole levies its own taxes, and is supported through the national government's Pacte Métropolitain, and resources from member communes.

Echoing concerns about the impact of restructuring on community identities and democracy in Dublin (discussed later), however, the Métropole has been criticised for concentrating power in the hands of communal Mayors, who make up the Executive. The system arguably creates an institutional layering effect, de-politicising development policy through inter-mayoral deal-making a step removed from direct citizen, councillor or communal influence (Griggs and Howarth, 2015).

If Nantes is a good example of metropolitanisation consolidating the city's position as a development dynamo, the study of Barcelona showed that this is a challenge for the anti-austerity left. In Spain, the Rationalisation and Sustainability of Local Administration (LRSAL) bill sought, as part of the national austerity drive led by the Partido Popular, to promote municipal mergers. According to Medir, Magre and Tomàs (2018: 136), the reform remained in a period of 'non-practical implementation' because local authorities and autonomous communities saw it as an imposition from the centre.

Barcelona is one of Europe's largest urban areas comprising more than 5 million people. In 2010, the Catalan parliament established the 'law of the metropolitan area of Barcelona' (MAB), setting up an entity encompassing the city and 36 surrounding municipalities, representing some 60 per cent of the metropolitan population. In the Spanish context, where there is no national drive toward metropolitanisation, the system is relatively advanced, with shared competences in planning, transport and infrastructure, water, housing and environmental services including waste. MAB also developed a non-binding strategic plan to guide municipal policy in a variety of areas (Tomàs, 2017). However, MAB subsists alongside other metropolitan authorities, notably for transport, has no direct democratic legitimacy and cannot levy taxes or make executive decisions (Tomàs, 2019).

This half-developed system means that supra-local service agreements are asymmetrical, often involving different constellations of municipalities and partners in different contracts. In the case of water, the privatised supply was contracted to a consortium involving the city and 22 other municipalities (March et al, 2019). This arrangement stymied attempts at re-municipalisation by Barcelona City Council. Similar barriers also existed for attempts to re-municipalise energy, discussed further in Chapter 5. In this instance, metropolitan collaboration was a barrier to de-neoliberalisation.

The main progressive arguments for small, powerful units of local government are related to democratic propinquity (John, 2009), whereas for larger units, if suitably endowed with resources, it is about greater political capacity and influence: potentially less granular democracy (albeit with potential for devolving authority and resources to district and neighbourhood entities), but more political power and, in theory, equity between centres and peripheries. Municipalist theory, with its libertarian socialist roots, is inherently sceptical towards upscaling and statification, instead privileging the devolution and diffusion of powers and the recuperation of marketised services at local or sub-local scales. However, March et al (2019) ask whether, in the case of water, it is desirable or practical to move towards a more devolved − arguably fragmented − system and suggest that some form of metropolitan collaboration is essential, if legal and political deadlock can be overcome (March et al, 2019: 373). In that sense, the dilemmas in governing Barcelona from the left suggest that the politics of city-regionalism are contingent, ambiguous and subject to multiple struggles (Scott, 2019).

The constitutional weakness of local government in Montréal is compounded by continuing inter-municipal fragmentation. Hill (1977) depicted the metropolitanisation of Toronto as the kind of successful venture needed to drive forward capitalist urban development, a 'mega-city' formally constituted in 1998 (Boudreau et al, 2007: 33). Montréal has followed a more tortuous path. In 2000, a municipal reform initiated by the Québec government amalgamated the 19 boroughs into a 'mega-city'. However, after a change of provincial government, a referendum in 2004 allowed the boroughs to recover some of their powers, on the condition that they participated in what is now the city's 'agglomeration council', Ville de Montréal over which Valérie Plante currently presides as Executive Mayor (she is also ex officio Mayor of the Ville Marie Borough). The mega-city was thus '"merged" and "de-merged" in short order' (Hamel and Keil, 2020: 113; also Boudreau et al, 2007). The fate of the Greater Montréal project possibly contributed to the sense of an urban political economy at the crossroads, because planning, infrastructure and economic decision-making amalgamations that might enhance its competitive position, have been thwarted by localist sentiment.

The picture in the UK was mixed. Urban areas were undertaking more-or-less formal collaborations, in some instances heading towards amalgamations. The UK government rolled out a range of 'city deals', 'devo-deals', 'Local Enterprise Partnerships' and 'combined authorities', through which funds and powers were delegated to supra-local consortia, provided they can reach agreement with the UK Treasury (Pugalis and Bentley, 2013). This was the latest chaotic phase in an ever-churning regional and city-regional policy, but oriented to driving local economic governance upscale to the city-region, or further. The most powerful city-regional entity created so far, is the Greater Manchester combined authority, presided over by a metro-Mayor, Andy Burnham, who was previously prominent in national Labour Party politics (Berry and Giovannini, 2018). The example of Leicester and Leicestershire, where political, demographic and agglomeration geographies do not favour such an arrangement, highlights the limitations of this concept, and the extent to which local government remains dependent on central government patronage and vulnerable to its political whim (Tomaney, 2016).

In 2016, Leicester and Leicestershire attempted to win government approval for a new 'combined authority' operating across city, county and districts of Leicestershire, to consolidate existing local economic development and infrastructure resources and draw devolved powers from the centre. The government rejected the proposal, because the city and county refused to countenance its demand for a new sub-regional 'Metro-Mayor'. Had Leicester agreed to this model, the City Mayor would have lost economic development powers, leaving his Office hollowed out and Leicester city beholden to a supervening authority with potentially different priorities. Said a public official working in local economic development 'unfortunately we are in one of the areas that is not wanting to have a directly elected Mayor, so our allocation of money is much less I think than it otherwise would have been' (Davies and Bua, 2016). As Copus, Roberts and Wall (2017: 180) concluded, after decades of central manipulation, experimentation and austerity, English local government was still at the wrong end of an 'abusive relationship' with the centre.

City-regionalism and combined authorities are but one way in which local government is becoming more remote from citizens, though the Brexit impasse also stymied progress. Austerity, combined with the ongoing government squeeze on non-statutory public services, suggests that local government is headed towards a model where the median municipality is larger than at present (units of local government are already very large), delivers little apart from statutory social services, and passes such economic development powers as it possesses to an even larger regional or sub-regional entity. The County of Leicestershire was considering alternative proposals to abolish the two-tier county-district structure and put a 'unitary county' in its place, around the city of Leicester. The rationale was to save money and create local government arrangements to counterbalance the neighbouring West Midlands regional combined authority (Robinson, 2018). The proposal reflected the national zeitgeist for downloading responsibility to scaled-up super-authorities in return for modest devolved powers and resources.

Over and above uneven developments in city-regionalism, there were other moves towards municipal mergers and amalgamations, linked to austerity, in Athens, Barcelona and Dublin. In Greece, the Kallikratis reform arose from the first austerity memorandum, though it was in line with what the PASOK government wanted to achieve anyway and expected to reduce national public spending as a proportion of GDP by 0.5 per cent (Ladi, 2014: 200). Kallikratis halved the number of municipalities in the Athens metropolitan area. It also transformed the regional administrative tier into a political one, assigning responsibilities for transport and urban planning (Chorianopoulos, 2012). However, policymaking powers were not devolved because the centre did not want to create obstacles to privatisation. Metropolitan governing powers therefore remained weak.

Ireland also went through dramatic local government restructuring. The country used to have a two-tier government system. The constitution now provides for local authorities organised into one tier following the abolition of town and borough councils in 2014, part of an 'efficiency' drive warranted by austerity. According to G. Murphy (2015: 555), residents 'fearful that their community will die around them' interpreted the rationalisation of local government as an attack on their identities and denial of democratic voice. It highlighted the intersection between territorial rationalisation, municipal upscaling and the hollowing out of political identity on one hand, and the downloading of the costs of the GEC onto local authorities and citizens on the other.

Despite a constitution recognising the right to local self-government, the 2014 Local Government Reform Act in Ireland merged 114 local councils into 31, with three unelected regional assemblies. The urban area of Dublin now comprises four authorities, including the City Council which serves a huge population of 553,000, further divided into five administrative areas. Between 2014 and 2019, more than 1/3 of the city council was made up of anti-austerity councillors. However, in a system where many statutory functions are invested in the Chief Executive or in ministers, and the leadership model is very weak, they had very little formal power (Gaynor, 2020). Moreover, decisions of the council were frequently overturned by national government (28 per cent of council planning decisions in 2015) leading to accusations that the city's own development plan was systematically ignored (Kelly, 2016). As indicated earlier, local respondents did not see 'reform' as having revitalised or empowered the City Council at all. Moore-Cherry and Tomaney (2019) went further, accusing the Irish government of 'metrophobia', its centralising and clientelistic tendencies leading it to eschew democratic metropolitanisation in a capital city, which drives the national economy. For them, the throttling of metropolitan government by a revanchist state was counter-productive to rational or sustainable development in the city-region.

In Australia, the number of municipal-level governments was cut from 869 in 1980 to 571 following merger policies initiated by several states, including Victoria in the 1990s under the austere rule of Jeff Kennett (Henderson et al, 2020). The severity of austerity policies and the breadth of the restructuring at that time, forms an instructive contrast with the relative fiscal and institutional stability of the post-GEC period. It reinforced the sense that in escaping relatively unscathed from both the GEC and austerity, Greater Dandenong was unique among the eight cities and that the temporalities of retrenchment, rescaling and revitalisation were very different.

Conclusion

Whether through coercively imposed 'revenue autonomy', squeezed fiscal autonomies, redistributed tax burdens, caps on borrowing, or deteriorating ratios between revenue and debt servicing costs, the political capacities of local government have, insofar as they derive from law and money, generally been eroded across the board. Nowhere, unsurprisingly, did we find restructuring processes, either centralising or de-centralising, that made it easier for cities to deliver anti-neoliberal or counter-austerity programmes. As might be expected, downloading from upper tiers simply compounded the pressure from diminishing transfers and shrinking or flatlining local revenues.

The research also disclosed widespread evidence of decreased fiscal autonomy, meaning that the capacity to compensate declining transfers through local taxes diminished, along with the capacity to decide on whom and for what purposes local taxes are levied. Borrowing autonomy varied (though aligned with the 'golden rule'), and in some the capacity to borrow was squeezed by upper tiers to further clamp down on spending, as in Athens and Barcelona. However, Baltimore shows that freedom to borrow is double-edged, because municipal and provincial debts were major drivers of fiscal retrenchment in a city with inadequate revenues, limited or no equalisation, punitive interest rates and high deprivation. As a political strategy, illegal deficit financing of the kind attempted by a small number of authorities in Britain during the 1980s is technically difficult, depending first on the unwillingness or inability of higher tiers to enforce the law and second on the support of a creditor.

Administrative upscaling was the indirect corollary of increasing stress on municipal resources and the drive for 'efficiency'. Mechanisms included voluntary amalgamations and mergers pursuant to metropolitan governance, to enhance the political weight of the urban area and create economies of scale with downward pressure on spending. However, despite rationalisation exercises city-regionalism was, for a host of locally specific reasons, relatively underdeveloped in terms of formal or semi-formal combines. The contrasting experience of Nantes brings the metropolitan governance 'deficit' into clearer view, as well as pointing to democratic deficits and distancing effects that can arise when it is executed. City-regional infrastructures and institutions appeared underdeveloped from the standpoint of neoliberal visions for creating (sub)regional investment magnets and generative agglomerations. Given the prominence of city-regionalism in contemporary urban policy discourse, and if the consolidated city-region is seen a barometer of economic efficiency (Parkinson, 2016), most of the eight cities had a long way to go to achieve optimal cooperation and integration; not least because of local inertia and resistance but also because of metrophobia. The findings chime with Scott's (2019: 17) observation that 'it is probably fair to say that no actual city-region in the world today has succeeded in constructing a stable, durable, and comprehensive framework of governance, no matter what its organizational form'. From a technical planning perspective, there appeared to be ample scope for further entrepreneurial governance innovations through rescaling to achieve scalar efficiencies, though these too can have unintended consequences (Ladi, 2014).

Conversely, the challenges facing Barcelona highlight dilemmas confronting anti-austerity activists in terms of what forms of supra-municipal collaboration could plausibly be congruent with a democratic, de-centralising and egalitarian governing ethos. Olin Wright (2019: 126) argued that democratically empowered de-centralisation 'rests on the idea that for many issues, problem-solving can be more effective when real decision-making power is given to democratic public authorities located closer to the problems'. The primary question, then, is how recipes for territorial, scalar, functional and administrative re-organisation contribute to fulfilling political goals, rather than the dominant economic rationality privileging the utility of urban areas for growth (Jonas and Moisio, 2018: 353). Factors such as political and cultural identity, representation, democratic control, spatial equity, propinquity and distributive justice provide a more helpful analytical compass for determining what political capacity (if any) supra-municipal and city-regional entities can and should exercise, in which spheres of public action.

The key message across the eight cities was that whether or not directly implicated in post-GEC austerity, municipalities faced a variable and increasing mix of upward and downward constraints depleting their formal political capacities. These arose from centralisation and de-centralisation processes alike, depending on how they were employed – the former to undermine political autonomy, the latter to increase financial responsibility. The research suggested that insofar as political capacity is concerned, whatever local tax powers may exist, there is no substitute for a generous equalisation mechanism capable of funding a full-spectrum of statutory and non-statutory municipal and urban governance functions and channelling the accumulated wealth of society into communities devastated by market failure.

Considered from the standpoint of governability, state rescaling in the period since the GEC tended to consolidate disciplinary neoliberalism, creating additional pressures on local governments to reinforce tax bases through place-marketing. One conclusion is that state rescaling since the crash makes it more difficult for most elected municipalities to diverge from austere neoliberalism. Rescaling has been far more about centralising political control, restructuring lower-tier authorities, and downloading costs and responsibilities than it has been about political empowerment.

From a Gramscian perspective, these processes make cities more 'governable' from the standpoint of national and provincial elites, pushing local state mechanisms into closer alignment with the administrative and financial priorities of upper tiers. Even if local political agendas diverge, as they often do, the capacity to act on them effectively has been curtailed. From the perspective of Stone's (2015) iron rule, where sustaining a governing regime requires that resources must be commensurate with the agenda pursued, these dynamics make it harder to mobilise them for egalitarian anti-neoliberal agendas. They also erode putatively progressive governance capabilities, insofar as these are contained by a legal framework. Cooperation around market-centred development is the path of least resistance for 'realists', notwithstanding that many cities are likely to fail and that longstanding policies, like city regionalism, often do not come to fruition. In short, state-rescaling has a strong tendency to reinforce the capacities of multi-scalar austerity regimes, while depleting the capacities of those that seek to govern differently. This does not mean that they can do nothing, as new municipalist experiments attest (Chapter 6), but that in the age of austerity, they have tended to operate in an increasingly hostile and debilitating environment. Nor does discipline and control within the state ensemble necessarily translate into the effective control of societies, or mitigate the crisis of governability diagnosed by Streeck (2016). The contrary may be true, with authoritarianism producing unintended consequences such as diminished co-optive powers and fuelling resistance. The remaining chapters consider these issues further, with Chapters 4–5 next exploring collaborative governance dynamics between state, market and civil society actors. The lesson from this chapter is that these cannot be considered in abstraction from scalar, spatial, jurisdictional and inter-governmental dimensions, which co-determine the powers and liabilities accruing to any urban regime-like formation.

Consolidating Neoliberal
Austerity Regimes

Introduction

Chapter 3 explained how various forms of state rescaling squeezed the formal political capacity for municipalities to contest austere neoliberalism. To the extent they are implemented successfully, these measures contribute to consolidating states and sub-national regimes in an integral sense: they make it easier to ensure that elements in the local state ensemble pull in broadly the same direction. Chapters 4 and 5 turn from state rescaling to coalitions among state, market and civil society actors, and the urban regime configurations that have arisen, or been challenged, in the post-crisis period. For this reason, the chapters proceed on a city-by-city basis rather than thematically.

One avenue in this account is the question highlighted in the introductory chapter of what happened to participatory governance, and what this in turn reveals about the trajectory towards more-or-less inclusionary and exclusionary modes of governing in and against austere neoliberalism, marshalling what co-optive and pre-emptive powers and incurring which liabilities. In exploring this issue, 'social partnership' is employed as a portmanteau term to encompass both the corporatist and post-corporatist modes of collaborative governance privileging, respectively, trade unions and 'civil society'. Both kinds played a significant role in austerity governance and resistance (Gaynor, 2011).

The research revealed significant variations and transitions in the powers and liabilities accruing to urban regimes, which attest to the importance of reading austerity governance through urban histories and traditions. This chapter explores the four cities in which regime consolidation was occurring around the intensification of austere neoliberalism, Athens, Baltimore, Dublin and Leicester. Chapter 5 discusses four cities deviating from this pattern, Barcelona, Greater Dandenong, Montréal and Nantes. Chapters 4 and 5 work with the conception of the 'local state' explained in Chapter 1, encompassing all governmental and quasi-governmental agencies situated within the city/metropolis and having the city/metropolis as their main concern (Magnusson, 1985), while disclosing the role of civil society fractions in constructing and contesting urban political (dis)orders. Following Jessop (1997: 64), they inquire into the operationalisation of austerity governance through strategically selective combinations of political society and civil society, collaborating around 'congruent' (aligned rather than necessarily identical) agendas (Stone, 2004: 9).

Athens: an emerging multi-scalar elite pluralist regime[1]

The Greek state tradition is associated with authoritarianism, weak local government, weak voluntary and community sectors and clientelism, all of which mitigated against the development of conventional urban regime politics in the pre-GEC period (Chorianopoulos, 2012). Greece acceded to the EU in 1981, after which it became eligible for the plethora of programme funds that, in countries like Ireland (discussed later) drove the development of collaborative apparatuses. Yet, as Chorianopoulos and Tselepi (2019) explain, lack of state capacity intersected with the prevalent cultural political economy to undermine reforms of this kind. Several rounds of local state rescaling and reform in Athens failed to establish the tapestry of collaborative governance mechanisms found in other European cities. The centralised and clientelistic political culture limited the capacity and enthusiasm of national and local state actors, while lack of interest and support – sometimes outright hostility – from within Athenian civil society created an enormous implementation gap (Chorianopoulos, 2012; Di Mascio and Natalini, 2015).

In the 1990s, Greece began to establish what scholars of industrial relations call 'competitive corporatism' (Kennedy, 2016). This model differs from classical corporatism. Where the latter traded full employment for wage moderation, competitive corporatism sought to win labour leaders to marketising principles underpinning structural reform and workforce flexibility. Kennedy (2016) argued that competitive corporatism failed sufficiently to subordinate or incorporate organised labour. Unlike counterparts in Ireland, for example, Greek unions continued to organise highly disruptive waves of mass strikes long after the GEC (see Chapter 7). The attempt to construct a social partnership was overturned by the austerity-driven imperative for radical labour market reforms. According to a trade unionist (Chorianopoulos, 2016):

> It wasn't just that collective bargaining agreements were abolished; it was also that all mediation, arbitration and conciliation for conflict resolution processes were abolished as well... The troika abolished all such processes even though they were not featuring high on the list of reasons explaining the limited competitiveness of the Greek economy. Now, this is not a conspiracy theory. You have one body, the employers, saying that social dialogue should be abolished, and this is one of the first things the Troika does.

In place of 'competitive corporatism', the post-GEC policy environment saw further reforms attempting to construct a post-corporatist governance landscape based on partnerships between state, citizens and the third sector, following the 'contributory principle' (Davies, 2012b). This model, explained in the introductory chapter, was popularised by third-way currents in the 1990s and 2000s and embedded in the conditions attaching to EU programme funding. It is based less on bargaining, negotiation and deal-making, and more on consultation, consensus-building and resource-mobilisation. Government, businesses and communities are supposed to invest together in building governing capacity and focus efforts on enhancing the competitive-yet-inclusive position of the city.

As Chapter 3 explained, the Kallikratis reforms accomplished a radical restructuring and rationalisation of local government, while slashing the number of municipal employees nationally by 50 per cent. Bertrana and Heinelt (2013) described the reform as taking advantage of the unique opportunity afforded by economic collapse and mandatory austerity to attempt a break with clientelism, in favour of a shift towards the managerial 'good governance' of EU, OECD and UN imaginaries. The effectiveness of this reform remains open to question both in terms of efficiency and culture change (Ladi, 2014; Di Mascio and Natalini, 2015). However, as a corollary of the austerity drive reform efforts sought once again to open up decision-making structures to state, business and privileged civil society actors in a new 'collaborative turn'. State-led, in some cases EU-funded collaborative governance reforms, included the mandatory establishment of 'Deliberation Committees' at the municipal and regional levels involving councillors, officials and nominated civil society groups. Migrant Inclusion Councils were established in every municipality for dialogue with newcomer groups about service provision and integration in Greek society. E-governance mechanisms including consultations on government policy and petitioning, were also introduced (Chorianopoulos and Tselepi, 2020).

These mechanisms had questionable efficacy in terms of both democratic inclusion and enhancing the co-optive powers of the local state. Because of the centralised character of the Greek state, and the overweening priority accorded to austerity, they were peripheral in the governance of Athens. For example, when questioned about deliberation committees, local politicians either did not know what they were, or saw them as unimportant: as one put it, 'I don't think that collaboration happens through committees... What does the Act know about deliberation?... about participation? Why should I have one committee and not more? The Act should have set the framework for deliberation and left it at that.' For a second respondent, 'it doesn't work like that. Deliberation is a difficult thing. You don't just choose people randomly and ask them to discuss and decide on things... Deliberation needs a lot of work in advance. You have to find topics of common interest, there are conflicting interests.' For a third, 'why doesn't it work? I would say, for various reasons. One is that the purpose of the Deliberation Committee is not clear. So, they've selected people without really knowing why or what for... So, it remains without people really caring or wanting to be there.' (Three politicians, cited in Chorianopoulos, 2016.)

Beyond these mechanisms, there has been a further cultural shift towards collaboration, seen by municipal officials as the only plausible option. One said in response to criticism from activists: 'They moan because we work with NGOs. OK, find us another way. It's not the memorandum or austerity; it's necessity that drives us' (Chorianopoulos and Tselepi, 2019: 89). A city councillor pointed to the collapse in the local authority staffing base: 'we had 12,000 employees and now we have 7,000, while reduction in force is complemented by a hiring freeze imposed by the state... What do you do in such a case? Do you shut the municipality down? You have to react, for sure, but within a framework' (Chorianopoulos and Tselepi, 2019: 88). Articulating the neoliberal orthodoxy espoused by Mayor Kaminis (Chapter 2), the councillor declared that local government should 'become less intrusive and invasive and more enabling; creating links and letting things happen... It should function as a monitoring and facilitating institution' (cited in Chorianopoulos and Tselepi, 2020: 45).

The municipal culture shift, rooted in functional understandings of the need to collaborate, spawned a variety of initiatives involving government, business and NGOs. Of particular interest from the standpoint of urban regime re-composition was the plethora of initiatives established through city partnerships with transnational civil society organisations linked to some the world's wealthiest families. These initiatives are to help alleviate distress, cultivate 'resilience' and coordinate the grassroots activities of community groups (Chorianopoulos and Tselepi, 2019, 2020). The Athens Partnership, sponsored by the Stavros Niarchos Foundation and 'with strategic guidance from Bloomberg Associates', was established by the City Mayor to facilitate 'high-impact partnerships between the Municipality of Athens and the private sector' (Athens Partnership, 2018: 5). It, in turn, established a variety of initiatives such as the 'Athens Tourism Partnership', involving the city, Aegean Airlines and Athens International Airport. INNOVATHENS is a public–private consortium established in 2014 with resources from the European Regional Development Fund supporting start-ups in the tech sector, engaging IT firms and co-funded by Samsung (Chorianopoulos and Tselepi, 2020: 45). synAthina is a municipal unit facilitating communication and activity coordination among community groups. This programme was funded by Bloomberg Philanthropies through the competitive 'Mayors Challenge Award' and run by the city's Vice Mayor for 'Civil Society and Municipality Decentralization' (Chorianopoulos and Tselepi, 2020: 47). The award of one million dollars supported day-to-day operations and facilitated networking. Community projects were not funded through this scheme but directed onwards to other NGOs and the private sector. An official explained the market for projects:

> we have developed a network of sponsors that supports these initiatives. We visit them and we present to them the projects that we have endorsed, and they tell us, in return, whether or not they'll support these proposals. Sponsors are primarily companies. 'Niarchos', for instance, funded a street performance in the city centre... 'Vivechrom' provided graffiti material... What we do is that we act as go-betweens... We facilitate citizens' ideas. (Municipal official, cited in Chorianopoulos, 2016)

The goal of the modest Bloomberg investment (like that of other investors such as Niarchos and Rockefeller Philanthropy), however, was to influence the culture and practices of local government: 'if outdated regulations are needlessly prohibiting the advancement of good ideas, for instance, our team will work with other departments in City Hall to update those regulations, policies, or procedures' (Municipal official, cited in Chorianopoulos, 2016). There were many other such initiatives to cultivate 'partnership' (Chorianopoulos and Tselepi, 2020).

This glimpse reveals several points about the changing governance of Athens. First, transnational civil society organisations, fronts for the missionary wing of the global ruling class, gained new and unprecedented influence in the city's governance, on the way the city council operates and the way it sees itself. Second, the rise of the transnational organisation (TNO) in urban governance marks a rescaling within Athenian civil society itself, creating a new configuration in which local organisations are dependent on the (highly conditional) largesse of billionaire sponsors, as well as legitimation through the austerity state. Third, however, if projects, like synAthina are seen as part of a hegemonic endeavour to attune Athenian society to the cultural practices of neoliberal entrepreneurialism, it has delivered little in the way of co-optive power. Alienation among grassroots organisations, discussed further in Chapters 6 and 7, attests to this. According to one community activist, contradicting Kaminis's position on the 2015 referendum (Chapter 2):

> The referendum wasn't about the Euro or Grexit. It was about austerity. You can't stand out as the main proponent of the 'yes' vote, as the Mayor did, knowing that what we stand for is negated by the 'yes' vote. That's why very many solidarity networks have pulled out from synAthina ever since. The networks don't trust the City anymore. (Cited in Chorianopoulos and Tselepi, 2020: 50)

Some respondents suggested that productive exchanges between grassroots civil society organisations and the state had become virtually non-existent. According to one from the voluntary sector,

> No, we don't collaborate with any state institutions. Yes, we're an NGO, but we don't want to be seen as yet another organization that's funded by the state to return a fraction of what it gets to the people in difficulty. This view might not do justice to many NGOs, but it's a strong one and we hear it all the time; '... ah, you're there, so you get a piece of the pie as well', so to speak. (Cited in Chorianopoulos, 2017)

In summary, a weak and hollowed out municipality sought to embrace 'collaborative governance', producing not participatory democracy but a newly regressive regime politics. As Chorianopoulos and Tselepi (2019: 81) put it, a 'deprivileged local authority is opening up to the influence of corporate and third sector organisations out of fiscal necessity, adopting a partnership approach that is best understood as a form of elite pluralism'. While practices of clientelistic and market-inefficient governance have by no means been excised from Greek politics, and authoritarianism is increasingly the norm following the reforms discussed in Chapter 3 and the return of conservatives to national and municipal government in 2019, the shift marks a significant departure from the pre-austerity period. TNOs and international corporations have achieved significant policy influence in Athens, constituted through an emergent, semi-formal multi-scalar elite pluralist regime (Chorianopoulos and Tselepi, 2019, 2020). The system has echoes of the longer standing arrangements in Baltimore, discussed later, and marks a substantial radicalisation of the feeble restructuring efforts undertaken in decades prior to the GEC. However, the co-optive power of this formation is limited, with bifurcation occurring within a rescaling civil society: TNOs seeking to lever austerity for the institutional and cultural transformation of urban governance on the one hand, resistance through local solidarity networks hostile to this endeavour and the continuing, if diminished, struggles of the trade union movement on the other. To further understand these rescaling dynamics, and their implications for the emerging urban political order in Athens, Chapter 7 explores the city's heroic resistance to austerity.

Baltimore: a racialised elite pluralist development regime

Chapter 2 explained that the experience of permanent retrenchment rendered the vocabulary of austerity largely redundant in Baltimore. Otherwise, its regime politics have notable similarities with those emerging in Athens, but with three key distinctions: they are longstanding and deeply embedded, egregiously racist and exceptionally repressive by conventional democratic standards. The formal racialised mapping of Baltimore began in the early 20th century with the residential segregation ordinance of 1910 (Rothstein, 2015). Legal segregation was supported by vigorous white activism. In 1925, white neighbourhood associations urged property owners to sign covenants prohibiting property sales to African Americans. City government supported white activism by sponsoring a Committee on Segregation, which enrolled more neighbourhood associations throughout the city. The Federal Housing Administration (FHA) contributed by subsidising loans to suburban developers excluding African Americans.

This racist regime prohibited black families from accumulating housing equity during the suburban boom from the mid-1930s to the mid-1960s. Post-war industrial decline combined with federally supported suburbanisation (highway construction as well as FHA activism) to compound depopulation and the spatial concentrations of dispossessed African Americans. Segregation was further enhanced by urban renewal and infrastructure development policies, restricting public high-rise developments to African American areas. The National Association for the Advancement of Colored People (NAACP) condemned this policy for placing 'the full strength of the Federal government behind a policy of rigid residential segregation' (Williams, 2005, cited in Pill, 2015). Legal segregation ended in 1954. However, the demography of the city continues to reflect racial and spatial injustices instantiated in the first half of the 20th century and sustained by the urban political economy of Baltimore to this day.

Davies and Pill (2012: 2204) argued that the election of Martin O'Malley to the Mayoralty of Baltimore in 1999 cemented the governance arrangements and priorities we see today, combining downtown development and gentrification programmes with attempts to encourage African American mobility. A key initiative was the introduction of the 'asset-based' model of resource allocation to neighbourhoods, which persists in modified form – the so-called 'housing typology' (Davies and Pill, 2012). This took the form of a triage system. 'Stressed' neighbourhoods were written off for purposes of investment and earmarked for housing demolition and site re-assembly. Displacement continues via housing mobility programmes to relocate black residents to suburban 'opportunity' neighbourhoods. Competitive neighbourhoods, at the other end of the continuum, were deemed not to require intervention, which was to be focused on the middling neighbourhoods to 'help the market', including measures to support home ownership (also Pill, 2020: 151).

Unsurprisingly, black activists detested these mechanisms. Chapter 6 discusses *The Uprising* in response to the killing of African American, Freddie Gray in April 2015. Speaking at Gray's funeral, Revd Jesse Jackson captured the underlying critique: 'there are two Baltimores – the one that includes the Inner Harbor and other tourist areas, and the Baltimore that features 16,000 vacant lots and thousands of lives often deemed expendable' in the neighbourhoods (report from Baltimore

Sun, cited in Pill, 2015). The city's revitalisation policy accelerated the dynamic, by concentrating investment in neighbourhoods deemed market-viable and writing-off those that were not. The 'city of neighbourhoods' discourse, was seen by activists as reinforcing racialised polarisation and fragmenting urban justice movements. Said one, 'we all need to be part of a whole city, not just our own little neighbourhoods' (Dvorak, 2015). The specific challenge of collaborative governance in this context was that of agitational rescaling from the grassroots, to overcome neighbourhood fragmentation through community organising and resistance, in pursuit of an inclusive 'One Baltimore' (see Chapter 6).

Despite *The Uprising* of 2015, the city continued to channel enormous public resources into downtown development. The waterside megaproject at Port Covington, an old railroad terminal, received $660 million in Tax Increment Financing. This was the biggest such subsidy in Baltimore's history, occurring alongside other forms of state support (Pill, 2020: 150). Anchored by international sportswear company Under Armour's HQ, this project was supposed to create a mixed-use development with homes, hotels, retail and leisure facilities. Community activists were incensed. Said one, 'we're disinvesting from places that need it the most... and the benefits promised don't materialise'. For a second, 'another private community [is created] where we're not even welcome' (citations from Pill, 2020: 150). In short, Baltimore is a city in which racial injustice, displacement, gentrification and iniquitous downtown development dominate the policy agenda to the exclusion of ameliorative, integrative and redistributive revitalisation programmes. Those programmes that did exist withered on the vine of federal retrenchment over the past 40 years.

Unsurprisingly in this environment, ideas associated with the European 'collaborative moment' did not travel. The governing agenda was rather driven by an inter-sectoral policy-setting elite converging around the state of Maryland, Baltimore City Council and local non-profits, or 'anchor' institutions. The prevailing mode of collaborative governance in Baltimore resembled the informal development regime disclosed by Stone (1989), except that leading partners were non-profits rather than corporations (Davies and Pill, 2012; Pill, 2020). As explained in Chapter 3, the configuration of sub-national government is typical of the US, where competences of local government derive from the state. Baltimore, a seemingly impregnable Democrat stronghold, is governed by a Mayor with a city council comprising 14 single member districts. Municipal power is concentrated in the Office of the Mayor, while the city's Board of Estimates exercises oversight of the municipal budget.

Although municipal power, such as it is, is concentrated in the Mayoralty and Board of Estimates, Mayoral and municipal leadership in the city was considered weak, partly because effective powers had eroded with the city's resource base and its spiralling debt. For one respondent, 'We have a tremendous amount of racism institutionally in how we've been planned as a city, how our institutions function as a city, and the lack of resources and leadership to really do some reconciliation that's necessary' (Pill, 2020: 146). For a community activist, 'though there are individuals who identify themselves as black in those leadership positions, if the agenda is not expressly black then it is a systems agenda in which the systems that be are expressly white, white supremacist' (cited in Pill, 2017). For another activist,

> Rich white philanthropists and developers with black faces like the mayor and the city council controlling where the money goes... the foundation world generally has a lot of power... large white philanthropic organizations... they drive the policy agenda for the marginalised communities right?... traditionally they set the agenda for criminal justice or police reform or social services. They essentially called the shots there. (Cited in Pill, 2017)

Non-profits, predominantly from the 'Ed and Med' sectors fill the perceived municipal leadership gap, 'working hard with each other because there's a vacuum in city government' (councilperson, cited in Pill, 2016). A Foundation-based respondent discussing economic inclusion initiatives since *The Uprising* commented, 'the great anchor institutions in our city have really stepped up and increased the climate of collaboration. And I think that all of us have realised that without collaboration – again, in spite of city leadership – without collaboration, we won't be able to accomplish our goals' (Pill, 2020: 152). Such comments attest to the distinctive and influential role of non-profits and philanthropies in the governance of the city (also Pill, 2019).

Unlike Athens, where TNOs have become significant actors, Baltimore's non-profits are locally embedded and a form of place-dependent capital. Key players include Johns Hopkins University and Medical System (the city's primary 'anchor institution'), the Annie E. Casey Foundation and the Goldseker Foundation. The President of Johns Hopkins was credited with special convening power. According to a councillor, Hopkins 'announced a lot of policies', 'setting a pattern of commitment back to the city that they are then promulgating amongst their other college and university neighbours. They're not trying to make us [city government] do it... they're taking the lead' (Pill, 2020: 150). Another community sector respondent echoed this sentiment: 'Hopkins doesn't have the best reputation. They have done some awful things... I get that but I'm also trying to create a dialogue with these people, because they are the 800-pound gorilla in the room... And we need to be able to work with them and they need to be able to know that we're not going to be calling them out every five minutes' (Pill, 2020: 153).

An activist pithily summarised, 'one of the biggest issues that we have in Baltimore... is a condensation of non-profit and foundation forces that then are allowed to produce policies' (Pill, 2020: 153). Together with the City Council and the state of Maryland, Baltimore's non-profits have formed the core of the urban regime the city since the late 1990s. As in other American cities, a further layer of Community Development Corporations was seen as having been enrolled to regime policy agendas in the period since the 1980s (McQuarrie, 2013). A CDC respondent verbalised the central logic of the housing typology: '[we are] an asset-based community development organisation, we don't work in the strong areas and we don't work in the weak areas, we work in the middle' (Pill, 2020: 151). Unsurprisingly, grassroots civil society actors found this governing architecture and the role of the 'non-profit industrial complex' to be highly exclusionary and anti-democratic. At a project workshop in Baltimore, for example, a participant pointed out that the community was not only not 'at the table, but 'we don't even know where the table is'. Another activist reflected on the prospects for an inclusive conversation: 'In Baltimore, those opportunities are rare. Those opportunities are thwarted intentionally, and they're restricted when they are available' (citations in Pill, 2017).

In summary, Baltimore was a city governed by a durable alliance between a fiscally orthodox and indebted Democrat municipality, a boosterish non-profit elite and downtown developers, in which grassroots organisations representing the working class black majority had very little leverage. The elite–pluralist regime formation that emerged from Reagan-era retrenchment, with its commitment to localised and privatised models of development (Davies and Pill, 2012), remains intact. However, its hegemony might be eroding. Chapter 7 explores *The Uprising* against police racism in Baltimore and considers how far it has diminished the co-optive powers of the urban regime, if not its immediate ability to govern.

Dublin: a revanchist national austerity regime

Local government in Ireland is very weak. Dublin City Council (DCC) does not have a strong political leader, but rather a figurehead in the person of the Lord Mayor. Municipal power, such as it is, is concentrated in the hands of managers. Moore-Cherry and Tomaney noted that despite being the centre of Irish national politics, 'the spatial entity of Dublin is relatively powerless' (2018: 365). The democratic deficit means that national members of the Irish Parliament, the Dail (TDs), attend more to local affairs than is typical of national parliamentarians and are often seen as the first port of call for citizens, leading to a centralised system in which TDs, ironically, are perceived to be excessively 'localist' in outlook and to behave more as leading councillors might in a stronger local government system (Spotlight, 2013).

Instead of 'devolution', austerity has meant further centralisation, together with functional downloading discussed in Chapter 3. Political fragmentation at the city scale compounds this tendency. In the 2014 elections Labour, complicit with austerity in much the same way as other mainstream social democratic parties in Europe, lost its position as the largest party to the Republican party Sinn Féin. In the subsequent administration, Sinn Féin held 25 per cent of seats on the council (losing half of them in 2019). Dublin has no formal councillor coalition, although informal issue-specific alliances occur. Radical anti-austerity parties achieved a significant increase in seats within DCC in 2014 and near 10 per cent of the vote, divided among three groups of which 'People Before Profit' was the largest with almost 7 per cent. However, the political re-composition of the Council towards the left had little practical impact in empowering it or shifting its stance on austerity, as indicated by its decision to apply the maximum rebate to the local property tax (Chapter 3). Sinn Féin and the anti-austerity left suffered setbacks in the 2019 municipal election, with the traditional centre-right governing party, Fianna Fail, and the Greens coming to the fore in a loose coalition.

Centralisation, through austerity, assumed a variety of cultural, political, fiscal and administrative guises. Several respondents talked about authoritarianism: 'death by bureaucracy has now replaced debt by economic austerity... there's a new authoritarianism' (community activist, cited in Gaynor, 2020: 82). 'They're supposed to be serving us. They don't serve, they govern... There's a new political class that has risen... An aristocracy rather than serving politicians'. As explained in Chapter 3, local planning decisions were frequently countermanded by the centre. A prominent theme was 'the collapse of any social contract between state and citizens, no matter how fragile it may have been in the past' (activists, cited in Gaynor, 2017). In this sense, Dublin echoed Athens. In both cities, socio-spatial distancing intensified; not only because of the fiscal squeeze, but also institutional reforms eroding links with citizens and third-sector groups, concentrating power in a revanchist state apparatus, albeit with diminishing co-optive power.

An Irish government white paper on the development of collaborative governance (Government of Ireland, 2000, cited in Gaynor, 2011) echoed the language of former UK PM Tony Blair (1998). It described the state in the then fashionable vernacular of partnership, as 'not the answer to every problem, but just one player among others', with the government's vision of society described as being 'one which encourages people and communities to look after their own needs – very often in partnership with statutory agencies – but without depending on the state to meet all needs'. This passage captures the spirit of the 'collaborative moment' in Dublin during the 1990s and 2000s, underwritten by EU programme funding.

As a small country, with a population little more than half that of London, Ireland constructed an elaborate 'Social Partnership' arrangement in the 1980s (at a time when Thatcherism had already eviscerated corporatism in the UK). Gaynor (2011) described these arrangements as having a 'solid corporatist core' of representation from business, labour and the state: to negotiate pay and also discuss a wider range of policies, along with a strong party-based relationship between the unions and dominant governing party, Fianna Fail. In the mid-1990s, the 'Social Partnership' was extended to a 'community and voluntary' pillar involving civic associational networks, meaning that corporatist and post-corporatist vehicles existed in tandem and overlapped. Dublin developed an extensive participatory apparatus aligned to the new pillar. 'So numerous and diverse were these mechanisms, that by the early 2000s it appears to have become difficult to pinpoint exactly how many categories and specific institutions existed' (Gaynor, 2015).

Built on state-centred and authority-based governing traditions as they were, the significance of these institutions for extending participatory democracy is debatable, when evaluated against demanding concepts like 'empowered participatory governance' (Fung and Olin-Wright, 2001). Whatever its strengths and weaknesses, however, this system was largely dismantled under austerity. For a local politician, there had been a time [the 1990s] when… there was a sense that local government was beginning to get closer to the people. And you had foras and, these came later, but the Policing Forum and all that kind of stuff came out of it. But In all cases, they were emasculated when people in government buildings of all parties said, 'Oh my God! This is a monster we better try and control. And they did.' (Gaynor, 2017)

Relatedly, retrenchment and re-composition in Dublin's VCS began in the period preceding austerity, with a first round of cuts in 2002. Under austerity, however, the process accelerated and state funded CSOs suffered drastic budget cuts, reportedly of 35 per cent between 2008 and 2012. The perceived political animus in this wave of retrenchment is notable. Many respondents were adamant that it was a deliberate strategy on the part of the state to discipline and re-purpose the more quarrelsome elements of Dublin's voluntary and community sectors. 'It felt like the civil servants were waiting in the long grass… It felt a bit like slash and burn… There was a bit, kind of, we'll teach you a lesson, and protect the core – the core being themselves, you know?' This impression was reinforced by a government official, who asserted that they were 'funding groups to deliver frontline services in the main, not to be there with megaphones leading' (citations from Gaynor, 2020: 81). At the national level, meanwhile, the corporatist arm of the Social Partnership collapsed when government imposed pay cuts on public servants and both unions and business confederations, for different reasons, withdrew. Chapter 7 discusses this episode in more detail.

In short, austerity destroyed the possibility of a participatory governance system capable of pursuing progressive, inclusionary or egalitarian goals. Dublin's 'collaborative moment', riding the Celtic Tiger, did not withstand the crisis as authoritarian and austere state traditions returned to the fore. Dublin differed from both Athens and Baltimore in that it was not governed by an 'urban regime' in the Stonean sense: an ensemble constituted by interdependent local state and non-state actors operating within the city and having the city as their main concern (Magnusson, 1985). Governing power was rather concentrated nationally, with a weak local governmental apparatus taking its cue from above. The story of austerity governance in Dublin is one of revanchism consisting in political centralisation, authoritarianism and repression, the rollback of once-extensive participatory institutions, and measures to discipline and hollow-out the voluntary and community sectors. However, the hegemonic grip and co-optive power exercised through this ensemble was limited, in the context of rising alienation and anger within a newly rebellious civil society. These processes saw the regime subjected to challenges from a surging anti-austerity movement, discussed in Chapter 6.

Leicester: a nationally mandated austerian realist regime

As Chapters 2 and 3 explained, local government in the UK, England in particular, has been severely weakened by austerity and fiscal restructuring, posing an acute challenge for deprivileged cities like Leicester. The forces of national state discipline and control, combined with the local politics of austerian realism (Chapter 2), kept the question of resisting austerity a long way from the local political agenda (Marcuse, 2015). Framed by the centralising traditions of central–local relations, austerian realism operated across different spheres of governance and in a variety of collaborative endeavours, constituting a potent, regime enabling disposition. Austerian realism is deeply entwined with the state-led reorganisation of local civil society, the reconfiguration of collaborative governance, and the tensions and crosscurrents in the governance of Leicester arising from these processes. The local state in the UK is an institutional and spatial–scalar jumble, meaning that notwithstanding municipal 'Stockholm Syndrome' (Copus et al, 2017: 180), governance is enacted through a plethora of formal, semi-formal and informal inter-governmental and multi-stakeholder collaborations.

The relationship in any particular policy sphere usually involves one or more national government departments exercising a direct or indirect policy setting role in conjunction with a sub-national entity. Functions beyond the jurisdiction of municipalities, such as hospitals, policing or workfare are delivered through territorially asymmetric units and answer to different authorities. Those decisions within the purview of the City Council itself tend to be led by the City Mayor in consultation with other senior political leaders on the Executive, but also informally through the convening power of the Mayoral office. One councillor explained that the Mayor did not require 'structures to get people around the table' (Davies and Thompson, 2016: 152). Local VCS organisations play a flanking role in the governance system, especially where they are commissioned to deliver state-funded contracts. Business leaders exercise policy influence in the sphere of local economic development, for example through the Leicester and Leicestershire Enterprise Partnership (LLEP). Its influence will grow if and when it assumes the power to veto local authority business tax increases.

Laden with idealised sentiments about the supposed potentialities in network governance, the politics of the British collaborative moment were also an attempt to deal with practicalities such as the spatial and sectoral fragmentation of urban governing capacity, and the emerging crisis of legitimacy in representative democracy (Davies, 2011b). Blairite Britain became a paradigm case with its 'third way' discourses and repertoire of participatory mechanisms. Like other cities, Leicester joined in the New Labour wave of institutional experimentation, establishing a city-level multi-stakeholder local strategic partnership (LSP) 'One Leicester' and securing one of its flagship New Deal for Communities packages, intended to revitalise the Braunstone neighbourhood on the Western fringe of the city and involving communities directly in decision making (the latter turned out to be anything but an advert for collaboration, regeneration and community empowerment (Broughton et al, 2013)).

For a time under New Labour, LSPs were viewed as the pre-eminent collaborative governance mechanism, bringing together a wide range of local actors charged with enhancing joined-up government and social inclusion. Leicester established a central partnership board, or 'hub', with thematised 'spokes' dealing respectively with issues such as health, education, economic development and the environment. Nationally, these institutions were much criticised for circumventing democratic accountability, re-creating departmental 'siloes' and failing to include or listen to anyone not bringing a can-do attitude to the table (Davies, 2007; 2009). They were also criticised for creating largely impotent local economic development coalitions (ODPM, 2005). As it turned out, and as was the case in Ireland, they had no durability either. Once Labour was evicted from office in 2010, and the age of austerity began in earnest, they disappeared without trace.

Though a paradigm case, the 'collaborative moment' in the UK never lived up to its billing as ushering in a new age of inclusive, joined-up governance networks based on trust, but subsequent developments put an end to any remaining hopes and expectations. The Conservative-led coalition elected in 2010 cut all the programmes that resourced state–civil society partnerships in the New Labour years and like LSPs, they disappeared in the early years of austerity. The whole New Labour apparatus collapsed, mostly unloved and unlamented. Said a Leicester councillor, 'even when they were very fashionable in the Blair years... I was intensely sceptical of them.' By the time Leicester's Mayoralty was established in 2011, 'the fashion had changed'. It was 'very easy to ditch the whole damn lot' (cited in Davies and Thompson, 2016: 152). Like Dublin, the institutionalised partnership apparatus of the New Labour era was short-circuited by the combination of austerity and changes in national political priorities. In Leicester, it was further sidelined by the new Executive Mayoralty, with its own convening powers and modes of leadership and engagement.

In the New Labour years, participatory governance was organised in part through neighbourhood community governance mechanisms, which also for the most part disappeared in the age of austerity. This completed an unravelling that had begun in the late New Labour period, with the territorial rationalisation of 'neighbourhood', as funding slowed and priorities shifted to larger units (Davies and Pill, 2012). The rollback of neighbourhood community governance in Leicester suggested that for all that the New Labour machinery was superficial and unlamented, collaboration between municipality and communities in the wider sense of a front-line relationship between citizens, public service 'users', service providers and community workers, had been badly damaged by austerity. One community worker commented, 'nine engagement officers have been cut to four covering the whole city. Their title has changed to ward engagement officer and their main role now is to support Councillors with their ward meetings. They have minimal contact with local groups' (correspondence). A second community worker reflected:

> We will be much more based in our buildings. We'll still be offering stuff, you know, things to the community, but it will be from our buildings, which will mean that there's far less contact with a wider audience. And there aren't the Community Engagement Officers, so we can have the time to talk to people about: 'So what's bugging you this week? And what's hurting in your life?' and things like that. I won't regularly see people to be able to get a wide view of what's happening in the communities. Makes me a bit sad. (Davies and Bua, 2016)

Austerity was seen by this respondent, and others, to be rationalising and bureaucratising community engagement and eroding molecular, everyday links between state and civil society groups resulting in greater distancing. So too was the increasing concentration of public contracts in large non-profits and with preferred contractors, with which small local voluntary and community organisations could not compete. The local third sector was being hollowed out and distanced from locality, with resources concentrated in ever larger organisations. The consequences remain to be seen, but one councillor made a powerful observation (cited in Davies, 2017b: 26):

> I think the cuts to the council's budget has more profound effect than people understand. And it may take a while before clearly you know something falls down. It maybe two or three years before you really realise that they would've sorted that if they've been here. They would've communicated with us about that if they've been here. But sooner or later and of course these things take ages to build up. To build up a strong civic society takes a long time. And then you cut it down. It's like planting a tree. It will take years for it to grow again.

The re-composition of state–civil society relations has been a crucial tool for channelling austerian realism and constituting the local austerity state. Multicultural Leicester has long been an important governance terrain (Machin and Mayr, 2007). The presence and economic activity of Black and Minority Ethnic (BAME) groups, credited with the resilience and entrepreneurship that keeps Leicester going through hard times, was a crucial part of the city's brand. According to one city councillor, 'people I know did not bring money with them but they brought their cultural ways, heritage, traditions. And now, the authority is so grateful to these Ugandan refugees – their economic contribution to the city – they have put it on the World Map' (cited in Davies et al, 2020: 62).

In Britain, as in many other parts of the world, struggles for gender and racial equality began to assert themselves as union militancy receded. In Leicester they overlapped in the famous strike, led by Asian workers, at Imperial Typewriters (Tuckman and Knudsen, 2016) and commemorated in a recent exhibition in the city.[2] Race and ethnicity came to be recognised, not only as a legitimate terrain of struggle for equality in workplaces and communities, but also as a form of competitive advantage. Leicester was among the pioneers embracing multiculturalism and celebrating the capabilities of BAME entrepreneurs became a crucial part of its governing ethos (McLoughlin, 2013). The politics of multiculturalism in Leicester are complex and multi-faceted in ways that are addressed more substantially elsewhere (for example, Hassen and Giovanardi, 2018). Many people we spoke to celebrate it as an intrinsic good, a matter of pride and a strength of the city, with high levels of positive intercultural association. Others suggested that multiculturalism has never been matched by interculturalism, and also that not all black and minority ethnic groups are treated equally. And, as Chapter 2 explained, much of the city's BAME economy is brutally exploitative (Hammer et al, 2015), with swathes of the garment industry implicated in practices of 'modern slavery' (LeBaron, 2020).

Austerity put the multicultural governance model established in Leicester in the 1980s under stress. Immigrant groups arriving in Leicester in the early 1970s, notably Ugandan Asian refugees, quickly won political influence and city leaders resolved to mobilise the knowledge and skills they brought with them. As part of Leicester's multicultural turn, an informal governance coalition emerged comprising LCC, statutory agencies, BAME community leaders and the local media. LCC provided infrastructure grants to umbrella groups, to help with integration, community building, service provision and communication. Interviewed in 2013, an official from LCC explained (cited in Davies et al, 2020: 67):

> We do have an active community and voluntary sector in the city and we do interact with them. Some of that is formal because we have contracts with organizations to help us engage with certain communities, for example, the Leicester Council of Faiths or the Federation of Muslim Organizations, the Guajarati Hindu Association, Race Equality Council – recognizing value those groups can bring in helping us understand/engage with those communities of interest.

These mechanisms became an important facet of regime building in the pre-austerity decades, involving valued resource exchanges: money and facilities to build community infrastructures, in exchange for engagement pursuant to integrating and marshalling the capabilities of new arrivals. However, a number of BAME umbrella organisations were de-funded under austerity, further justified on the grounds that they were no longer fit for purpose and that newer communities in Leicester had not received the same support. One major umbrella group, the African Caribbean Citizens Forum, collapsed as a result.

It is important to emphasise that the multicultural ideal remains strongly embedded in the politics of the city and its continuing celebration of 'diversity' as the source of economic resilience, entrepreneurship and cultural vitality. Nevertheless, austerity posed a challenge for the informal community governance coalition established in the 1980s. Considered side-by-side, the balance between the two dimensions of multicultural coalition governance, occupying the spheres of economic development and community organising, have tilted towards the former. In both cases, the shift was warranted by the politics of austerian realism.

Austerity in Leicester, to summarise, was delivered through a nationally mandated austerian realist regime, exercising pre-emptive power throughout the local state in its inclusive sense. The research revealed a favourable conjuncture for austerity in the legacies of past crises, struggles, defeats and political re-orientations. These created a potent strategic, institutional and ideological bias towards implementing austerity, which at the same time hollowed out networks and eroded political voice and communication. As Chapter 7 shows, although the governing regime has not solved the social crises engendered by austerity, and previous rounds of neoliberalisation, it has proven adept in containing, and muting resistance, as entrepreneurialism became more pronounced. The combination of rescaling and regime composition under austerity highlighted the potential for radicalising Harvey's (1989) entrepreneurial city. The co-optive apparatus associated with the 'collaborative moment', on the other hand, was radically scaled back.

Conclusion

The four cities discussed in this chapter encapsulate several ways in which authoritarian neoliberal regime politics evolved in the age of austerity. In Baltimore, though the scale of its debts increased significantly post-austerity, and retrenchment intensified accordingly, the core of the governing regime – the developmental alliance between city and major non-profit anchor institutions – had been in place for a generation. Baltimore's continuity regime was served by its informal character, the pervasiveness of neoliberal groupthink and the centrifugal dynamics unleashed by the city's racialised and fragmented system of neighbourhoods, whose community groups lacked the resources needed to win access to decision-making. In Athens, the dynamics of austerity and the realpolitik of the municipality, gave rise to a new governing regime somewhat resembling that of Baltimore, under the disciplinary impetus of austerity. This was anchored in the relationships between state, city and TNOs, which grassroots organisations were unable, and did not seek to influence. These developments contributed to bifurcating and rescaling civil society. In both Leicester and Dublin, the politics of austerity, driven by determined conservative governments at the national level, consolidated disciplinary urban regimes and rolled back the participatory mechanisms that were fashionable in the neoliberal boom when 'civil society' was summoned to the fore in partnerships with the state. Socio-spatial distancing resulted from the de-funding and hollowing out of the local VCS and in the dismantling of partnership apparatuses.

These cities varied significantly in size and influence, but in each case the persistent lack, and further diminution of political capacity described in Chapter 3 contributed to the cooption of the municipality and its ostensibly centre-left political leaders. In each, multi-scalar regime politics contributed to rendering neoliberal austerity governable, a political expression of 'crisis-displacement' (Theodore, 2020), and to disorganising and disrupting fractious elements within civil society. In Athens and Leicester in particular, but also Dublin with the reflation of its financial bubble, the governing arrangements discussed in this chapter and in Chapters 2 and 3 point to the qualitative radicalisation of austere neoliberalism. This is a point upon which Chapter 8 reflects further in discussing the concept of 'late entrepreneurialism' (Peck, 2017a; 2017b). What ultimately made these regimes successful was their capacity, if not to prevent resistance then to contain it within parameters that meant austerity could be delivered without serious impediment. However, as Chapters 6 and 7 further explain, consolidating neoliberal regimes also incurred liabilities in terms of weakening hegemony, as their co-optive reach diminished.

Regime Divergence and the Limits of Austere Neoliberalism

Introduction

The cities of Montréal, Nantes, Dandenong and Barcelona diverge in several ways from patterns of consolidation in austere neoliberalism discussed in Chapter 4. This chapter first discusses Montréal and Nantes, as two cases of established urban regimes dealing with policy failure and coming under strain from internal contradictions. The second part of the chapter explores Greater Dandenong and Barcelona, cities with very different political orientations and traditions, but where constructive regime building activities were occurring, respectively at a distance from and against austere neoliberalism.

Montréal: a development regime interregnum?

Chapters 2 and 3 contextualised the discussion of regime politics in Montréal, explaining the policy of *rigueur* at the provincial level, measures to centralise political and administrative control and the economic development dilemmas facing the city in recent decades. The government of Québec is a regime agenda setter, in the dual sense of controlling key public service budgets and, through austerity measures, downloading problems to other actors in the statutory and third sectors (Hamel and Autin, 2017). Hamel and Keil (2020) emphasise that *rigueur* was not only about cuts, but a state restructuring project amounting to a revanchist attack on the collaborative, democratic and deliberative traditions of the city.

Between 2013 and 2017, the city of Montréal was governed by an electoral coalition, *Équipe Denis Coderre*, which took a pragmatic stance towards Couillard's agenda. One the one hand, it made its own budget cuts and workforce reductions, but on the other hand accommodated the trade unions and community organisations by providing support, beneath the radar, to those resisting austerity (Hamel and Keil, 2018). Municipal managers and planners not typically sympathetic with austerity, were in an ambivalent position and imbricated in complex 'mechanics of adaptation, resistance and cooperation within the turbulent context created by austerity' (Hamel and Keil, 2020: 116). If the provincial government (despite its euphemistic language) had an 'austerian idealist' flavour, Hamel and Keil compare the city's disposition with the 'austerian realism' of Leicester, concluding that actors in the governance of Montréal were immersed in 'a governmentality that rested on the partial acceptance of the ground rules of neoliberalism even by opposing actors', though this was challenged vigorously by disputatious forces within civil society (Chapters 6 and 7). Like Athens, Baltimore, Dublin and Leicester, the relatively weak and fragmented local government in the city-region of Montréal limited the prospects for convening regime power around a new and distinctive agenda. How far this situation would change following the election in 2017 of a progressive electoral coalition led by Valérie Plante remained to be seen as the study concluded.

The austerity drive from provincial government led directly to the erosion of participatory governance mechanisms. As part of the fix arising from the Quiet Revolution, the newly assertive Québécois developed a collaborative approach known as the Québec Model (Hamel and Jouve, 2008). The model evolved into a more neoliberalised form over time, but captured the widely shared commitment to egalitarianism, solidarity and strong community organisation, anchored by a redistributive state (Hamel and Keil, 2020). From the beginning of the 1980s community groups in Montréal sought to build collaboration around local economic development through a series of initiatives to reverse the deterioration of industrial neighbourhoods (Hamel, 1991). These projects emerged from community activism, rooted in the housing settlements movement and in the culture of community organising specific to Québec. Bua and Bussu (2020) distinguish 'Governance Driven Democratization' from 'Democracy Driven Governance', which in Montréal occurred in tandem. Montréal's tables de quartier (neighbourhood tables) provide a flavour of the city's participatory traditions. These are multi-sectoral entities pursuing a variety of economic and social objectives, linked to social inclusion.

There were 30 in the city organised into La Coalition Montréalaise des Tables de Quartier (CMTQ).

In some ways, these were similar to the state–organised entities characteristic of the 'collaborative moment' in Europe. In Kraemer's (2012) translation of Lachance et al (2004: 198), the discourses are familiar. The tables 'address local issues by means of a multidimensional and multi-problem approach, in an integrated neighbourhood development perspective'. They are formally constituted, but relations with the local state vary. Some, rooted in community organising traditions, long predate the collaborative moment, and keep government at arm's-length. Others were created through state sponsorship in the 1990s, in which instances public agencies were full decision-making partners (Kraemer, 2012). Each was supported by the 'Montréal Initiative for Local Social Development', itself a partnership involving the CMTQ, Montréal's regional public health department, and Centraide, a local philanthropic organisation dedicated to fighting poverty and social exclusion. The local importance of these mechanisms was captured by a coordinator of the Coalition, 'In the regions, there aren't all those structures like in Montréal, and they don't have all these networks like we already have in Montréal, it's not the same way of working either' (Hamel and Autin, 2017: 182). Hence, while collaborative resources struggled to cope with social needs aggravated by *rigueur*, the Tables were able to function and remained one of the enduring legacies of the Québec Model.

At the same time, *rigueur* was perceived as an attack on the democratic and deliberative culture of the city, and the capacity of community groups to act as tribunes. Several respondents made this point. Said a trade unionist:

> Austerity, it doesn't necessarily touch strictly economic policies. Indeed, we're restructuring the State also so that there are less spaces of dialogue, or less possibilities of cooperation. Because if we take out all those possibilities... I don't want to say that cooperation or collaboration always happen in happiness, joy and harmony. But now, we're completely wiping out those possibilities.

Another respondent from a community group commented,

> How I see it: those who manage austerity feel like it's a bad time to go through, we close our nose and we do it. We don't listen anymore, because we feel like everyone will be

against it. So there's no listening, hardly any cooperation or collaboration... Coiteux [Minister of Municipal Affairs and Public Security], right now, he doesn't listen to anyone. So there is no collaboration. (Hamel and Keil, 2018)

A third respondent made a different point about the erosion of professional expertise needed for individuals to make an informed contribution to consultation.

There is still some consultation, on education, that was inaugurated yesterday by the Minister of Education... So there's something like a game here and I think it's sick. It's sick in two ways: for citizens and at the level of public administration because you're going to throw away proficiencies that you'll hire again in 6–7 years because you'll rebuild these services. But in the meantime, you've deprived yourself of these abilities. So, then... The knowledge of the people, that you deprive yourself of, here, you don't have it anymore and you have start all over again. (The preceding citations from Hamel and Keil, 2018)

This observation echoes points made in Athens and Dublin about austerity constituting a political attack on expertise, public intellect and institutional memory, and in Leicester about the undermining of communication channels between local state and citizens. Collaboration is further hollowed out by the territorial scaling up of governance institutions. For example, local centres of health and social services were replaced by larger integrated services. Local structures where citizens could at least express a view were dismantled. Scaling up is useful in that it costs the government less to deliver services, distances it from immediate political scrutiny, and closes a channel of potential resistance or, at least, dissent within civil society.

Professionalisation of and downloading to the voluntary and community sectors have also been persistent features of neoliberalisation over decades. As these organisations largely depend on government funding, they often end up dealing with the fallout from austerity and, at the same time, trying to resist it. This creates dilemmatic, even contradictory imperatives. A community worker commented:

We find, again, this outsourcing of the state towards the community sector... The relationship to the state... is a love/hate one, a conflicting collaboration where we tell ourselves 'We have a mission, in the interest of the public, so public funds should finance what is in the interest of the public'. And at the same time we are very jealous of our autonomy even though the accountability mechanisms are harsher than ever. (Cited in Davies 2017: 34)

Finally, successive governments since the early 2000s eroded neo-corporatist bargaining arrangements associated with the Québec model (Pineault, 2012: 39). However, they had not dispensed with them entirely, and bargaining between trade unions, employers and provincial government continued. As Chapter 7 explains, these mechanisms were double-edged. They gave the unions powers that elsewhere disappeared or were downgraded, but also served as a vehicle for containing and sectionalising labour, while fragmenting anti-austerity forces (Hamel and Autin, 2017).

So far, there is little in this story to distinguish Montréal from the themes explored in Chapter 4. Yet, as Chapter 2 explained, regime consolidation around neoliberal goals and mentalities had not translated into a strong development dynamic. Hamel and Jouve (2008) record how the urban regime that emerged during the 1980s shifted economic strategy away from major events towards a place-marketing agenda positioning Montréal as a 'world class' city based on financial and digital economies. They explain how the Consultative Committee on the Development of the Montréal Region (1986), chaired by a senior business academic at McGill University, produced a report recommending the 'world city' approach, aiming to attract new corporate HQs through the city's UN networks. The Committee garnered support from key business interests, including the 'presidents of the Montréal Stock Exchange, the Chamber of Commerce, the Board of Trade, Power Corporation, Beaver Asphalt, the Hudson Institute of Canada' and the construction sectors (Hamel and Jouve, 2008: 25).

This coalition was sustained through the 1990s, but more through continued goal alignment than tangible achievements. Between 1999 and 2012, for example Montréal lost almost 30 per cent of its head offices (Leduc, 2014, cited in Hamel and Keil, 2015). The rollback of the 'mega city' project discussed in Chapter 3 further weakened the 'world city' brand. The governance predicament, therefore, was continuing regime stagnation, while alternative social forces were excluded from debate about the city's future. Echoing Loopmans (2008), Montréal appeared to be caught in an interregnum characterised by both structural failure and weak hegemony. As the study concluded, there was evidence of an economic upturn in the city, driven by construction and housing booms and a growing knowledge economy sector (Moser et al, 2019). The administration of Valérie Plante was also advancing positions associated with the Green New Deal, and Plante herself participated in a huge rally in support of the global climate strike in September 2019. At the same time, she adopted a vigorously boosterish economic strategy dubbed 'Accelerate Montréal', echoing the attempt to marry sustainability with growth in Nantes.

Montréal is a story of long-term regime weakness, unresolved struggles and political fragmentation. The key issues have been threefold. First, the radicalisation of austere neoliberalism through retrenchment and restructuring has been executed, albeit with mitigations and concessions further discussed in Chapter 6. Second, however, the austere neoliberal medicine did not solve the city's governance crises nor translate into a productive governing regime dynamic: either through a tenable business agenda, or the incorporation of significant fractions of civil society into the local state. Rather, the collaborative model was rolled back, with revanchist overtones of the kind seen in Dublin. Third, despite the nebulous progressivism of the Plante administration, the search for a distinct and generative model of social solidarity had yet to bear fruit (Hamel and Keil, 2015). As Chapters 6 and 7 explain, resistance to austerity was creative and vibrant, but also fragmentary and vulnerable to recuperation.

Nantes: a corroding sustainable development regime?

The 1980s industrial crisis in Nantes took the form of a collapse in the shipping industry and re-location of port industries to neighbouring St Nazaire in the Loire estuary. In the decades since, this period of retrenchment has been employed to frame representations of Nantes as a city of rebirth, renaissance and revitalisation. What became known as 'system Ayrault', a powerful coalition driving the governance of Nantes, began to emerge, even in the midst of retrenchment, through an inter-sectoral modernisation forum, the 'Kervégan Institute', convened by Jean-Joseph Régent, chair of the city's Chamber of Commerce. It brought together political, economic, cultural and academic figures to configure a new agenda for Nantes (Renard, 2000, cited in Griggs and Howarth, 2015). When he became Mayor in 1989, Ayrault further energised the development coalition, gradually assuming a leadership role across city and metropolitan region.

Griggs, Howarth and Feandeiro (2020: 98) explain the core principles driving the development of Nantes under System Ayrault: attractiveness, sustainability and participation. In this regard, there were affinities with the post-Franco Barcelona model, discussed later, as well as the Plante agenda in Montréal. The impetus for public participation, as a governing principle, came from the development coalition itself with additional encouragement from higher tiers of government. In the 1970s and 1980s, the Nantes football team was a source of pride for its fast, fluid passing game, which became known as the Jeu à la Nantaise (Nantes Game) (Griggs et al, 2020: 98–9). According to its architect, team manager José Arribas, the Nantes game worked because players understood that the team was greater than the sum of its parts. 'This is why, much more than a game system or organisation, it is a game design that needs to be talked about in Nantes. Or if you prefer a state of mind that I can translate as follows: "everyone tries to blend in and trust the partner"'. Borrowed from the footballing ethos, Jeu à la Nantaise became embedded in the governing discourse of the 'citizen city'.[1]

For nearly three decades, the governing coalition under Ayrault's leadership proved durable, exemplified by its success in driving forward the Métropole project and its emblematic status, as Nantes was awarded the status of European Green Capital in 2013. The former illustrated its convening power, the latter the way Nantes was recognised as a model city worthy of emulation on the international stage. Community participation was always important to Ayrault, who saw it as a way to re-engage residents on the public/social housing estates in Nantes, many of whom defected to the far right in the early 1980s. In the pre-GEC period, moreover, Nantes outperformed many other French cities in terms of economy, infrastructure development and population growth (Griggs et al, 2020: 96). For a considerable time, conditions allowed the three elements of attractiveness, sustainability and participation to 'cohere, thus securing legitimacy and popular consent for the resulting policies and practices' (Griggs et al, 2020: 105). For example, the EU defended Nantes against claims that the international airport project at Notre-Dame-des-Landes was incompatible with the European Green Capital award, on the pragmatic grounds that sustainability and growth had to be coupled in innovative ways):

> We looked at this closely, but it is not a point that penalised
> Nantes. In Frankfurt, which is one of the most important

crossroads in Europe, the management of negative impacts is very important for the population. Here it is different; the airport close to the centre is transferred to a more remote zone. It is always necessary to find a compromise between economic need and negative impacts. It is important to ensure that the grounds of the current airport are revitalised.[2]

In the period since the GEC, and particularly the election of Johanna Rolland to the Mayoralty in 2014, the participatory strand of the Nantes Game has been rebooted through mechanisms to support 'co-production, shared governance, citizen dialogue and open and participatory governance', construed as being 'at the heart of [its] projects', where 'attractiveness and sustainability are rhetorically placed at the service of social cohesion and the quality of life' (Griggs et al, 2020: 98). One public official declared that in Nantes 'the ball circulates a lot between different actors, for a project that is a collective one'. In the words of another, 'participation: it's in our DNA'.[3]

Chapter 2 suggested that narrations of 'crisis' in Nantes tend to face upwards and downwards and away from the city itself, while identifying multiple dislocations: a crisis of French politics and republican values, a crisis of social exclusion, construed in Nantes as 'décrochage' (the notion that poor neighbourhoods are uncoupled from 'the economic motor of the city'), and a crisis in traditional modes of service delivery (a widespread international issue) (Griggs et al, 2020: 100). The renewed emphasis on collaborative governance formed a crucial element in the city's response to these perceived crises, occurring alongside the gradual incursion of challenges associated with national austerity and slow growth. In the city's press kit on citizen dialogue, Rolland highlighted the crises of representation, trust and legitimacy, which she saw as a serious threat, while pointing to potential remedies in the proximity of citizens with city institutions, and the expertise of citizens as potential innovators.[4] The suite of initiatives revived the 'collaborative moment' to an extent not seen in the other European cities. Ostensibly, with its established governing coalitions and relative insulation from harsher forms of neoliberal retrenchment (Chapter 2), Nantes was better resourced than most to pursue the inclusionary and democratic dimensions of regime building.

Yet, Griggs et al (2020) show that the collaborative apparatus has less solved the crises identified by Rolland than it has internalised them. Cynicism was widespread among civil society respondents. For example, one of the big debates held up by the city to testify to its participatory credentials, about the future of the Loire valley, was dismissed by one civil society group: 'the mountain brought forth a mouse'. Moreover, 'so-called participatory democracy is in fact a technique to attempt to manipulate public opinion. We call that a "smokescreen"'. According to a trade unionist, 'we cannot highlight a participatory democracy which does not exist and for the moment... it does not exist despite the statements'. Moreover, in the neighbourhood forums, 'people who are truly in vulnerable positions are not in the know, or do not keep themselves in the know, or are not free, for these types of things... they do not go to these meetings' (citations from Griggs et al, 2020: 101–102). The suggestion was that property owners had a much stronger voice in neighbourhood forums than social/public housing tenants.

Critics of the Nantes approach suggested that they were neither interested nor welcome in participatory forums. The City Council did not want to hear certain messages, 'so (the dialogue) becomes completely stuck in these meetings'. Where consensus could not be reached, or inconvenient challenges were mounted, public authorities cited the Republican ethos, where their authority as educators and arbiters of the general will superseded any participatory, democratic and collaborative ethos. For example, the city council espoused its educative function, where citizens receive a 'foundation document' setting out the context. This 'aims to be pedagogic' (citations from Griggs et al, 2020: 103). Officials could thereby try to negate or de-legitimise opposition groups deemed to be promoting sectional interests. But this approach brought contradictions into play. It invoked a Republican theory of the state to legitimise regulating the participatory apparatus and de-politicising the city's development agenda. Yet, the participatory apparatus was supposed to ameliorate the crises of this very Republican ethos. Thus, this expression of the Nantes Game was reproducing the same crises and conflicts that it was supposed to mitigate, situating the three core goods – attractiveness, participation and sustainability – in an increasingly antagonistic relationship. Griggs, Howarth and Feandeiro (2020: 105) conclude:

> as the continuity of the political system has begun to corrode, reflecting its endeavours to confront the eruption of various dislocations and crises in the city and the country, and as the fiscal tightening begins to have some impact on the regime, so the component parts have begun to creak and groan as they rub against one another. Instead of cohering

in a reasonably stable way, they have begun to exhibit signs of tension and contradiction.

The struggle over the future of the Nantes Game took on a more overtly politicised form in the battle over the proposed, now abandoned, airport development at Notre-Dame-des-Landes, which was supposed to replace Nantes Atlantique. The cancelling of this project, while outside the boundaries of Nantes Métropole, signified a blow to the growth agenda, and risked widening the disjuncture between the goals of attractiveness, participation and sustainability. The growth regime, and its participatory strategies, were much derided by opponents of the airport development. 'Nantes Nécropole' was the chosen title of one prominent campaign, an astute critique of the brand projected by the Métropole (Griggs and Howarth, 2020).[5] President Macron's decision to cancel the project was certainly a victory for tenacious long-term mobilisation against what campaigners condemned as unsustainable aviation-driven growth. Though not directly linked to austerity, it was among the most important instances of successful resistance to neoliberalisation in the eight cities. Chapters 6 and 7 discuss this struggle and its limitations.

Through the Jeu à la Nantaise, Nantes built a successful multi-stakeholder governance regime, centred on can-do local elites from the state, corporate and civil society sectors, enabling it to emerge dynamically, as an early adaptor, from the industrial crises of the 1970s and 1980s. For a long time, it sustained the three primary goods of attractiveness, participation and sustainability in a constructive relationship. This became more difficult in the post-GEC period, despite the city's confidence in its ability to sustain the growth model and navigate austerity. The renewed and intensified emphasis on collaboration did not reinforce regime coherence, but rather internalised the dislocations it was supposed to resolve while alienating many grassroots organisations and trade unionists. City leaders compensated for stakeholder disgruntlement by accentuating the Republican state tradition – itself one of the pillars of the French state considered to be in crisis. Although, Mayor Rolland remained strong compared with potential rivals, handily winning the 2020 municipal elections, the cancellation of Notre-Dame-des-Landes, as the study concluded, posed questions about the continuing viability of the Nantes Game. Nantes re-animated its participatory apparatus to sustain and reinforce the capabilities of its governing regime, but with limited effect in extending its co-optive reach into organised civil society. Any incipient urban regime crisis was not of prolonged duration, like that of Montréal, but had begun to pose similar questions about the future of this distinctive expression of entrepreneurialism, the limits of hegemony, and the potential alternatives discussed in Chapters 6 and 7.

Greater Dandenong: a state-led intercultural revitalisation regime

Like other cities, Metropolitan Melbourne has been subjected to waves of industrial retrenchment, urban decline and austerity, the latter most notably under the federal government led by Jeff Kennett between 1992 and 1999 (Painter, 1998: 33). One official commented, 'with the impacts over the years of the downturn in manufacturing Dandenong started to lose its place. So, it ended up as a place – and it still does have issues – with high unemployment and all the social issues that go with that' (cited in Henderson et al, 2016). The Greater Dandenong case study focused on the governance of economic restructuring in this disadvantaged city to the South East of the Melbourne city-region, at a time when a period of 'austerian idealism' seemed a real possibility. However, as Chapters 2 and 3 explained, the threat did not materialise and Greater Dandenong became an outrider to the initial parameters of the project, as a city exposed to neither recession nor austerity. This did not make it immune from wider international trends and pressures, or from neoliberalisation; notably the privileging of efficiency, fiscal conservatism, consumerism and market-driven growth. Henderson et al (2020: 125) argue that in Greater Dandenong, the approach partly reflects 'progressive fiscal conservatism', or what Harvey (2005) called 'neoliberalism with a human face', through its state-sponsored economic and social revitalisation programmes.

Greater Dandenong has a small city council with 10 members, eight of whom represented Labor. The Mayor is more a figurehead than an executive, but there is no official council leader either and, like Dublin, the city council was not configured for strong political leadership. This model also reflects the relative positional weakness of the municipality in a system directed, financially and politically, by federal and state institutions. The Revitalizing Central Dandenong (RCD) programme was initiated by the state of Victoria in 2005 in a period of Labor government, to address structural weaknesses and economic disadvantage in the area. It began with an 'unprecedented' investment of AUS$290 million, to support land acquisition, staff costs and infrastructure delivery. It further leveraged private investment and local government spending of approximately AUS$120 million in complementary improvement projects (Henderson et al, 2020: 127).

As a state-driven programme, RCD has been vulnerable to political vicissitudes, highlighting party-political differences between Labor, which treads a line between social investment and fiscal restraint, and the Liberal National Party, with its more fiscally conservative outlook (Henderson et al, 2020: 130–1). When the LNP was elected in 2010, state support for RCD dropped. According to one respondent, referring to the agency that then became 'Places Victoria', the LNP's 'rhetoric around VicUrban was it had grown fat, it had grown lazy, it was wasting money… VicUrban's got to live within its means' (Henderson et al, 2016). At the same time, like austerity regimes operating in and above other cities, State Premier Ted Baillieu committed to surplus budgeting. The rhetoric echoed that employed to warrant austerity elsewhere, but without overt retrenchment of the kind envisaged during the Premiership of Tony Abbott. For a period after the GEC, private investment in Central Dandenong slowed, though it picked up again thereafter – a figure of $700 million dollars was claimed as the leverage on public RCD investment. Labor took the reins once again in 2014, led by Daniel Andrews. His administration backed RCD as part of its strategy for a more strongly poly-nucleated city-region, re-distributing some of the economic heat from downtown Melbourne. According to Gavin Jennings, Minister for Priority Precincts, 'From the centre of Dandenong, the benefits of renewal will resonate throughout this vibrant and fast-developing community and we're proud to be leading such an important initiative.'[6]

The governance arrangements constructed through RCD were not solely about state funding, state direction, city-regional development priorities or progressive fiscal conservatism, though they made little sense outside this framework. The RCD programme was rather generative of a new coalition dynamic, centred on the city's cultural pluralism and commitments to racial equality, drawing from the developmental resources of intercultural governance. Henderson, Sullivan and Gleeson (2020: 140) argue,

> Though this scenario still broadly reflects the relatively weak nature of the municipal layer in the Australian federation, we note the growing assertion and significance of other actors in the revitalization effort, including, in particular, the municipal government as well as the private sector and culturally aligned NGOs in the latter stages of the study period.

There were affinities between the stories of multiculturalism in Leicester and Dandenong insofar as it had also become a resonant tool for place-marketing and claims on attractiveness in the latter. Key differences were twofold: the public investment climate in Dandenong, compared with severe retrenchment in Leicester, and the sense that multiculturalism might be characterised by stronger intercultural solidarity. According to the 2016 census, the majority of the city's population had a migrant background. Some 60 per cent were born outside Australia, and 75 per cent spoke a language other than English at home. According to one respondent, 'the sheer weight of difference has helped ensure that nobody is a majority and the norm is you come from somewhere else'. This provided a 'starting point for community interaction', where residential mixing prevented the spatial concentration of ethnic groups (Henderson et al, 2017). According to Sullivan, Henderson and Gleeson (2019: 29), 'everyday encounters and negotiations that occur between people helps to break down barriers of difference and build intercultural understanding, leading to a sense of belonging and inclusion'.

Food production and consumption provided an example of intercultural governance. It was used by the municipality to encourage dialogue and mutual understanding: 'If you make some flat bread, you all get sit around and talk. And so, we've used it as a mechanism of engagement. In other words, food is recognised as a... social unifier to bring together' (Sullivan et al, 2019: 31). Food was a key driver of intercultural place-making and for trying to create a local tourism industry through collaboration between the municipality, state governments and different cultural groups. To this end, revitalisation created cultural precincts, such as an Afghan Bazaar and Little India. According to one former state official, 'not only are they fantastic from a social cohesion point of view, they're also destination drivers to Dandenong... to celebrate the diversity of the place, the diversity of the food offering' (cited in Davies, 2017: 31).

The idea of multiculturalism was embraced by business, and both tiers of sub-national government. According to one local government respondent, 'diversity is not seen as a threat; it's a great thing and we want to praise it and celebrate it and remove any stigma of it'. Said a representative from the local interfaith network, Dandenong is a place where there is "freedom to go wherever you want" and you will find "diversity and cohesion" with "no fear," only an "openness, trust and invitation" to interact. 'People are very proud of the diversity and want to preserve it. They see it as healthy' (Davies, 2017b: 30). The research team encountered these sentiments repeatedly (Sullivan et al, 2019: 28).

As in Leicester, many inward migrating groups established themselves in the commerce of Dandenong and from there gained political influence. Trading and community groups flourished and were able to influence local policy through engagement, advocacy and lobbying. 'They've grouped up and they have a strength that was unimagined in the 1980s when the Indo-Chinese groups came. By grouping up, they have developed a voice in the community' (elected national politician, cited in Sullivan et al, 2019: 29). Membership of the City Council had a strongly multi-ethnic, multi-faith flavour. One indicator of inter-cultural regime building was that community leaders from a variety of different faith and ethnic groups had been elected to the Mayoralty in preceding years.

The re-composition and activism of local civil society over time – both commercial and non-profit sectors – was a major influence on the politics and culture of the city and also changed the composition of the city-central economy. In the vocabularies of Gramscian regime politics, RCD invested in strengthening a multicultural civil society that in turn cultivated its own resource base feeding back, constructively, into regime capacity. In addition, despite the constraints of the Australian system, the municipality had become resourceful, proactive and savvy in cultivating relationships and navigating relations with state authorities and the corporate sphere. According to a respondent from the business activist group, the Committee for Dandenong (C4D),

> local government is constrained by what it can say and how it can say it and who it can say it to... We're not constrained by that though, and clever people in local government understand that we're not constrained by that and would like to see us make statements or fight for things... the Committee for Dandenong and its constituency lobby both State and Federal Government, to try and get their attention. (Henderson et al, 2017)

The potency of this ensemble as a vehicle for equitable revitalisation should not be exaggerated. Many socio-economic indicators for Dandenong attested to continuing inequality and deprivation. Equally, the city was not immune from racism displayed very publicly by prominent Australian politicians. At the same time, the revitalisation agenda drew from entrepreneurial city and attractiveness menus. What Dandenong demonstrated, in a way that other cities did not, was that in the age of austerity a revitalisation programme driven by intercultural entrepreneurialism could produce a multi-stakeholder and multi-scalar regime politics imbued with the spirit of the collaborative moment, albeit in a more organic form and without the idealised character expressed by Mayor Rolland in Nantes, or in earlier European variants of the third way. The ethos of intercultural revitalisation generated affects and shared goals that bore little resemblance to the equalibertarian solidarities born of anti-austerity struggles discussed in Chapter 6, but they arguably overflowed or were supplementary to neoliberalism as well. Nor were they imprisoned by system drivers prominent elsewhere. Despite talk of looming crises, discussed in Chapter 2, and the widening disjuncture between revenues and demands, the revitalisation regime appeared to be in a constructive phase, facing no obvious challenges from governmental or civil society actors in the city or other tiers. As preceding quotes demonstrate, respondents tended to be optimistic, drawing from the well of positivity cultivated in a vibrant intercultural governing space. This is not to suggest that there were no political conflicts (for example, Sullivan et al, 2019: 23), but that unusually, the revitalisation programme did not provoke outright resistance. In Dandenong, social entrepreneurialism was in a more vigorous phase, driven by an activist state nurturing a proactive civil society and sustained by a felicitous economic conjuncture. The contrast between this story of urban governance and the nadir in public trust in the Australian government was very stark (Cameron and McAllister, 2019, particularly pp. 15–16).

Barcelona: a new municipalist challenge to austere neoliberalism

The regime politics of Barcelona have been much debated in the post-Franco period (for example, Blanco, 2015a), with the characteristics of the 'Barcelona model' a significant point of contention. Blanco et al (2020) explain that like other cities, Barcelona experienced industrial decline in the 1980s, with the 1992 Olympics becoming a pivotal event in the transformation of the city into a growth machine, attracting investors and tourists of all hues, from alt-lifestyle seekers and gap-year travellers of minimal means to the super-rich yachting elite. Barcelona has fared much better as a post-Olympic city than Athens or Montréal. It has become richer than many of its Spanish counterparts (Degen and Garcia, 2012). OECD data shows that between 2001 and 2015, for example, its per-capita GDP as a percentage of national per-capita GDP rose from 121.5 to 143.9 per cent, while Madrid's declined from 137.2 to 135.4 per cent.

Depending on who uses it, in what context, the term 'Barcelona Model' refers variously to the powerful public–private growth coalitions driving forward urban development, the participatory governance mechanisms that arose after Franco and/or the emancipatory spirit of Barcelona's radical political traditions born in the early 20th century. In this sense, it has evolved and is contested in much the same way as the Nantes and Québec models. In the decades before the GEC, under the leadership of the PSC, Barcelona established a dense ensemble of participatory governance mechanisms with many formal or semi-formal channels of engagement and collaboration involving local government, public agencies and elements of civil society involved with social assistance, community organising and neighbourhood representation. As Blanco et al (2020) explain, the credibility of these participatory mechanisms was always a bone of contention among those who saw the system as a vehicle for democratic inclusion and those who saw it more as a vehicle for absorbing civil society into the growth machine. Viewed from the perspective of Barcelona en Comú, it had evolved in a similar way to the Québec Model: 'Barcelona is today synonymous with the Barcelona Model: a way of making a city that has been dominant for almost three decades and that, beyond its democratic beginnings, has ended transforming Barcelona into the Mediterranean paradise for neoliberal urban policies' (cited in Blanco et al, 2020: 27). Blanco (2015a) argued that the participatory apparatus did influence social policy and service delivery, but that it had neither access to nor leverage on economic development. He proposed that there were dual circuits of regime power operating in the city, respectively in the spheres of economy and social reproduction, an idea that chimed with the view of Stone et al (2001) that it is easier for organised citizens to influence non-economic domains of public decision-making and action.

The political configuration changed as the 'age of austerity' got underway. In the first instance, between 2011 and 2015, the three tiers of the Spanish state aligned behind austerity (see Chapters 2 and 3). The social-democratic PSC dominated the politics of Barcelona for 30 years after democratisation, but imploded after the crisis. In 1991, the PSC won 21 of 41 seats on the City Council and 42.95 per cent of the vote. By 2011, its share had declined to 22.14 per cent and 11 seats, losing office for the first time since the first democratic elections in 1979, to conservative Mayor, Xavier Trias. In 2015, the PSC experienced a further dramatic collapse, winning only 9.63 per cent of the vote and four seats, for fourth place (Davies, 2017a: 14). At the same time, the radical left saw an equally dramatic revival through the Barcelona en Comú coalition, replicated in other Spanish municipalities and by the rise of Podemos on the national stage. Podemos is currently the junior partner in coalition with the Spanish Socialist Party, the Partido Socialista Obrero Español (PSOE). Like social democratic counterparts PASOK (Greece) and the French Socialist Party, the PSOE vote collapsed after the GEC – by more than 50 per cent at its nadir in 2016 – and remains much depleted despite leading a new government from 2019.

The research highlighted four key dynamics in this period, pulling in different directions: unashamed celebration and turbo-charging of the growth machine by political and economic elites; eroding the participatory apparatus through 'institutional layering' (reducing the scope for influence while leaving the mechanisms in place); growing activist disillusionment with participatory governance, and the rise of multi-faceted, durable and militant urban and national movements against austerity, drawing inspiration from and radicalising longstanding political traditions in the city associated with cooperativism and libertarian socialism (Davies and Blanco, 2017). Consequently, the boosterish austerity regime tightened its grip on the apparatus of state and economy, but at a significant cost in terms of diminishing hegemony. Diminishing hegemony, in turn, was signalled by four main factors: the strengthening Catalan independence movement, the rise of increasingly confident and well-organised anti-austerity movements such as the Indignados and the 15-M mobilisations in 2011, the collapse of the PSC and the victory of Barcelona en Comú in the 2015 elections, propelling housing and anti-eviction activist Ada Colau to the Mayoralty.

Since 2015, Barcelona City Council has spearheaded the international 'new municipalist' movement, which is diffuse and heterodox (Thompson, 2020) but anchored by the common objectives of overcoming austere neoliberalism and instantiating a new politics of equality and solidarity through resistance, co-production, 'new urban activisms' and – when in office – urban policy (Walliser, 2013; Russell, 2019; Barcelona en Comú, 2019). The new municipalism is certainly a challenge to the neoliberalised Barcelona model, but by no means overturns it completely. It rather generates renewed tension between the dual circuits of regime power disclosed by Blanco (2015a), as the social and political spheres seek to transgress upon the economic. Whereas Trias sought to constrain the participatory apparatus, Barcelona en Comú has sought to radicalise it. Blanco and Gomà (2020: 396) summarise the main mechanisms: rebuilding neighbourhood governance through de-centralising policy and enhancing lateral cooperation, the co-production of urban policy involving lay citizens and community organisations, promoting community engagement as a vehicle for collective political action, open and inclusive management mechanisms for the provision of public services and the management of urban spaces, and promoting cooperative forms of social innovation in policy arenas such as housing, energy and culture. Blanco and Gomà argue that the ethos of new municipalism involves promoting and supporting these practices, while attempting to extend them upwards to higher tiers of the state and outwards to other municipal jurisdictions.

Part of the city's strategy has been to challenge austerity by asserting the right to housing in the face of post-GEC dispossessions. The growth machine has been challenged by curtailing the tourism boom, for example limiting Airbnb and legislating against the conversion of residential properties for hire by tourists. The City Council also suspended licenses for new pubs, restaurants and nightclubs in tourism-intensive neighbourhoods. Municipal privatism was challenged by a new policy for public procurement, which encouraged co-production between municipality and progressive civil society groups and sought to re-municipalise strategic services, such as energy and water.

Colau summarised the impact of her administration, arguing that 'citizens have noticed a change in the political agenda, in the way of doing things, with a much closer politics... We have put social issues above all other concerns... We have clearly changed the priorities of the city.'[7] Her leadership role should not be understated either. Though considered to have moderated her approach in office, her rhetoric remains powerful. She has used the Mayoralty to make a series of principled, radical and internationally inspiring calls to action, challenging neoliberal, environmental, sexist and racist orthodoxies head-on. Chapters 6 and 8 reflect further on the significance of these interventions.

Whereas the 2011 elections resulted in scalar convergence behind austere neoliberalism at the city, regional, national and EU levels, 2015 fractured it three ways. As Barcelona en Comú took the reins of municipal power, a new coalition committed to Catalan independence assumed control of the Autonomous Community. After a turbulent period following the September 2015 regional elections, Carlos Puigdemont (later to be exiled) took the Catalan Presidency and set in train the November 2017 independence referendum. Under the direction of Partido Popular PM Mariano Rajoy, himself deposed in 2018, the forces of the Spanish austerity state employed violence and intimidation against voters, invoking the constitutional inviolability of Spain as its warrant. By 2016, state power in and above Barcelona was divided among three different political fractions: austere neoliberalism coupled with Spanish chauvinism at the national level, what turned out to be a hopelessly naïve and out-manoeuvred pro-independence administration at the regional level, and a new municipalist coalition in Barcelona allied to anti-austerity movements in Spain and internationally (Blanco et al, 2020: 31–2). The Colau administration supported the right of Catalans to decide, but otherwise took an ambivalent stance towards the question of independence. At the same time, it formed a coalition with the collapsed PSC rather than the main left-of-centre independence grouping, Esquerra (The Republican Left of Catalonia). It did so again in the more challenging political climate of the 2019 municipal elections, which it narrowly lost to Esquerra. The three positions overlap at various points, but they were significant crosscurrents in the urban politics of Barcelona, around which different civil society forces coalesced. This made it difficult for the radical left to build a wider hegemony (Blanco et al, 2020: 31–2; Zografos et al, 2020). At the same time, it was subjected to predictable attacks from the forces of the right: media, corporations, the courts, legal restrictions, conservatism within the municipal bureaucracy and blocking tactics by coalition and opposition councillors. Chapter 7 discusses these constraints.

Following an extended period of mass mobilisations against austere neoliberalism, both before the GEC and after, Barcelona en Comú was able to form a municipal coalition led by the radical left, with (increasingly) critical support from the movements in which it was born. By comparison with other administrations, this one made significant inroads, utilising the resources of both municipal apparatus and allied civil society groups. With Colau as Mayor, Barcelona en Comú shifted the parameters of the Barcelona model in a direction that de-privileged dispossession through development, and re-asserted democratic and economic rights. This particular state–civil society configuration continues to carry weight in the city, and far beyond. The unanswered question was whether, in the changed circumstances of the 2019 mandate, further inroads could be made through re-radicalisation, the engagement of new social forces, or a period of stagnation – perhaps reversal – would ensue. Chapter 6 further discusses strengths in the new municipalist approach, while Chapter 7 illustrates how regime capacity has been limited, both by institutional and structural constraints on local government and the conflictual architecture of urban civil society, with its own class, ethnic and territorial pre-occupations. The impediments appear greater than in 2015, not least because of the relative isolation of Barcelona within Spain after the widespread electoral wipe-out of the municipalist platforms in 2019. The unknown factor was whether Colau and Barcelona en Comú could overcome these limits and re-mobilise the rebellious spirit that propelled them to power (see Afterword).

Conclusion

This chapter has explored the governance of four cities that do not sit straightforwardly within the compass of consolidated austere neoliberalism discussed in Chapter 4. Montréal, Nantes, Dandenong and Barcelona all encounter familiar challenges with economic restructuring, and all have been exposed to waves of ideology, policy and state restructuring associated with austere neoliberalism and competitiveness. Yet, in the post-GEC period they moved in different, if inter-related, directions.

The regime configurations in Montréal and Nantes had quite different characteristics and objectives, but in both cities a hitherto durable governing regime now lacked efficacy, posing the question for future studies of what might come next. Montréal's overtly neoliberal 'world city' agenda never achieved great success. The 'Nantes Game', on the other hand was successful for a period but began suffering setbacks in the context of a wider breakdown in the congruence of regime objectives, tied up with the political crises engulfing France. The government of Québec deliberately undermined participatory governance mechanisms, while Nantes extended them. But neither approach seemed to be enhancing regime capacity, entrepreneurial or otherwise. The strategy of the Plante administration begs the question of whether a new regime can be built in Montréal, based on principles not unlike those beginning to lose traction in Nantes.

Dandenong and Barcelona point, respectively, to the potentialities for regime construction and transition beyond the parameters of austere neoliberalism. It would be misleading (and Euro-centric) to suggest that Dandenong was aping forms of governance envisioned in Europe in the halcyon days of the 'collaborative moment' before the crash, or that it wished to proceed down the same path as northern counterparts. It might be more accurate to suggest that in the shadow of the Chinese boom, and in a positive investment climate, Greater Dandenong was constructing the kind of stakeholder-based social investment regime that many European cities aspired to, but failed to achieve. Australia was fortunate, both politically and economically, to have avoided the kind of recessions and retrenchment seen in the northern hemisphere. As Sullivan, Henderson and Gleeson (2019: 41) commented, 'Central Dandenong shows the international community a political alternative to austerity'. Nevertheless, as Davies and Msengana-Ndlela (2015) observed, beyond felicitous circumstances urban regime building also requires political effort. The intercultural revitalisation regime in the city-centre exemplified the potentiality for constructive stakeholder politics, built around an ethnically plural notion of what 'social inclusion' means within the compass of market-led development. It was able to mobilise resources and fulfil the agendas of collaborators in a way that did not exhibit the pathological traits which Peck (2017b) identifies with 'late entrepreneurialism'. It was suggestive of a generative, localised hegemony project with significant co-optive powers.

Barcelona, finally, demonstrated all the traits of a dynamic growth machine in the post-Olympic period, shuddering to a halt after the GEC. The crash did not put an end to extravagant boosterism or to the celebration of extreme wealth – far from it. The city sought to radicalise this approach under Mayor Trias. The neoliberal variant of the Barcelona model did not falter because it had necessarily hit structural buffers, but because the politics of the city intervened to set it on a different course. For all the formidable barriers it faced, the conditional alliance of local state and anti-austerity actors shifted the polarities of the Barcelona model some way back towards democracy and equality. Whether this approach can further overcome and transcend austere neoliberalism will depend on the revitalisation of the spirit mobilised during 15-M and after. Chapters 6 and 7 turn to the question of urban resistance and alternatives to austere neoliberalism.

6

Resisting Austerity: Resonant Solidarities and Small Wins

Introduction

After this study commenced in 2015, Crouch's (2011) conjunctural question concerning 'the strange non-death of neoliberalism', was answered, to a point, by overlapping waves of re-politicisation and reaction. The consideration of urban political (dis)orders problematises three momentous shifts concentrated in, but not limited to, Europe, North and South America: the rise of neo-reactionary forces, with an overtly neo-fascist right, the collapse of austerity-complicit social democratic parties in Europe, and the uneven, tentative, intermittent rise of a heterodox anti-austerity left including prominent anti-capitalist currents. Further episodes of re-normalisation in the previously dominant hegemonic project of neoliberal globalism – what Tariq Ali (2018) dubbed the 'extreme centre' – could occur, though even with the election of Joe Biden to the US Presidency, this seemed unlikely at the time of writing. On the contrary, global events continually add weight to May's (2017) suggestion that political time is speeding up, and intervals between acute episodes of instability are diminishing. These eruptions are signs of a Gramscian interregnum, signalling the iterative breakdown of old regimes of hegemony-domination. This uneven process of disordering is contested by passive revolutionary forces to the right and far more tentative and transient forces to the radical left. However, as the discussion of Greater Dandenong in Chapter 5 illustrates, political contagion was not universal. It remains to be seen whether escalating conflicts and geo-political tensions, now exacerbated by COVID-19, will turn repeated political-economic and environmental crises into a poly-crisis of more general and globalised proportions.

Chapters 6 and 7 explore patterns and trajectories of resistance to neoliberal austerity, and its impact on the governance and governability of the eight cities. The objective is two-fold: to consider the extent to which resistance has weakened neoliberal austerity within the state apparatus, or itself been weakened; and to explore the impact of contentious politics in reconstituting civil society as an 'autonomous' terrain of anti-neoliberal and potentially counter-hegemonic politics. Whereas Chapter 6 focuses on the productive relationship between resistance and solidarity, Chapter 7 looks at how resistance was muted, contained, disorganised or coopted. As a case of regime transition, many of the issues pertaining to resistance and containment in Barcelona were introduced in Chapter 5. In this chapter, we delve further into the political characteristics that made the city a source of inspiration to the international municipalist movement and potentially enhance its transformative capabilities.

Chapter 1 discussed Gramsci's famous observation that he was 'a pessimist because of intelligence, but an optimist because of will', a variation on Marx's idea that people make history but in circumstances they inherit. According to Burawoy (2011: 73), pessimism of the intellect discloses the 'structural determination of social processes, setting limits on the possible'. 'Politics, on the other hand, requires optimism, concerned as it is with collective will formation, dissolving limits and striving for the impossible.' Gramsci also commented (1971: 54–5; Q25, §2),

> The history of subaltern social groups is necessarily fragmented and episodic. There undoubtedly does exist a tendency to (at least provisional stages of) unification in the historical activity of these groups, but this tendency is continually interrupted by the activity of the ruling groups; it therefore can only be demonstrated when an historical cycle is completed and this cycle culminates in a success. Subaltern groups are always subject to the activity of ruling groups, even when they rebel and rise up: only 'permanent' victory breaks their subordination, and that not immediately.

The disruptive activity of the ruling groups has certainly been effective in the neoliberal era (Anderson, 2000; Crouch, 2011), but the completion of a putative historical cycle is knowable only in retrospect and then perhaps only from a considerable distance in time and with attendant controversies around methodology, evidence and interpretation. However, Gramsci points to phenomena immediately familiar in the 21st century. The non-linear and episodic waves of anti-neoliberal, anti-authoritarian and anti-capitalist struggle; the tenuous unity between struggles, fragmentation among forces opposing austerity, and the tendency of insurgencies to subside; sometimes with gains, sometimes in defeat, sometimes restoring the semblance of a prior 'normality' and sometimes creating space for reaction. Peck (2017a: 16) commented on the tasks of conjunctural urbanism:

> In principle, 'noisy' moments of contestation and the much quieter creep of consolidation ought both to be within the ambit of such critical, relational modes of analysis, although in practice the roles of active resistance on the one hand and incremental normalisation on the other have not always been accentuated.

Chapter 1 argued that the study of normalisation and upheaval has synchronic and diachronic aspects. The former interrogates the balance of forces at a given moment, while the latter situates it in its historical context (Rosenberg, 2005). In the diachronic dimension, mounting system pathologies in quiet periods set the tone for noisier moments of contestation, crisis, reaction and transformation. Resentments, festering in slow time, but with little immediate effect on the conduct of politics, punctuate normality in all sorts of explosively insurgent and reactionary ways, something to which the ambiguously contentious politics of the Gilets Jaunes testify (Bristow, 2019). Synchronic analysis captures dynamics of normalisation–contention in real-time and weighs their significance for reproducing and disrupting political orders. This chapter casts light on recent perturbations, reflecting on what they reveal about the conjuncture, and the agency incubating within cities embroiled in the rolling international crises of neoliberal globalism. The conjunctural question introduced in Chapter 1 is, if we survey patterns of resistance and disruptive agency in the period since the Battle for Seattle, held by many on the left to mark the return of radical left politics to the West after two decades of defeat in the initial neoliberal insurgency (Bornstein, 2009), are there signs that they are coalescing into something durable and transformative? Or, is this still a period of experimentation in which austere neoliberalism persists, albeit with diminished hegemony, while uprisings come and go, with little left behind in the sense of emerging counter-hegemonic apparatuses or other durably transformative legacies? Chapter 8 returns to these questions. The remainder of this chapter explores productive struggles and solidarities encountered in the eight cities, highlighting strategic internationalism, the feminisation of urban politics, the reconstitution of contentious civil society through struggle, and the potential for 'up-loading'.

Strategic internationalism

Chapter 5 explored the movements and political re-compositions leading to Ada Colau becoming Mayor of Barcelona in May 2015, under the banner of Barcelona en Comú. Respondents were acutely aware of the strategic and structural limitations of the local state project. Barcelona en Comú took initiatives to mitigate them, among which agitation for international solidarity was perhaps the most resonant. Barcelona has special international significance as a source of inspiration for new municipalists across the world. Recognising its position as such, Barcelona en Comú established an International Committee to communicate lessons and foster dialogue (@BComuGlobal on Twitter). Barcelona en Comú exercised considerable convening power globally. New municipalists across the world gathered in Barcelona in June 2017 under the hashtag #FearlessCities. Leading activist Laura Roth (2019) explained the internationalist philosophy:

> The municipalism we are talking about is not parochial, but rather has an internationalist or global horizon. The new municipalism is conscious that what affects us at a local level depends to a large extent on what happens at other levels, ranging from the regions to the national state and the rest of the world. Accordingly, it also recognizes that municipalities have a great responsibility and capability to confront global problems, and that municipalist organisations and governments must support one another in order to reinforce themselves at other levels. It is for precisely this reason that the Fearless Cities movement is working as a network at the global level.

Ada Colau's speeches and council documents were replete with references to planetary geo-political challenges: 'Speculation is a threat to cities, as is climate change for the planet. We prioritise life or allow speculation: we choose life.'[1] 'We are ashamed that thousands of people die at the borders of Europe. It's not appropriate for cities and states that want to be the First World and examples of democracy and human rights. If Europe wants to remain an international benchmark for human rights and democracy, it must radically change its policy.'[2]

Barcelona's historic pro-refugee mobilisation in 2017 captured this sentiment, mobilising a slogan condensing anti-fascist and anti-neoliberal politics into one: 'tourists go home, refugees welcome'. Some see strategic internationalism as part of a 'left wing populism' (Mouffe, 2018), constructing a political imaginary dividing 'us' (the 'people', regardless of their origins) from 'them' (economic and political elites). As Blanco (2017) put it, 'the "us" becomes very inclusive and leaves little room for xenophobic attitudes'.

One open question is how far networks constituting the ebb and flow of a municipalist internationalism can be channelled into supporting and augmenting specific municipalist programmes. Some 200 leading figures on the international left from a wide range of political traditions signed a letter declaring support for Ada Colau's re-election campaign in May 2019. They included among many others, Debbie Bookchin, Judith Butler, Bill de Blasio, David Harvey, Chokwe Antar Lumumba, Toni Negri, Dilma Rouseff, Richard Sennet and Yanis Varoufakis.[3] The letter highlighted the allure of Barcelona in the political imaginaries of the international left, regardless of otherwise substantive differences between the signatories. Developmental processes associated with planetary urbanisation are more often than not hostile to equality and solidarity. But in this instance, they pointed towards the potential for practical inter-urban solidarities constituted through several modes of exchange. As activists projected the figurative Barcelona through the digital, infrastructural and economic connectivities created by neoliberal 'glocalisation', the planetary aspect of urbanisation assumed an emancipatory form far removed from the corporate, technocratic mode of integration associated with neoliberal globalism. It was rather conceived in terms of a plural, open ended, dialogic process of world-making in pursuit of equality (Madden, 2012: 778). From this perspective, Barcelona might be viewed as the subject-object of a libertarian socialist globalisation enacted through the city, at once demonstrating, calling for and summoning international solidarity, notably in the struggles for racial and gender equality.

The feminisation of urban politics

Like other literatures, the gendering of austerity was a prominent theme in this study, showing that women tend to be more exposed to public service cuts and disadvantaged by state restructuring, both as users and employees. M.P. Murphy (2015: 226–227, cited in Gaynor, 2020: 78), explained the impact of Irish austerity in terms that resonate in many countries: 'Simply put, more women are employed in the public sector, more women use public services and more women claim social welfare payments.' At the same time, women have been at the forefront of anti-austerity struggles, most prominently in Barcelona and Dublin but also in Montréal where the student movement of 2012 set out demands for 'direct democracy, feminism and ecology' as the basis for 'a radical renewal of and extension of Québec's social democratic exceptionalism' (Pineault, 2012: 52).

Women have been central to the fight against austerity in Barcelona, and across Spain. The significance of what activists call 'feminisation' is the subject of considerable attention. For Russell (2019), it refers to nothing less than the 'transformation of power itself', from its traditional masculine, adversarial and conflictual forms towards a constructive, communicative form. According to an activist cited by Russell (2019: 1005–6), '[To feminise power] is not to take power, but to build a new kind of power, from the bottom up, a power to do with others, a power as a creative power and collective capacity to change things.' Ada Colau exemplified this feminised style of leadership. Under her Mayoralty, the City Council's executive comprised a majority of women in leading roles overseeing citizen participation, urban planning, mobility, health and international relations. It established a new Office for Feminism and LGBTI Affairs to promote equality and respect.

The deep political resonance of feminisation in Spain was captured in the mass strike, of possibly unique historic proportions, on International Women's Day in 2018, dubbed the 8-M mobilisation. These events represented a new high water mark in the rise of a global 'feminist-public sphere' (Felski, 1989), which has produced many militant events including a victorious strike against the so-called 'Law and Justice' government's anti-abortion bill in Poland in October 2016. On some counts, the strike of 8-M 2018 involved more than 5 million people. In another stirring intervention, Colau explained that the strike was to 'show that without women, the world really does stop... As people in public positions, we have the duty to mobilise on behalf of those who can't go on strike. This is the century of women and of feminism; we've raised our voices and we won't stop. No more violence, discrimination or pay gap' (cited in Jones, 2018).

The 2018 strike occurred following the repression of the Catalan independence referendum. According to one activist (cited by Beatley,

2017) after the crackdown: 'The Spanish state and all of its institutions are patriarchal, and they're founded on the basis that men are positioned above women. And clearly, their security forces adopt that patriarchal mentality.' If the realpolitik of city hall moderated municipalist aspirations, the events of 8-M suggested that the institutional turn had not itself chilled the climate of urban mobilisation or prevented city leaders contributing to it. To this extent, there remained a strategic connection between new municipalist leadership, activism and repeated waves of mobilisation around internationalist and feminist causes. Here too, Barcelona sought to fuse local and global struggles into a generalising emancipatory politics.

Whereas Barcelona channelled and amplified the globalisation of feminist struggles, the 'water wars' in Dublin empowered a more localised feminism, through rebuilding community-based solidarities. As the research commenced, the revanchist national state regime (Chapter 4) seemed to have had a deadening effect on resistance to austerity and Dublin, much like Leicester, was an antithesis to rebellious Barcelona. For Hearne, Boyle and Kobayashi (2020: 235), Ireland was seen as having an 'extraordinarily moderate and passive society', in which Irish people were 'stoical', doing collective penance for their alleged excesses in the pre-2008 period (see Chapter 2). This stereotype overlooked the rich traditions of mobilisation and resistance in Ireland from the Easter Rising onwards, but by the time the study concluded, the political context had blown it away.

As part of the bailout agreement in November 2010, the Irish government introduced a metred household water charge to be implemented by a new company, Irish Water. The Right2Water campaign against the charge launched in Dublin in October 2014, with a demonstration of some 120,000 people. This was a vast number in a small country of 4.7 million, equivalent in size to the London demonstration of 1.5-2 million in February 2003 against the looming war on Iraq. Though it had something of a *deus ex machina* quality from the 'passive society' perspective, the new movement was fuelled by myriad inchoate resentments and smaller mobilisations accumulating over years, fomenting in the neighbourhoods, and culminating in a widespread sense that austerity had gone 'too far' (60 per cent of surveyed protestors) and ordinary people were being forced to pay for the speculative excesses of the rich. 'The government did not stand up to the bullies. It chose to stand up to the weak' (social researcher, cited in Davies, 2017: 18). The charges were perceived to have been 'the straw that broke the camel's back'. If 'introduced 10 years ago, they probably would have been passed. The timing of the water charges was like, "let's kick people and continue to kick them for as long as we like and they'll never do anything'" (activists, cited in Gaynor, 2020: 85). While the EU celebrated Ireland as the 'poster-child' of austerity (Hearne et al, 2020: 234), traumatised citizens were to be dealt another brutal blow.

The movement deployed a variety of tactics, including mass demonstrations, non-payment and civil disobedience, with physical resistance to the installation of water meters. Non-payment was sustained at high levels. In 2015, 56 per cent of taxable citizens failed to pay the charge, with a corresponding revenue shortfall (Hearne et al, 2020: 239). In July 2016, the government suspended the charge, later accepting the recommendation of a special commission that access to water should be considered a human right, and household water consumption funded from general taxation.

Together with the abandonment of the airport development at Notre-Dame-des-Landes discussed later, this episode marked the clearest single instance of a victorious struggle against neoliberalisation encountered in the eight cities. It echoed the defeat inflicted on Margaret Thatcher's Conservatives by the UK anti-Poll Tax movement but promised to exceed it in political significance. Unlike the anti-Poll Tax movement, the anti-water charges movement was generative of further struggles, particularly in the field of housing. Four features are of particular interest for understanding emergent solidarities in anti-austerity and anti-systemic protests.

First, its explosion onto the national stage in 2014 endowed the water charges movement with some of the characteristics of 'urban rage' (Dikeç, 2018), becoming a 'nodal issue' for a wider set of grievances (Griggs et al, 2020: 103). This point was made repeatedly: 'people wanted something to voice their concern. People wanted something to voice their anger. And they saw this as a mechanism. But it's not in any sense just about water.' 'We were fooled with the whole Celtic Tiger business and the fact that the poor people were made disproportionately to carry the costs, I don't think anybody would argue with that, right? And, you know, we were duped. And "We won't be fooled again", as "The Who" said' (citations from Gaynor, 2020: 87). Police violence further contributed to transforming the water protest into a site of generalised political grievance, compounding alienation and anger against the Irish state, and reinforcing the sense of austerity as a new authoritarianism (Chapter 4). The Irish government sought to criminalise civil disobedience and used police to enforce the installation of meters. According to an elected politician cited by Gaynor (2020: 84):

The level of Garda mobilisation of some of the localised water protest served as an eye opener for people where they felt that the Guards were policing austerity... they prioritise that over the policing of crime and stuff... So, people draw conclusions from that, in terms of how the state has an oppressive apparatus which it uses as a means of containing anger and opposition.

Second, the water wars brought a new layer of people into political activism. A survey in 2015 of 2556 people involved in the protests found that 54 per cent were new activists (Gaynor, 2020: 85). One of the most striking features was the central role played by women. While mobilising the city's working classes too, many leading activists were middle-class women, reflecting the fact that elements of this stratum had been hurt by austerity. Irish austerity was gendered in several ways, from brute economic impacts to its political construal as the theft of family and motherhood. Austerity caused significant net outward migration of Irish citizens. A woman activist captured the pain of separation (Gaynor, 2017):

The biggest blow was when our son decided to go to Australia. Now, he was in employment. He'd been in the construction industry. Obviously, that went bust. Then, he was working in a call centre and it just sucked the life out of him. It was just so soul destroying. And so, him and his partner made the decision they were going to Australia. And I suppose that's really when austerity hit me. It wasn't the financial inequity. It was the emotional, the family ties. So, from there, I was very angry.

Another respondent observed,

mainly women with children will be totally anti-austerity because... there has been nothing progressive for their children. And most working men and women who find that they're paying the massive Universal Social Charge. Their wages have been cut. They have no pension to speak of. And they say 'well, that's austerity'. (Politician)

When asked about motivations for becoming active, women repeatedly expressed concern about the lack of opportunity and absence of hope for their children (Gaynor, 2020: 86).

In juxtaposition with Barcelona, the Irish movement reveals that the feminisation of urban politics has many different qualities. It is notable, for example, that the explosion of resentment against austerity was inflected with family values. However, it became detached from historic associations with conservatism and religious deference in Ireland. As one respondent observed (Gaynor, 2020: 87),

> I think there's something fundamentally that's changed in terms of people's psyche in terms of how they see the world. Where previously they would have accepted it, a bit like the [Catholic] Church... Now they say, 'Hold on,' you know. 'The emperor has no clothes.' And once you switch that on in people, they start to see other things.

The third significant feature of the water charges movement was that it fortified intercultural solidarities and transformed the physical proximity of neighbourhood into an enriched propinquity (Russell, 2019; Gaynor, 2019: 13–14). Once again, women activists were central to the process. According to one (cited in Gaynor 2017),

> Women would bring food down in the afternoons so that, when children would come home from school, that they would stop off and they would have a stew or they would have something before they went home. And I thought that was really lovely. I thought actually that was really, really special... And the amazing thing is after a few weeks of doing this, businesses started to drop up food to us... The local chippers got involved, they started dropping up pizzas to us. The Chinese dropped up with chicken curries and... and you know, local supermarkets would bring us scones.

Diverse acts of collective resistance, solidarity and support were also seen as healing and rebuilding fractured communities. For a female politician, 'The anti-water charges campaign is kind of... Like first of all, incredibly hopeful... it has been very useful in places... where there is a diversity of people living, in bringing together new residents with older residents around a common cause' (Gaynor, 2020: 87). An activist enlarged on this theme, observing that,

> The extraordinary thing about the water charges movement I think is the very organic, if you like, level at which people got involved in it. And I think that fed their own sense of

confidence about it. And by that and, quite specifically, I mean at the act of being able to sit on or stand over their water meter, doing their knitting or in a group – you know, in a very defensive mode saying, 'No, you're not going to put that meter in here.' (Gaynor, 2017)

These new, granular solidarities rolled forward, fourthly, into further campaigns. This aspect should not be exaggerated. Gaynor (2020: 88) points to the dissipation of momentum in the period since the water charges movement (also Hearne et al, 2020). However, there has been no return to the passivity stereotype. The combination of austerity and the renewed growth bubble fomented further intense social crises leading the Dail to declare a national housing emergency in October 2018.[4] Protests, if not on the scale of the water charges movement, were large, vibrant and angry, opening a new arena for political struggle.

Dublin's 'water wars' demonstrate how the hegemony-dominance of austere neoliberalism can fragment, and neighbourhood mobilisations around the struggle to subsist gain traction, and with durable effect. In this sense, the movement signified a rupture with the old order, ushering in a phase of politicised disruption and re-composition in civil society. Together, the politics of Barcelona and Dublin demonstrate how anti-austerity struggles that propel women into positions of leadership (formal or informal) can foster more generalised struggles, projecting upwards onto the international and global scale, and downwards into the reconstitution of granular solidarities. In this sense, women-led and -influenced struggles were generative of substantive equality claims and substantive equality gains.

The politics of Barcelona and Dublin diverged in two notable ways. First, the wave of struggles in Barcelona were shaped and inspired by enduring traditions of struggle, while those in Dublin were born of pent-up resentment and anger and, in many ways, alienation from traditional modes of struggle rooted in (male-dominated) corporatism (Chapter 7). Second, Barcelona was at the forefront of the international municipalist movement, while municipalism had little resonance for anti-austerity activists in Dublin. Among the main reasons for this contrast were the extreme weakness of the city council in Ireland's small revanchist state, and political inertia within the council itself (Chapter 4). Though anti-austerity councillors won an electoral voice, the propulsive forces required to resist austerity were concentrated outside and against the governing regime. They eroded its hegemony and caused it to retreat on a nodal issue but without defeating it, making incursions into its institutional space or establishing alternative hegemonic apparatuses.

Re-constituting rebellious civil society

The research disclosed three further processes through which rebellious forces in civil society reconstituted themselves against austere neoliberalism: the development of grassroots solidarity networks, the politics of rescaling and redefining the city, and the tentative emergence of new vehicles for inter-sectoral solidarity.

New urban activisms: collaborative governance at the grassroots

The idea of a transformative partnership between the municipality and organised anti-austerity forces combines traditional left commitments to social and spatial equality with politicised expressions of co-production and commoning (where 'commons' refers to not-for-profit resources held in trust for, belonging to or affecting a whole community, but not under state control). A council official in Barcelona offered this definition (cited in Davies, 2017: 15):

> The Commons aren't spaces owned by the public sector, but they represent a shared and common wealth. The attributes of universality, redistribution, accessibility... characteristic of the Public are missed in many public administration projects. This is why I think that the Commons are more capable of acting as the Public than the public administration itself.

The relationship between democratic process, public ownership, everyday making and commoning remains controversial (Thompson, 2020). So too is the extent to which 'co-production' is economically and politically empowering, a form of privatised neoliberal 'responsibilisation', each in succession or both. These questions play out in debates about utopias, real (Olin Wright, 2019) or envisioned (Bell, 2017). In Barcelona, however, many examples of commoning emerged from the anti-austerity grassroots after the GEC, often of brute necessity. Myriad agroecological consumer cooperatives, food banks, clothes banks, community gardens and social economy initiatives appeared, inspired by longstanding cooperativist traditions. They built solidarity networks and were enmeshed with anti-austerity movements. To support these activities, the City Council introduced a measure to enable community management of public facilities and spaces. These vehicles were also tolerated or even encouraged by regional authorities, provided they did not infringe marketable property rights (Davies and Blanco, 2017). Born of necessity, they also had a distinctive political content in Barcelona. Though situated in an ambivalent relationship with the municipality, they constituted part of the new municipalist ensemble if this is conceived in a Gramscian, inclusive sense. An explosion in the number of diffuse 'solidarity networks' was also evident in Athens, but these were more-or-less wholly disconnected from the austerity state apparatus, and illustrate a contrasting point about disorganisation, discussed in Chapter 7 (Chorianopoulos and Tselepi, 2020).

Rescaling and redefining the city

Chapter 4 explained that Baltimore has been governed as a racially organised 'city of neighbourhoods' for a century, a political geography that continues to shape it today. In April 2015 a young African American, Freddie Gray, died after receiving severe injuries in police custody. Activists dubbed the seismic events that followed *The Uprising*, a term that for them had positive connotations (for example, Pratt-Harris et al, 2016). This consisted in an escalating mix of rioting and organised street protests. The Governor of Maryland declared a state of emergency, and deployed state troopers. *The Uprising* provoked solidarity demonstrations in other cities, part of a national stirring of urban rage led by the USA's African American citizens that began with the killings of Trayvon Martin in 2012 and Michael Brown in Ferguson in 2014 (Cobbina, 2019) and launched the first wave of the #BlackLivesMatter movement.

Like the water charges movement, *The Uprising* became a nodal issue, spurring more general claims on social justice. A community activist explained that 'the unrest awakened many people... talking about things they've never talked about before' (Pill, 2020: 156). The emergence of a more assertive strand of community, social movement and labour organising has been one legacy. The first wave of #BlackLivesMatter did not achieve the highest profile in Baltimore, but a resonant message was that African American activists 'trained outside of the local non-profit formula' (Pill, 2020: 154) were becoming more vocal and assertive. A voluntary sector respondent commented, 'these young African American males who use technology... to get their point across and they are starting to get a following... And so, you're starting to sort of get this grassroots community-driven young folk, energetic constituency that is starting to gain momentum and have a voice' (Pill, 2017).

The wave of resistance and renewal in community organizing within Baltimore assumed a spatial character in the aftermath of *The Uprising*, the challenge to dominant discourses and practices representing a struggle for rescaling from below (Smart and Lin, 2007). The historic discourse of a 'city of neighbourhoods' had long dominated revitalisation and gentrification-displacement agendas, articulated in the city's housing typology (Chapter 4). The neighbourhood apparatus had itself been an impediment to city-wide mobilisations and the emergence of a sustained collective voice. In this sense, the past and present of Baltimore echoed Hatherley's (2017: 112) description of the poor, black neighbourhoods in Washington, DC as a 'secret city', with 'no part in the city's official layout and monumentality'.

Baltimore's history of racial segregation therefore made activist language significant in re-politicising urban space. The critical notion of 'parallel tracks' or 'two cities' challenged the 'city of neighbourhoods'. For example, 'Port Covington, a neoliberal city' was contrasted with 'a parallel structure, a parallel narrative... [a] vision of community empowerment from the grassroots up, as opposed to seeing black folks as appendages of a neoliberal wave' (Pill, 2020: 157). For another respondent, Baltimore was a 'tale of two cities... one doesn't have anything to do with the other, other than its geographic proximity. Well, *The Uprising*... shows that there is a connection. Just ask anybody who is trying to run a business downtown or at the inner harbour during a five-day curfew' (Pill, 2015). During *The Uprising*, Baltimore's 'secret city' forced itself into the light and activists hoped there could now be 'a counterweight to the political, social, and economic hegemony of that neoliberal common-sense stuff' (Pill, 2017).

Mayor Rawlings-Blake announced her own alternative 'One Baltimore' initiative shortly after *The Uprising*, as 'a comprehensive and collaborative public–private initiative to support ongoing efforts to rebuild communities and neighbourhoods'. Her 'one city', unlike 'parallel tracks', stressed the need for 'civic dialogue and a process for ongoing engagement' with Baltimore's 'underserved neighbourhoods' (cited in Pill, 2015). The stated purpose was to 'build and sustain trust' but also 'generate resident created and led solutions'. Some side-payments were attached to this rhetoric. The multi-agency partnership, Project Core (Creating Opportunities for Renewal and Enterprise) deployed resources in 'stressed' neighbourhoods, but there was no deviation from Baltimore's downtown development agenda (Pill, 2020: 154).

The politics of 'one city' could therefore be seen as an attempt to counter the activist construal of 'two cities'. Nevertheless, through new organising practices, and marginal policy gains, *The Uprising* generated a political afterlife, beyond the fleeting moments of socio-spatial centrality achieved in the event itself. Baltimore saw revitalised community organisation (propinquity) and new claims on the right to the city (centrality and nodality). However, Chapter 7 argues that these new political forces as yet had little impact on the regime politics of Baltimore, strictly 'business as usual' (public official, cited in Pill, 2020: 154). In this sense, like Dublin, the reconstitution of a more rebellious strand in civil society diminished the co-optive power of the dominant regime, but without overturning it, or significantly disrupting its capacity to govern.

The politics of Nantes further illustrate how campaigns around specific issues can channel anti-systemic grievances and pose political questions about the future of a city and a nation. The decision in 2018 of President Emanuel Macron to abandon the long touted international airport development in the extra-urban location of Notre-Dame-des-Landes near Nantes, exemplified this. Griggs and Howarth (2020) explain how, although sitting outside the boundaries of Nantes Métropole, the proposed airport was a significant strand in the city's development strategy, as well as at regional and national levels. It attracted sustained opposition from the outset. The campaign brought together farmers, residents, politicians and environmental activists, mobilising a powerful counter-expertise in legal and planning processes, while drawing support from across France and, indeed, internationally where campaigns against airport expansions cross-pollinated and worked across borders.[5] Protesters at Notre-Dame-des-Landes set up camps and took over vacant compulsorily-purchased farms on the proposed site of the airport, transforming the government owned 'zone to develop' into a 'zone to defend'.[6]

Like Dublin's anti-water charges movement, and Baltimore's *Uprising*, the campaign against the airport simultaneously won its proximate struggle and became a nodal issue, presenting a new challenge to the dominant model of governance and development in Nantes. Demonstrators linked the campaign against the airport to adjacent grievances and demands. Christine Poupin, a leader of the Anti-Capitalist Party generalised accordingly: 'there is a moment when it becomes necessary to say 'STOP'... STOP to the airport obviously, but also STOP to its world, and its world is the same as that of the state of emergency as that of the destruction of the employment law.' Students protesting in Nantes against the reform of labour rights drew similar links, reported in the media: 'they shout against police violence, the airport, capitalism, government, bosses' (citations from Griggs et al, 2020: 103).

Griggs, Howarth and Feandeiro described the airport development at Notre-Dame-des-Landes as an 'ideological battle', challenging both the Nantes economic model, and the republican legitimacy of the French state, leading to demands for the city to reprioritise spending towards social housing and homelessness. These demands were couched in terms of a challenge to attractiveness and the 'prestige' projects that served this goal, articulated by the subversively resonant counter-signifier 'Nantes Nécropole'. Such considerations pose the question of where an alternative vision for the city might come from, particularly given the legacy of the Gilets Jaunes and the wave of mass strikes against Macron in late 2019 and early 2020, which forced him to retreat on his signature pension reform. According to Griggs and Howarth (2020: 31), the subversive discourse of the 'slow city' incubated in the airport campaign, was beginning to percolate into Nantes itself, such that 'the movement of the countryside has led to a questioning of the dominant logics of urban governance and policy'. Nevertheless, as Chapter 7 explains, an alternative project had yet to crystalise due to political fragmentation within the city itself.

Intersectoral solidarities: students, workers, communities and voluntary groups

Viewed from the author's UK standpoint, where organised resistance to austerity was of limited scope and durability, the contentious politics of Montréal and Québec were intense. There occurred multiple waves of militant resistance to neoliberalisation in the post-GEC period, and to Couillard's *rigueur*. Québec's students, with their long-standing organising traditions were at the heart of these mobilisations, notably in the so-called 'Maple Spring' uprising of Spring 2012, which achieved a partial victory in preventing a tuition fee rise (Boudreau and Hamel, 2017). *The Coalition large de l'association pour une solidarité syndicale étudiante* (CLASSE) mobilised around a tri-partite master-frame, echoing Barcelona in asserting a politics of 'direct democracy, feminism and ecology' (Pineault, 2012: 52). Student strikes recurred in different forms, with different intensities, and around a variety of goals since the Maple Spring (Collombat, 2014). They were a reference point for other mobilisations involving both community and worker organisations. Unions had a more prominent role in Montréal than in other cities. As one respondent explained (Hamel and Keil, 2016), the difference between Montréal and the rest of North America is that it has a higher rate of unionisation. For this reason, salaries are way higher than in the rest of North America and, therefore, there is less precariousness. There is a strong presence of the CSN. This makes a huge difference, compared to other cities.

After the Maple Spring, the peak moment in worker struggles against Couillard occurred in December 2015, with a general strike under the banner of the 'common front', a slogan first raised in the general strike of 1972 (Graefe and Rioux Ouimet, 2018). The Common Front agreed a deal with Couillard, celebrating it as a victory. However, critics argued that it had delivered only marginal gains while more militant unions fought against ratifying the deal, to no avail. Activists saw the major unions folding their hand in this way as a betrayal (Graefe and Rioux Ouimet, 2018: 179), an issue Chapter 7 discusses further in relation to the influence of 'social partnership' traditions on anti-austerity struggles.

In an action unique in this study, 1300 community organisations went on strike against funding cuts on 2 and 3 November 2015, with a mass demonstration in Montréal, eliciting concessions from the government (Smith, 2015). Just as the depth of union organising in Montréal marks it out as unusual in the North American context, so too does the density of its voluntary and community sector networks and organic collaborative traditions, discussed in Chapter 5. A significant organisation in these mobilisations was 'La Coalition Main Rouge', a group originally established in 2009 to oppose privatisation and service charges, to which some 100 groups were affiliated. The Coalition organised community groups, trade unionists, students and feminist groups. According to one community organiser, this form of organising 'allows a reunion of the Left; allows the trade unions and community organizations on the Left to meet. Those meetings are the ones that permit the creation of potential solidarity movements' (cited in Hamel and Keil, 2020: 118). The recognition of common cause between community-based movements, student and worker struggles extended to wage struggles for precarious immigrant workers. An activist explained: 'we're part of a fight for a $15.00 minimum wage. In this fight, we're developing alliances with various groups – such as the workers of Montréal's Old Port, for example – who are on strike, fighting for the same thing. We've adopted a collaborative strategy with trade unions' (Hamel and Keil, 2020: 119).

From the standpoint of examples of alternative institutional ensembles emerging from inter-sectoral struggles, the Coalition Main Rouge stands out. Chapter 8 discusses the potential significance of such formations in relation to Gramsci's conception of the hegemonic apparatus, introduced in Chapter 1. This instance captures something of the continuing ebb and flow of resistance in Montréal, its durable 'infrastructures of dissent' (Sears, 2014), and the attempt to construct new solidarities. The city demonstrated the continued vitality of inter-sectoral organising traditions, legacies of political traditions evolving over many decades. It combined traditional and novel forms of struggle and was one of the cities in which resistance delivered tangible – if modest – gains. In 2017, furthermore, the 'progressive' Projet Montréal achieved unexpected electoral success under the leadership of Valérie Plante. Further electoral success for the left came in the provincial election of 2018, when eight Montréal representatives of Québec Solidaire, were elected to the regional assembly.

Despite these accomplishments, Chapter 7 discusses three main weaknesses. First, despite tactical concessions Couillard was able to deliver most of his austerity agenda. Second, instances of unity, union and community struggles remained fragile and vulnerable to fragmentation. Finally, in the provincial context, Montréal was isolated by the election in 2018 of a provincial government, Avenir Québec, led by the 'populist' François Legault.

Uploading: policy pressure on upper tiers

Barcelona City Council was far from immune to criticism for moderating its radicalism particularly after the electoral compromise of June 2019 (Chapter 7). Shortly after her election in 2015, Colau argued that it was 'common sense, to keep what works and to improve it as much as possible' and that it was 'optimal for a city like Barcelona that there is maximum collaboration between the public and private sector, but the role of each must be clear' (Blanco et al, 2020: 28). This orientation meant that the relationship between city council and militant grass-roots organisations could be conflictual, but the constructive elements were also important. For example, the City Council approved a new housing policy, deemed 'historic', imposing a rule that 30 per cent of units in new developments and large regeneration projects must be public housing. The policy was an example of pressure translating from the movements into the city council and from there to regional government. According to Escorihuela and Domingo (2018) (translated in Blanco et al, 2020: 33), asserting the importance of the movements,

This is neither a measure of the Government, nor of Ada Colau and any political group. It is La PAH of Barcelona, the FAVB, the ABTS, the Sindicat dels Llogaters, and the Observatory DESC that presented it in the municipal plenary session in February, together with three more proposals for widening the public housing stock, supported by all the municipal groups except the PP. It is a new tool that is important to guarantee the right to housing in the city, but it isn't the only one.

At the same time, pressure further exerted by the movements, and the City Council, resulted in the Housing Agency of Catalonia adopting a Rental Price Reference Index, as a voluntary regulation mechanism. This concession was deemed 'absolutely insufficient' by activists, because it was unenforceable, and took no account of spatial concentrations of poverty (Blanco et al, 2020: 33). However, these measures demonstrated that city government can ally with social movements to exercise pressure on upper tiers of government, counteract pressure from opponents, and create a little space to deliver its own housing and planning policies. This is to suggest that policy assertiveness, built on provisional alliances of city council and civil society groups, can at least modestly enhance municipalist regime capacity.

Conclusion

The foregoing discussion highlights three ways in which resistance to austere neoliberalism acted positively in and against neoliberal regime politics. First, in the specific case of Barcelona, resistance propelled anti-austerity forces into office, and despite limitations discussed in Chapters 5 and 7, consolidated municipalist regime capacity through discourses, practices and mobilisations around international solidarity, anti-racism and feminisation. Here too, the leadership of Mayor Ada Colau played a powerful role in marshalling active citizens and international audiences to the cause. Moreover, Barcelona had modest successes in building a constructive relationship with forces engaged in new urban activisms and, led by social movements, pushing policy innovations upwards. These informal coalitional powers should not be exaggerated, but they were important in accruing modest gains to the new municipalist programme, to making Barcelona governable. Barcelona shows that while municipal power is always limited in a market economy and hostile state environments, it is more effectively exercised in a conditional dialogue with radical anti-austerity forces, whose autonomous activism enhances regime capacity and moderates the drift to conservatism in the state apparatus. The strategy of principled internationalisation is another way in which recognising the limited powers of an incipient municipalist regime is less a force for conservatism than a medium of political generalisation, with productive feedback into solidarity.

Second, the chapter discusses numerous instances in which acts of resistance served to politicise and reconstitute civil society forces organising against austere neoliberalism. These forced concessions of greater or lesser import, such as in Baltimore, Dublin, Montréal and Nantes, though without necessarily positing alternatives. But even where resistance does not disrupt regime power directly, it can strengthen rebellious civil society as a parallel force, as it did in Baltimore and Dublin, and briefly at least in overcoming sectoral fragmentation in Montréal. In these cities, struggle generated new, granular solidarities and contributed to further weakening the hegemony of austere neoliberalism and the co-optive reach of its governing regimes.

Third, there was a noteworthy trend towards political generalisation, where specific grievances give rise to systemic grievances and critique – what Griggs, Howarth and Feandeiro (2020) called 'nodal issues'. Nodal issues become the focal point for more general and widespread critiques of a political order, while the issues disclosed through critique then proliferate. This process of generalisation was particularly evident in Dublin with the water wars channelling a multiplicity of grievances and educating a new generation of (notably women) activists, whose energies translated into the struggle for housing justice. It was also evident in the struggle against the airport at Notre-Dame-des-Landes. In Baltimore, The Uprising in response to the killing of Freddie Gray translated into a revitalised politics of community activism, mobilising around the critique of 'parallel tracks', an expression of generalisation with clear anti-neoliberal overtones. The globally contagious impact of radical municipalist ideas was evident in the inspiring and educative role played by Barcelona. These features are all important in demonstrating how moments of protest and upheaval can achieve a sustained political afterlife, serve as a bulwark against re-normalisation, establish grounds upon which future upheavals might occur, and spread horizontally from local to global scale (May, 2017). Chapter 7 considers the limitations of resistance and the containment mechanisms employed by regime actors to divide, de-mobilise and deflect.

The 'Activity of Ruling Groups': Containment, De-mobilisation and Fragmentation

Introduction

Chapter 6 explored resistance from the perspective of its capacity to deplete the governability of austere neoliberalism, construct solidarities, incubate alternative political economies in local state and civil society, and channel particularistic grievances into a more generalised anti-neoliberal or anti-capitalist politics. From a Gramscian regime theoretical perspective, it focused on what organising resources forces opposing austere neoliberalism were able to mobilise, whether they act directly on the (local) state apparatus or capacitate and empower rebellious forces within civil society. This chapter returns to the problem of containment, de-mobilisation and fragmentation, dimensions of urban governance that mitigate against both antagonistic and constructive forms of resistance. This endeavour casts light on a number of issues: first, the means by which urban regimes contain and enclose resistance, and insulate themselves from potential impacts; second, the chilling and divisive effects of social partnership traditions; third, structural and institutional limitations on regime transition through new municipalism; and finally, the recuperative power of neoliberalising and reactionary forces, consolidated respectively through Syriza in Greece (Chapter 2) and Britain's Conservatives in the struggle over Brexit.

Containing and deflecting resistance

The relative normalisation of austerity in Leicester was notable for having occurred in the context of a sustained national government offensive since 2010, leading to a deeply regressive restructuring of the local state (Chapters 3 and 4), and real-terms spending reductions potentially greater than those in any other city (Chapter 2). Even so, the experience of crisis and austerity was less sudden and dramatic than in Athens, Barcelona or Dublin. Unlike previous recessions in the 1980s and 1990s, foreclosures and house price falls were limited, as were corporate bankruptcies, mass redundancies and rises in unemployment. The effects of the crisis tended to be incremental, though cumulatively devastating. Poverty, precarity and under-employment increased, particularly among younger people, while central government subjected those excluded from work to a harshly authoritarian workfare regime. According to a council official interviewed in 2013, the 'cost of living crisis has been attenuated a little by... the low levels of inflation... fall in oil prices which is no doubt welcome in many households and indeed businesses' (Davies et al, 2020: 69). For a councillor interviewed the same year, 'actually for most people most of the time this doesn't affect them very much and they don't want to do anything different much from what they are already doing... for most people life goes on' (Davies et al, 2020: 69). Though millions of people suffered falling incomes, they were offset to a degree and for a time, by rapidly falling mortgage and energy costs. A significant percentage of the population was not fully exposed to the crisis of social reproduction and for this reason was mostly unaffected, at the personal or household levels, by austerity. This segment of society largely escaped the fallout from the GEC.

With the help of the parliamentary Labour Party, which refused to oppose it, this combination of circumstances made it much easier for the UK government to deliver austerity without impediment. The situation changed significantly as the impacts of austerity accumulated, and the UK became re-politicised around austerity and Brexit. However, it provides important context for understanding the limited resistance to austerity in Leicester and the UK, reinforced by the local politics of austerian realism discussed in Chapters 2 and 4. The key to understanding the influence of austerian realism in Leicester lies in the struggles of the 1970s and 1980s and the shadow they continued to cast over anti-austerity politics. Leicester's civil society mounted energetic campaigns in defence of local services, including libraries, hospitals and fire-stations, some of which were successful. However, austerian realism, anchored by the instructive experience of defeat in previous generations of struggle, operated as a functional containment mechanism. The 'activity of ruling groups' in and outside Leicester contributed significantly to muting resistance (Davies, et al, 2020: 68–9), while it remained difficult for individuals trapped in the workfare cage, battling through each day, to find the time and headspace for collective action (a point also made in relation to Athens, discussed later).

The memories of defeat among trade unionists and municipalists in the 1980s cast a shadow not only over local government, but also anti-austerity activism. A voluntary sector respondent captured the pessimism anchoring austerian realism in commenting on the lack of militancy: 'Well, it's a bit... a losing game, isn't it really. I mean when die-hards tried in the past, it hasn't succeeded really. It's ended up losing what power it had, so that's like picking a fight with no chance of winning it' (Davies et al, 2020: 68). This quote encapsulates the perspective dominating the UK trade union movement since the 1980s and mirrors that of Labour municipalities. Responding to a proposal for a legal 'no cuts' budget from the white-collar and municipal union UNISON in 2017, the City Mayor dismissed it as 'pure fantasy'. He insisted that the city council 'going bust will not lead to the Tory Government crumbling'.[1] Davies et al (2020: 69) concluded:

> As the resources of austerity governance joined up, so resistance was weakened, contained, and disorganized. Explanation for this outcome cannot be reduced to the lessons of the 1970s and 1980s, but it is intelligible only in the long shadow they continue to cast. Resistance was durable in Leicester, but austerian realism contributes actively to the spatial containment of resistance and to the muting of contentious politics.

The granular politics of crisis containment and management had variable characteristics in UK cities (for example, Lowndes and McCaughie, 2013), but the situation in Leicester was replicated across the country to the extent that resistance was everywhere muted, and austerity delivered without sustained urban or national uprising. Crisis rather crystalised in other forms of which the right, after decades of neoliberalisation and re-acculturation, took decisive advantage, in part latterly by recuperating elements of Labour's anti-austerity platform (see later discussion). The containment of urban resistance through the austerian realist regime ensemble links to the widespread sense that the Labour Party, and Labour administrations delivering retrenchment at the front line, had betrayed long-suffering supporters. This sense of betrayal forms part of the explanation for the Conservative triumph in the British General Election of December 2019 (for example, White, 2020).

For all that *The Uprising* in Baltimore revitalised grassroots organising and altered the governing rhetoric of the city, it did not disrupt the core of the governing regime (its powers of pre-emption) or the continuing waves of perma-austerity inflicted on the city from within and above. In her $2.8 billion budget proposals for 2019, Mayor Catherine Pugh signalled business as usual. The police department, which absorbs the largest proportion of public spending, was to receive an increase of $16.9 million to $510.7 million, while the capital improvements budget was to be cut by $443 million. The goal, said Pugh, was to 'attract and retain businesses and residents', thus decreasing the property tax rate (Bonessi, 2018). The signs were that the administration would do little to disturb the basis of a socio-spatially iniquitous 'fix' that had endured, with incremental regime shifts, for a century (Pill, 2020). The Port Covington development continued. In contrast Sandtown in West Baltimore, the locus of *The Uprising*, was earmarked for demolitions and re-development in line with the housing typology (Chapter 4). As one activist commented, 'the conversation may have changed but the systems aren't changing'. Moreover, the crucial issue in a starkly divided city was still policing:

> Police-community relations... I think everything else is so minor... that developer developing Port Covington don't have absolutely nothing to do with my day-to-day existence... But I'm getting those kinds of conversations in my life all the time now – so and so got shot the other day... Why would anybody think those kinds of conversations in America are acceptable? They have become the norm and I don't want them to be the norm. (Community activist, cited in Davies, 2017: 13)

Chapter 6 explained that *The Uprising* in Baltimore spawned a renaissance in community organising, alongside conscious attempts to overcome spatial fragmentation. However, impacts on urban development policies were marginal. The contested 'parallel tracks' and 'one city' discourses show that different social forces were aware, in a quasi-Lefebvrian sense, that re-defining space and scale is fundamental to their struggles (Kipfer, 2002). However, these processes had yet to alter Baltimore's developmental trajectory. The alliance of a perma-austerian fiscal regime with a boosterish non-profit elite and downtown developers was not significantly disturbed. In this sense, resistance was kept at arm's-length from regime power. As the public official quoted earlier commented, it was 'business as usual' for the city (cited in Pill, 2020).

The governing regime, with its commitment to localised and privatised models of development (Davies and Pill, 2012), therefore remained intact. Yet, its hegemony was weakened and as events demonstrate, the USA is a re-politicising society in which new movements continually arise in cities and states, and a vocal democratic socialist constituency grows in influence, with increasing public support for socialist ideas (for example, Palmer, 2019).

Greater Dandenong was, once more, an exception; not only because it had not experienced recession or austerity in the post-GEC period, but also because revitalisation did not provoke the kinds of resistance seen in other cities. The RCD programme was not the subject of overtly contentious politics, despite the typically disputatious character of revitalisation programmes (for example, Broughton et al, 2013). As Chapter 5 explained, aspects of the programme were controversial, but contentious politics were confined to advocacy and election campaigning. According to a local politician (Sullivan et al, 2019: p. 29), for example, newly arriving ethnic minority groups influenced local policy through 'advocacy, lobby and engagement' – the 'grouping up' discussed in Chapter 5.

The relative lack of contentious politics around revitalisation does not mean Greater Dandenong was a city devoid of political and economic struggles. Small workplace struggles over wages and conditions could be heated. For example, around 90 Australian Workers Union staff at Fletcher Insulation went on strike for 97 days during 2017, resisting a management attempt to erode pay and conditions through a new 'enterprise agreement'. On finally reaching agreement with the company, the union claimed significant gains (Neill, 2017). However, pockets of worker struggle did not impinge on the revitalisation programme or trigger wider political struggles around the future of the city. The future was still framed by positivity, the long-term relative stability of the Australian economy and constructive regime-building efforts.

Scalecraft and spatial containment

Leicester City Council employed a variety of tactics to mitigate crises of subsistence and inoculate it against the sense of a political crisis induced by austerity and local state restructuring. This was the objective anchoring austerian realism. Tactics included making cuts early and without fuss (Davies and Blanco, 2017: 1522), rationalising services, seeking efficiency gains and allocating discretionary assistance and advice to cope with workfare reforms, through funding pots first slashed and then devolved to local authorities. They also included scalecraft (Papanastasiou, 2019) or scalar activism to dilute resistance. Leicester's programme for transforming neighbourhood services exemplifies this. The objective was to mitigate the impact of cuts by merging municipal functions into new multi-service hubs thereby enhancing efficiency, for example, by co-locating libraries in community centres. The programme proceeded through a series of public consultations, with the city divided into six programme areas. A council official reflected on lessons drawn from other cities (Davies et al 2020: 68).

> What we learned was that we didn't want to do the whole thing in one go... because that seemed to generate concern, protest, anger all over the place and it took a long time for people to even accept what had happened. So a different approach was taken, which was... to divide the city up into five or six areas.

The idea was to roll out the programme in the least challenging areas and draw lessons that could then be applied in more quarrelsome neighbourhoods. One neighbourhood did generate significant resistance to the proposed closure and sale of the local library building. This was a strong community-based intercultural campaign with support from local politicians. Soon after an angry meeting of more than 300 residents observed by the research team, the Council reversed the closure; a notable victory for campaigners. However, such vocal protests did not occur elsewhere in Leicester. An activist in the campaign explained how the LCC strategy for delivering reforms fragmented and contained the resistance:

> Well, I think we hear about things at different times. So... the different libraries were closed before ours was and we didn't know it was gonna come to us. So, I think in an ideal world yes, we would all stand together. But the reality is services are not cut in one swoop, because then you would have the whole city up in arms against you if you were the council. (Davies et al, 2020: 68)

Second, though 'super-diverse', Leicester is relatively residentially segmented, with working-class predominantly white neighbourhoods concentrated in the West, minority ethnic groups East and North East of the centre. These demographics posed questions about the extent to which multiculturalism generates interculturalism in the sense of affinities described in Greater Dandenong, especially in the political sphere. Said a focus group participant, 'some areas are totally monoculture... I mean, if you go into Belgrave, if you go into Highfields... there are fewer white areas now. But they can be... incredibly white. But actually, as a city, we're not at all. But where they're incredibly white, there's a fracture arising, you know.'

Critical respondents further linked residential separation to the lack of organised resistance, attributing this in part to the effects of official multiculturalism. Talking about the weakness of anti-austerity protests, a voluntary sector respondent commented, 'one of the benefits of Leicester being so diverse in terms of the various communities, it helps in it not happening because you'll be able to speak more forcibly if everyone was working together'. Relatedly, 'there is a possibility that because of the nature of the different communities in the city with the difference in terms of the way that they address what's happening to them economically, that you don't see the whole explosion. You might see an explosion of one particular group' (cited in Davies et al, 2017). This reference to the way different ethnic groups cope with economic dispossession gestured to influential ideas about Asian entrepreneurialism (Chapter 4) and to the resurgence of the right in the UK.

Leicester showed how the scalar and territorial activism of an austerian realist municipality can produce what Brenner and Elden (2009: 354) called 'territory effects': the normalisation of austere neoliberalism through political work on socio-spatial relations. The spatial governance of the neighbourhood services programme, construed as the 'activity of ruling groups', interrupted resistance and reinforced the local state through politically efficacious territory-making activities. In Lefebvrian language, the governance of these reforms produced 'abstract – homogenous, fragmented and hierarchical – space' (Kipfer et al, 2012: 123) through which the most vocal elements in civil society were contained. From the standpoint of public officials, themselves ardently committed to a public service ethos, but also mired in austerian realism, this approach signified good, pragmatic governance. From the activist perspective, however, it was divisive, undermining potential for citywide resistance. In the second instance, spatial segmentation, reinforced by the privileging of entrepreneurship in multicultural discourse, made it harder to articulate working-class experiences collectively, though austere neoliberalism had a dire impact on African, Asian and white working-class women and men alike. The spatial and entrepreneurial logics of official multiculturalism (always to be defended against racist currents) constituted part of the hegemonic apparatus of austerian realism, inhibiting the potential for inter-neighbourhood resistance outside the workplace, where resistance was also very muted.

The chilling effects of late corporatism

Anti-austerity struggles are beset by familiar dilemmas and weaknesses. Hill wrote of divisions among subalterns (1977: 88–9):

> Thus central city relations of revenue accumulation, production and distribution increasingly foster an urban politics characterized by an intensifying triadic struggle between (i) discontented taxpayers, (ii) increasingly militant municipal unions, and (iii) insurgent community groups. At present these segments of the urban working class are largely locked into a mutually antagonistic set of social relationships. Taxpayers rebel against the lack of efficiency and effectiveness of municipal expenditures, the service claims of the relative surplus population and the wage and benefit demands of municipal unions. Insurgent community groups attack budget priorities, the lack of accountability of service bureaucracies and municipal unions, and the unequal distribution of city services and employment opportunities. Municipal unions castigate 'community witch-hunters' and 'tight-fisted' taxpayers alike. Central city politics, one observer recently noted, is akin to a bucket of crabs.

The past 40 years have not entirely dated this perception and the research pointed to a multitude of centrifugal tendencies among anti-austerity forces contributing to the governability of austere neoliberalism. One of the most notable features, reflecting trends explored in other literatures, was the locus of resistance in communities and neighbourhoods and in the spheres of social reproduction (for example, Federici, 2012). This may partly reflect the analytical predilections of authors who see Marx's proletariat as obsolete or irretrievably recuperated (for example, Day, 2005), but it also reflects the outcomes of neoliberal restructuring and the effects of austerity in decimating trade unions. In many parts of the world, the organised working class has been severely weakened by restructuring, legal constraint, and the millstone of its own political traditions, so that other forces have come to the fore in anti-austerity struggles. The study cast additional light on these processes, suggesting that corporatist traditions maintained a chilling effect on trade unions, making it harder to build and sustain unity between movements in and outside the workplace.

In Montréal, patterns of resistance and containment had roots in the politics of the quiet revolution, bringing together the Québecois national project, extensive Keynesian interventionism and a social compromise between the labour movement and Francophone economic and political elites. This confluence formed the basis of the Québec Model discussed in Chapter 5. While the Québec Model mutated, bargaining arrangements between trade unions, employers and government remained in place (Hamel and Keil, 2015). These mechanisms were double-edged in the age of austerity. They gave workers a voice, and maintained wage pressure, but also served as a vehicle for containing and fractionalising labour, while undermining unity with more militant anti-austerity forces. Under Couillard, the government of Québec conducted negotiations with public sector unions in siloes. For Hamel and Autin (2017: 181), the unions were thus trapped in an 'iron cage' of state bureaucracy, partly of their own design. One respondent commented on the state of the struggle (Hamel and Autin, 2017: 184):

> On the side of the trade unions, we feel there is anger and discontent, we feel more people are ready to lose part of their salary for their convictions. We see it with the teachers. But I don't think we're on the brink of having trade union movements going on indefinite or illegal strikes with their members ready to follow a general mobilization. We're not there yet. After all, the rubber band hasn't snapped yet. And as long as some players will come winning out of all this, it will be difficult.

Even as it delivered gains and limited losses for individual unions, sectionalism undermined solidarities built in the struggles of 2015, and ultimately damped them down (Savard, 2016).

In Barcelona and Dublin, partnerships and compacts were more damaging for union involvement in anti-austerity struggles. Unions led some of the early resistance to the impact of the GEC in Ireland. However, the strategy thereafter was largely defensive, and they focused on closed-door negotiations with government around pay cuts and freezes, recruitment embargoes and no-strike agreements in return for guarantees against compulsory redundancies (Cannon and Murphy, 2015), an instance of what Gaynor (2011: 519) described as 'cosy relations'. They were not to remain so cosy.

Ireland's 'Social Partnership' collapsed, when the government imposed swingeing pay cuts on public servants and both unions and business confederations, for different reasons, withdrew. However, even under the duress of austerity, Ireland's trade union federation did not wholly abandon the partnership ethos, offering concessions through the so-called 'Croke Park Agreement' at which it conceded a veto on industrial action and further reforms and savings, in return for a moratorium on compulsory redundancies and pay cuts (Teague and Donaghey, 2015). The unions, also closely affiliated with the pro-austerity Labour Party, were thus unable to resist effectively when the austerity offensive began in earnest. A nadir occurred in 2013, when leaders of the two main public sector unions urged members to vote 'yes' to a deal that would have cut a further 7 per cent from the public sector wage bill, when public sector workers had already suffered a reduction of 25 per cent since 2009 (Erne, 2013). Though this proposal was rejected in a ballot, the capture, neutralisation and marginalisation of Ireland's trade union movement contributed to explaining the composition of the anti-austerity movement, discussed in Chapter 6: its movement-based focus on subsistence struggles and roots in community-based organising led by women, sceptical if not hostile towards male-led bastions of perceived failure.

Until 2010 the planning of employment policies in Barcelona was organised through pacts between the city council, the two largest trade unions of the city (and Spain) and the two main employer associations. While Spanish unions also mounted a response to austerity, including well-supported general strikes in 2010 and 2012, these were seen as tightly managed, and subordinate to the politics of partnership and pact-making characterised by cosy relations between the unions and the austerity-complicit PSOE/PSC. These relations during the PSOE administration set the scene for the further marginalisation of the unions during Rajoy's premiership (Balbona and Begega, 2015), when the Catalan wing of the PSOE, the *Partit dels Socialistes de Catalunya* (PSC) was also imploding. Unable to defend organised workers, and viewed with some disdain by elements within the Indignados and 15-M movements, the unions struggled to engage displaced, unemployed and precarious workers. These gravitated to grassroots neighbourhood and movement-based campaigns, including the *Mareas* (Las Heras and Ribera Almandoz, 2017). The *Mareas* (tides of change) organised around themes, each allocated a colour such as *Marea Blanca* against health service cuts and *Marea Violeta* against gender violence and restrictive abortion laws (Weiner and Lopez, 2018: Chapter 2). They involved workers and strike actions, but often with limited engagement from the mainstream union blocs. Despite Barcelona's prominence in international anti-austerity struggles, the organised working class had little resonance as a political subject (Blanco et al, 2020: 25).

The case of Greece was very different. Kennedy (2016) argued that the system of 'competitive corporatism' in that country had been overturned for 'embedded austerity' (Chapter 4). Greece, Athens in particular, was at the forefront of organised working-class resistance to austerity after the GEC. The long years of struggle since undoubtedly depleted energies from union-led resistance. A union activist captured the core problematic: 'during the last years we organised more than 40 general strikes and... I personally think that because of the crisis, unionism suffered a strategic defeat; we couldn't offer an alternative to austerity, a way out' (Chorianopoulos and Tselepi, 2020: 48). Despite heroic resistance at a high level over a prolonged period, these struggles were contained, did not escalate into full-scale anti-systemic revolt, and could not prevent Syriza from implementing the Troika-national austerity programme. As the respondent in Montréal put it, the 'rubber band' did not snap. Waves of union-led resistance continued, but they diminished. The scale of the strategic defeat and the absorption of the left into the austerity regime restored to power by Syriza in July 2015, only grew. After several years of centre-left 'austerity idealism' under Mayor Kaminis, conservatives won the 2019 Mayoral election in Athens, the governorship of Attika and the national election. The fascist party, Golden Dawn, suffered major electoral and judicial setbacks, but the new city Mayor quickly took up the authoritarian mantle launching fierce police attacks on spaces of intercultural solidarity with refugees in the renowned Exarchia neighbourhood (Crabapple, 2020). Events in 2015 and 2019 bookended a period of retreat for all traditions on the Greek left.

The main lesson from Barcelona, Dublin and Montréal is that the social partnership of the corporatist imaginary made governing austerity easier, either by weakening the unions, discrediting them for their cosy relations with employers and parties of the centre-left that delivered austerity, or undermining precarious solidarities within the 'bucket of crabs'. Older, larger unions are particularly vulnerable in austere times when they are on the defensive, leaving them weakly positioned as either junior actors in austerity regimes, or as regime antagonists, and in an ambivalent position in relation to both roles. The lesson from

Athens was simply that the frequent repetition of one- or two-day general strikes and mass street protests was not sufficient to defeat austerity. The GEC, and draconian austerity measures that followed, left unions wrong-footed and exposed to unprecedented attacks on jobs, wages and pension rights, often implemented by ostensible political allies. For Molina and Fausto (2016: 1), the prospects for a revitalisation of tripartite social dialogue in Spain were 'very weak'. Koutroukis put it even more strongly in the Greek case (2017: 81), arguing that 'bipartisan or tripartisan partnership in pertinent reforms has become meaningless'. In November 2012, unions in Greece, Italy, Portugal and Spain undertook the first transnationally coordinated general strike (Helle, 2015). What this one-off event achieved in projecting working-class struggle onto the international stage was squandered in the underlying mode of organising through social partnership and its national-level capitulations and defeats.

The theoretical conclusions to be drawn are debatable. Some leading social theorists and urbanists dismiss the organised working class as an agent of transformation, precisely because its traditional institutions are locked into narrow, instrumental politics of wage bargaining – a structural limitation (Day, 2005; Holloway, 2005). They see greater potential for political re-subjectivation in other spheres, not least struggles over urban space and the right to the city. Nevertheless, Hobsbawm observed of labour history that growth in unionisation is likely to be discontinuous, 'because if unions are to be effective, they must mobilize, and therefore seek to recruit, not numbers of individuals but groups of workers sufficiently large for collective bargaining. They must recruit in lumps' (Hobsbawm, 1984: 155). Whether unionisation in lumps can recur after decades-long decline and periods of strategic defeat, and in a very different global labour market, is open to question. Moody (2017) argues that it can, charting the rise of new rank and file movements across the US working class. He suggests that these revivals could be harbingers of a new upsurge in labour militancy and union recruitment. Tentative moves towards the organisation of precarious workers in companies like Deliveroo, Uber, and outsourced cleaners in British universities, by new unions unencumbered by social partnership traditions or legacies of defeat, pose similar questions about the potential for a new unionism incubating in the economies of the 21st century, with women again taking prominent leadership roles (Fishwick and Connolly, 2018). Recurring waves of mass strike in France in recent decades, show that organised workers are still a force to be reckoned with. There have been many false dawns in the fight against global neoliberalism across the spheres of production and reproduction, and Moody's point remains moot. In Davis's (2018: 22) Gramscian turn of phrase, 'self-organized proletarian civil society likewise can reinforce class identity in either a subordinate, corporatist sense, as a subculture in orbit around bourgeois institutions, or in a hegemonic, anticipatory sense, as an antagonistic counterculture'. Nevertheless, in a far-reaching review of global anti-regime protests over the past 120 years, Dahlum, Knutsen and Wig (2019) concluded that worker involvement has been by far the most decisive factor in democratisation struggles. Struggles with organised workers involved outperform all others, as recent mass strikes against pension reform in France also attested. Worker organisation could yet have the potential to escape the 'iron cage' of state bureaucracy (Hamel and Autin, 2017: 184). In place of epochalist assertions about the demise and rise of social subjects, a cautious conclusion seems appropriate: if the corporatist, co-optive model of social partnership encountered its nemesis in the form of austere neoliberalism, the potential for worker organisation as such is by no means exhausted.

Community disorganising

Chapters 4 and 5 explored reconfigurations of organised civil society and their contributions to consolidating and undermining urban regime governance and governability, while Chapter 6 looked at evidence of resonant solidarities in anti-austerity struggles. This section explores factors limiting solidarity within the sphere of community organising, and between community and other forms of organising. Chapter 6 showed how, in Montréal, voluntary and community groups opposed austerity with great determination and energy (Hamel and Keil, 2020). Albeit with concessions, the provincial government was able to cut the recurrent funding of community organisations substituting it for project-based contracts (much like Leicester). This increased the insecurity and instability of organisations now required to spend more time looking for new sources of funding (such as philanthropies). These processes undermined both financial and political autonomy. At the same time, there was increased pressure on the community organisations to pick up the slack from the squeeze on public services. In this familiar context of downloading, community organisations struggled to find time and resources to effectively contest and resist austerity. Whereas sectionalism undermined solidarity in the organised working class, the struggle for subsistence, and the risk of biting the hand that feeds them, weakened it in the community sector. As Hamel and Keil (2020: 117) explain:

> For grassroots organizations and community groups there are no easy solutions. Trapped between, on the one hand, the bureaucratic constraints inherent to state support and, on the other, political, ideological and ethical convictions, these actors do not enjoy a large margin of operation. And in addition to this tension, they must face intersectional contradictions in relation to class, race, sex/gender, and/or cultural identities.

Equally, as Hill surmised, there remained an asymmetry between the VCS focus on communities facing spatial, racial and economic marginalisation and the union pre-occupation with wages and working conditions. Many community organisations were caught between managing and contesting austerity, creating a tension between providing a service in the name of solidarity, and substituting for the state in the manner envisioned by neoliberals. Constructing a new and encompassing model of solidarity is difficult under such circumstances. Different actors have to cope with and contest austerity policies and, at the same time, strive to survive. These processes tend to drive fragmentation. Hence, Hamel and Keil (2020) conclude that just as the city sought a new development model, so activists in Montréal continued experimenting in the quest for new forms of social solidarity.

Nantes faced similar challenges. Looking beyond the campaign against the airport development, and discontent about the growth model, contentious politics within the city itself had less traction, reflecting the spatial locus of the former struggle outside the urban area and its social composition. If the continued efficacy of the Nantes urban regime was now open to question, the conclusion that reproduction of the everyday city in Nantes 'does not appear to come up against challenges articulated by counter-powers' also seemed to resonate (Griggs and Howarth, 2015). Perhaps less a 'bucket of crabs' and more 'ships passing in the night', forces organised around the airport campaign on the one hand, and deprivation and marginalisation in the city's neighbourhoods on the other, had yet to discover common ground. Griggs and Howarth (2016) noted that protests against the airport were spearheaded by middle-class environmentalists, peasant farmers and anarchists. Urban neighbourhoods affected by the financial crisis reflected class and ethnic divisions. Hitherto, the politicisation of grievances in the former battle had yet to produce common struggles involving the latter. Griggs et al conclude (2020: 102) that 'such forms of resistance and demands have not become a counterpower or counterproject, because they represent fleeting and sporadic forms of mobilization that have not gelled into a viable counterhegemonic discourse'. One outstanding question was whether the enormous forces mobilising against President Macron's 'reforms', through the Gilets Jaunes, waves of general strike action, the rise of municipalist electoral platforms, and the percolation of 'slow city' discourses into Nantes might challenge this diagnosis (Griggs and Howarth, 2020). Hence, although the urban regime was faltering, and the contentious politics of Nantes remained fragmentary, here too, the search for new modes of social solidarity and new counter-hegemonies continued.

Some of the same differences of tradition and focus were evident in Athens but in this case, there was an additional challenge of network fragmentation in the community organising arena itself. Athens' anarchist tradition came to the fore in the occupied squares movement, especially in the period when the international 'Occupy' movement was peaking alongside the rise of the Spanish Indignados and the Arab Spring in 2011 (Mason, 2012). Accounts of Athenian resistance further record the role of territorial claims and struggles inspired by autonomism and the philosophy of pre-figurative politics, 'be the change you want to see' as in the neighbourhood of Exarchia (Cappuccini, 2017). This mode of resistance-transformation also diminished in scale and coherence since the peak and was under direct attack by the state. However, its relative importance increased partly because of the decline in worker struggles, partly because any institutional gateway to transformation was slammed shut in July 2015, and partly because of dire necessity.

Like the 'new urban activisms' in Barcelona, solidarity networks in Athens tended to operate at the boundaries of assistance and resistance, creating distribution mechanisms for basic goods while opposing austerity. On some accounts, more than 2,500 grassroots schemes emerged in Greek cities during the crisis. According to a community activist (Chorianopoulos and Tselepi, 2020: 48):

> During the last three years [2013–16], grassroots initiatives in Athens more than doubled, while a total of 70% of the networks that existed prior to 2013, do remain active. These are groups that operate informally on principle, and only a few turn into NGOs. They don't want to have any dealings with the state or with handling funds. They just want to offer a way out of the crisis. That means a lot as we see a different civil society emerging; different from the one that surfaced in the 1990s because of EU funds.

For an indication of variety, Kavoulakos and Gritzas (2015: 346, cited in Chorianopoulos, 2017) mapped 68 social medical centres, 84 alternative currency initiatives, 71 education collectives, 58 'no middlemen' markets and 140 cooperative enterprises in Athens.

A significant contrast with Barcelona was the relationship between grassroots networks and the emerging urban regime. Whereas in Barcelona, the networks developed an ambiguously constructive relationship with the City Council in certain activities, reinforcing municipalist regime capacity, the reverse was true in Athens. Respondents suggested that eight years of austerity had demolished bridges with the local state. The study did not encounter a single grassroots' group or network participating in a municipal collaborative arrangement, despite attempts by the city to reach out through mediating mechanisms, like synAthina. Said one activist (Chorianopoulos and Tselepi, 2020: 50):

> there's this growing realization that we're on our own, under no protective umbrella of any formal authority or institution. Not only that, but that we're actually against them. Hence the shift towards self-organisation... The election of SYRIZA and the great disappointment that followed it shattered any remaining illusions that there's a chance for a way out via formal politics and institutions.

While vehemently opposed to austerity and further engagement with the state, the new wave of solidarity networks struggled to combine in ways that might signal a newly organised vehicle for opposing austere neoliberalism. Athenian solidarity networks were predominantly small-scale, run by a few people with their energies focused on managing the human crisis. According to a community activist, 'In the City, you have to go with a portfolio of eligibility papers in order to claim assistance. Same thing with NGOs. If the documents are not good enough – unemployment cards, tax certificates – then you come to us' (Chorianopoulos and Tselepi, 2020: 49).

Such traits made the reconstitution of anti-austerity struggles very difficult. Part of the explanation was the lack of time and headspace for organising: 'when the "what can we do" issue comes up, the answer is "small things, small acts", and the reason is a very pragmatic one. We don't have the time and the energy for anything more; we try so hard on a daily basis to simply make ends meet' (cited in Davies, 2017: 9). Another respondent commented, 'Back then, in 2010, I could see what was happening at the neighbourhood level, I could see it multiplying, reaching the city level. I'm not sure that neighbourhood initiatives can do that anymore.'[2] The solidarity networks were in the gritty business of securing subsistence and survival. Yet, it was also argued that 'volunteerism is a form of resistance. It's a statement, exposing the absence of the authorities from where they are needed; it's a way to show and deal with the problems the city is facing' (cited in Davies, 2017: 8). The widespread refusal of grassroots organisations to engage with collaborative mechanisms sponsored by transnational organisations and the state signified that austerity remained highly politicised, and that the grassroots co-optive power of the emerging and increasingly repressive urban regime was very limited.

Limits of new municipalism

In the municipal elections of 2019, Barcelona en Comú was narrowly defeated by *Esquerra*, led by Ernest Maragall. The radical left suffered substantial defeats in several other Spanish cities, including Madrid where a right-wing coalition, including the proto-Fascist *Vox*, overturned the Mayoralty of Manuela Carmina. That the Spanish municipal elections of 2019 were a blow to the international municipalist movement is undeniable. But unlike Carmina, Colau managed to hold onto office in Barcelona by cobbling together a coalition involving the PSC (as before) and relying on the vote of the centrist anti-independence councillor, Manuel Valls, in the Mayoral vote. Valls previously served as French PM under the austere presidency of François Hollande. The political consequences of this deal for the new municipalist programme, and its fractured relationship with left-leaning pro-independence forces, remained to be seen. The risk was that it further undermined the potential for dialogue and bridging to the left of the pro-independence movement.

The forces of the right and the economic development circuit of power imposed more familiar limitations illustrated most graphically by the suppression of the independence referendum. The attempted re-municipalisation of the city's water services highlighted several impediments at once. First, the process was derailed by opposition within the council, notably from coalition partner the PSC. With only 11 of 41 seats in 2015, and 10 in 2019, the coalition assembled by Barcelona en Comú could not be relied upon to enact legislation. Second, as discussed in Chapter 3, where re-municipalisation of the water supply is concerned, the contract was organised through a metropolitan partnership, meaning that the hands of the municipality were tied by prior scalar 'efficiency' measures as well as ongoing legal actions (March et al, 2019). Energy companies also waged a judicial battle against the city, which sought to build a non-disconnection policy into tendering requirements for organisations bidding to run the electricity contract. The courts overturned this policy on the grounds that it breached EU procurement law. One activist commented, 'there is a harassment and constant takedown to any measure taken by the City Hall' (cited in Blanco et al, 2020: 31). This did not only apply to the judicial system. Resistance was also encountered within the municipal bureaucracy, despite the appointment of Mayoral allies to head key departments. According to a journalist, 'I think they (Barcelona en Comú members) appeal too much to the fact that they do not have enough councillors, which is true. But, even if they had 10 more, the City Council machine would have been equally counterproductive' (Blanco et al, 2020: 30).

As anticipated in Marxist theory (and in a positive way by Weberian state theorists), the local bureaucracy was seen as a force for inertia, even when senior posts were occupied by loyalists. Hence, the election of a left governing coalition, allied to social movements, marked only a point of departure in transforming the local state apparatus (Davies and Blanco, 2017). As a journalist commented (Blanco et al, 2020: 31), 'So can we witness the beginning of change of anything? Perhaps, being optimistic, I would say yes, but the most powerful actors are still the same, in the same places, in the same formal or informal organizations in the city, I think. In this regard, I am pessimistic'. Those contemplating the systemic position of Barcelona en Comú, unsurprisingly, viewed the question of municipalist regime power in sceptical terms:

> The tools are very tiny, and the expectations are great. How can the City Council of a city that is globally located on the map of the relevant cities in the world, which attracts migratory flows, capital flows... how can it manage a power that it does not have? The City Council does not have the power of the city. It is a very small portion of power. (Blanco et al, 2020: 31)

Barcelona is of special interest from a Gramscian regime perspective, as a study in the possibilities for inaugurating urban regime transition by capturing and transforming an established state apparatus, in a conflictual urban polity with additional hostility from national and international political and economic actors. It is precisely because of its international prominence that reactionary powers, mostly confined to the shadows in periods of strong hegemony, become more active and visible under conditions of threat – most graphically in the suppression of the referendum and subsequent persecution of leading activists. The experience of Barcelona suggests several ways in which the capitalist state, and the multi-scalar ensembles of economic and political power through which it is enacted, constitute pressing barriers and threats to new municipalist programmes. An authentic planetary urbanism, in the revolutionary Lefebvrian sense, confronts enemies from without, from above, and within the city as well as its own strategic limitations. At the same time, Barcelona was the place in which these very issues were most effectively and thoughtfully politicised.

Brexit and the new conservative hegemony?

Explosions of resistance and reaction in the UK during the age of austerity did not manifest primarily through urban mobilisations, though these certainly occurred and sometimes achieved gains as discussed earlier. They rather crystallised on the national stage: the wave of strikes, demonstrations and occupations in the 2011–12 period, the enormous crisis of political authority facing the British state and further aggravated by the Brexit vote in June 2016 (Jessop, 2016), and the rise of democratic socialist Jeremy Corbyn to the leadership of the UK Labour Party from 2015 to 2020, underpinned by an explosion in national party membership. The tendencies towards crisis in the UK regime of austere neoliberalism were reflected less in than above Leicester's regime ensemble, where the politics of austerian realism operated as a mediating mechanism for the austerian idealism of national governments.

At the same time, what Jessop (2016) diagnosed as the organic crisis of the British state after the Brexit vote, was becoming very intense when viewed through the lens of its fragile accumulation regime, stagnant wages, crumbling government, growing control deficit and mounting alienation. The de-stabilising Brexit process and the rise of Corbynism left the British ruling class divided, but without translating inchoate discontent into fully-fledged and sustained political mobilisations against austerity or for an alternative programme. The term 'interregnum' seemed particularly apposite in relation to the political economy of the UK, at least until the general election of December 2019 swept a pro-Brexit Conservative government to power and destroyed Corbynism as an electoral force, and seemingly as a political force within the UK Labour Party.

Until COVID-19 diverted attention, much ink was spilled in explaining the severity of the electoral defeat inflicted on Labour, the role of Brexit and the politics of Jeremy Corbyn (White, 2020). This was a disorienting and divisive period for the British left, perhaps especially on the question of whether Labour should have honoured Corbyn's commitment to a 'People's Brexit', or liquidated itself into the Remain operation. However, there is no reason to believe either course would have won the election, since Corbyn himself had been successfully toxified by the right, with the active connivance of some Labour MPs, and his Brexit might have been represented as betrayal, or Brexit In Name Only (BINO).

Two factors seem relevant in the context of austerity and resistance. First, the highpoint of Corbynism was Labour's glorious defeat in June 2017, when the long decline in the Labour vote was sharply reversed. Otherwise, the party had been on a downward spiral, like its social democratic counterparts on the European continent, since Tony Blair's huge victory in 1997. Surfing the neoliberal boom, Blair rode a now-unimaginable wave of optimism about the potential for a more inclusionary market economy, with widespread establishment backing. However, the parliamentary mathematics of his three election victories obscure the fact that by 2005, Labour had lost four million votes. Nearly a million more had been lost by 2010, when Labour endorsed austerity and lost office to David Cameron's coalition.

The reason for the brief Labour renaissance under Corbyn was, undoubtedly, the popularity of the party's anti-austerity manifesto and its slogan 'for the many not the few' and his qualities as a mass campaigner. By December 2019, the Conservatives had squeezed the life from the political imaginary underpinning Labour's promise to end austerity, partly through pledging to do so itself while promising Brexit supporters a decisive break with the EU, and partly by neutralising Corbyn as a popular political figure. By depicting him as the leader of an anti-Semitic party, and as an establishment Brexit-blocker, the right was able to establish equivalence, casting him as just one more dirty and dishonest politician in the larger universe of dirty dishonest politicians. In such a universe, any politician claiming not to be dirty and dishonest must be a fraud, making them doubly dirty and dishonest, and doubly worthy of public contempt. Dirty and proud carried the day with Boris Johnson. Johnson added only 300,000 votes to Theresa May's 2017 tally, itself impressive by historical standards, but insufficient for a majority given the Corbyn surge. But this time the electoral bloc was sufficient, given the collapse in the Labour vote, to extend Tory influence into places harbouring a multitude of grievances, not least against the Labour Party for its many betrayals (White, 2020). It is therefore timely to ask how far the austerian realism of Labour municipalities might also have contributed to the swell of resentment against Labour, the failure of the Corbyn project, and the long term decline in the Party's vote.

The second factor was the restoration of the UK Conservative Party, perhaps the most formidable political party of the modern age, and its transformation from a neoliberal globalist entity (with a vocal conservative-nationalist fraction), into a conservative nationalist entity, in which the ethos of globalization is marginal and talk of austerity taboo for the time being. Like the absorption of Syriza into the international austerity regime, it was conceivable that the transformation of the Conservative Party heralded a conjuncturally decisive moment in the reconfiguration of the British state, in the sense of at least potentially executing a managed transition between distinct accumulation regimes (Morton, 2011). In 2005, after two huge Blair wins, Wheatcroft (2005) asked whether we were witnessing the 'strange death of Tory England'. The answer to Wheatcroft 15 years on is a resounding 'no'. After 10 years of weak Tory government, a government with a large parliamentary majority now holds office, and need not face an election until the end of 2024.

Does this government mark a resolution of Jessop's organic crisis of the British state? Could it turn its electoral bloc into a political *rassemblement* (Jessop, 2016: 1), a hegemonic bloc recuperating enough of the establishment and enough of a disgruntled capitalist class, while integrating segments of the volatile middle and working classes? It arrived at the beginning of 2020 as a strong government, credited by supporters for enacting Brexit, which had already altered the course of British history. The political tools at its disposal (including 'alt-right' style lies, propaganda, scape-goating and chaos-mongering) seemed formidable. It had apparently resolved the interminable Tory schism over EU membership, by downloading it and turning it into national crisis, from which it alone benefited. On the international stage, it complemented the neo-reactionary forces spear-headed by Trump, with able support from Bolsonaro, Orban, Le Pen, the *Alternative für Deutschland* (AfD) and others. Through the first phase of the COVID-19 pandemic in Spring 2020, the UK government enjoyed unprecedented levels of support.

At the same time, it faced growing tensions and contradictions. Though the question of EU membership was formally resolved, there remained significant divisions between hyperglobalist 'chlorinated chicken' and 'Buy British' Brexiteers. There was always likely to be a huge gap between electoral pledges to 'level up' and actual spending plans. The government faces enormous barriers to its attempt to reconstitute British capitalism including the climate rebellion, the threat of conflict with Scotland over independence, and now the economic devastation and conflict arising from COVID-19, over which the government squandered much of its early support in dealing with the virus, and became increasingly divided. There is also the possibility that Britain will not forever remain immune to social explosions recurring across the globe (see Afterword). Such contradictions continue to mark the intensifying crises of neoliberal globalism and they pose threats to conservative-nationalist regimes too (for example, Foley, 2019).

Conclusion

Chapter 1 argued that to understand the potentialities in counter-hegemonic resistance, it is also necessary to recognise limitations and evolving means by which pro-systemic forces organise and exercise powers. This chapter suggests, first, that these have been quite considerable, exercised both through dramatic conjunctural shifts and low-key exercises in scalecraft (Papanastasiou, 2019). Seen to a much greater and devastating effect in Baltimore's 'city of neighbourhoods' over a century, scalecraft through spatial salami-slicing also contained and depleted the resources of anti-austerity activists in Leicester.

To borrow from Marx, second, elements of the past continue to weigh nightmare-like on the politics of the living. Chapter 2 highlighted the prominence of economic rationalism in austerity construals. Austerian realism in Leicester was also reinforced by memories of defeat in past generations and fear of national government. At the same time, the weight of tradition impeded organised working-class resistance. The social partnership logics of corporatism constituted potent mechanisms for containing and diffusing union militancy, but also reinforced divisions, sometimes conflicts, between forces contesting austerity across the spheres of production and reproduction. Where union struggles did play a leading role in the struggle against austerity, in Athens, they were worn down over time and did not break with old traditions and constraints. Political and spatial–scalar unity remains a fundamental challenge, though new forms of work-based class organisation were emerging beyond the late-corporatist straitjacket.

Third, the unevenness and targeting mechanisms of austerity itself can make organising more difficult. For some forces, it is extremely difficult to focus on anything beyond narrow domains and responsibilities, augmenting the asymmetries between different spheres of struggle and, in the case of Athens, limiting the potential for atomised solidarity networks to cohere. The multiple tendencies driving the fragmentation of subalterns were partly to do with the 'bucket of crabs', but also 'ships passing in the night', where different struggles were mutually unaware, mobilised different class fractions or simply did not connect and could not, therefore, constitute unities-in-action signified by egalitarian claims such as 'we are the 99%', or 'we, the people' (Dikeç and Swyngedouw, 2017: 9).

The chapter finally highlights the resilience of capitalist state apparatuses to counter-politics. In Baltimore, renewed community activism brought black civil society to the fore, undermining the co-optive powers of the development regime, but without blowing it off course. From the vantage point of holding office, Barcelona en Comú was acutely aware that in addition to formidable state and corporate adversaries, the levers of power within the municipality were unreliable and difficult to wield. Barcelona was a reminder that if 'socialism in one country' is impossible, 'socialism within one city' is a fantasy (Harvey, 1989: 16). The nature of and means by which urban counter-power is exercised, and how the threat of reaction can be resisted, are ever-present challenges for municipalist internationalism, itself subject to the mundane ebb and flow of election cycles.

8

Reading the Conjuncture: (Dis)Ordering Dynamics in the Crises of Neoliberal Globalism

Introduction

This final chapter reflects on the question of governability, from the standpoint of the mooted interregnum in the hegemony of neoliberal globalism. It first recapitulates the positioning of each city in relation to austere neoliberalism and the urban political (dis)orderings disclosed by the research. The remainder of the chapter discusses five political-economic characteristics of the post-GEC conjuncture, interwoven unevenly through the eight case studies: pervasive economic rationalism(s) (Chapter 2), weakening hegemony (Chapters 4 and 5), the retreat to dominance (Chapters 3, 4 and 5), weak counter-hegemony and politicisation through radically contagious struggles (Chapters 6 and 7). The first three characteristics contribute to explaining the fate of 'the collaborative moment' in the age of austerity, and to reviewing the concept of late entrepreneurialism. The fourth and fifth characteristics, weak counter-hegemony and contagious politicisations, capture both powerful resistance dynamics and impediments to more decisive transformations. Weak counter-hegemony suggests that anti-austerity, anti-neoliberal and anti-capitalist forces continue to encounter barriers and limitations prevalent in the 20 years since the Battle of Seattle (Bornstein, 2009), while politicisation dynamics, arising from and further weakening hegemony, are signified by combustibility and tendencies towards generalisation and internationalisation through nodal struggles against austerity.

Urban regime characteristics and governability

It will not surprise readers familiar with the processual, variegated, hybridised and contested character of (de)neoliberalisation to learn that austerity is governed, resisted, averted, rejected and deflected in a multitude of ways that only reinforce the importance of urban research into multi-scalar governing configurations. Appreciations of urban history and tradition, locality, place and region are required to make sense of patterns, similarities and divergences. The form and impact of the 2008 crisis varied in kind and tempo, as did political construals of the period. Some characteristics resonated, with differing tonalities, in all the cities most notably the ubiquity of economic rationalism(s) (Henderson et al, 2020). The retreat to dominance and weakening hegemony were also prominent features in most of the cities. Other characteristics were unique, and most of the cities can be positioned as outliers from a certain perspective: for example, Barcelona as a new municipalist regime, Greater Dandenong in largely escaping the GEC and austerity or Nantes in its 'Keynesian' positioning. The research team did not know these cities were to become outriders at the point of case selection, but as outriders they highlight (partial) exceptions to the dominance of austere neoliberalism, while clarifying conditions in which it operates most forcefully.

Chapter 4 explained how Athens, Baltimore, Dublin and Leicester were governed by consolidated and consolidating multi-scalar regimes enacting harshly austere variants of authoritarian neoliberalism, each however in the context of weakening hegemony. Montréal and Nantes had longstanding urban regimes with a more complex relationship to austere neoliberalism. Both were rooted in historically and geopolitically distinctive governance 'models', seen as progressive, now under duress on account of contradictions, strategy failures and weakening hegemony. Nantes sought to position itself against austere neoliberalism, whereas Montréal was subjected to austerian idealism from above, and governed pragmatically from within. Montréal is distinguished from the consolidating neoliberal regimes primarily by the sense of a long-term unresolved crisis in its development model, in relation to which the GEC itself was a marginal issue.

Barcelona and Greater Dandenong were in regime-building phases, respectively against and at a distance from austere neoliberalism. The former was seeking, under a variety of constraints, to lead and advance the new municipalist cause while the latter represented an experiment in an inclusionary model of market-led development, long abandoned in the austere heartlands of Europe and the USA.

Montréal and Nantes posed the question of whether governance models originally articulating distinctive urban political identities and principles can survive, while Barcelona begged the question of whether the democratic origins of a recuperated model might be retrieved and radicalised. In Greater Dandenong, the question was how robust and durable its revitalisation regime would prove to be in the face of global headwinds. Table 8.1 summarises this reading of urban regime configurations. The next part of the chapter explores five cross-cutting political-economic characteristics influencing the grounds of (un) governability in the age of austerity.

Pervasive economic rationalism

Chapter 2 demonstrated that what Henderson, Sullivan and Gleeson (2020) call 'economic rationalism', an expression of *homo oeconomicus*, was a prominent, multi-valent current across the eight cities. It was predominantly an ordering or stabilising factor in the reproduction of austere neoliberalism. The most widespread and frequently overlapping valences of economic rationalism were twofold. It was constituted first by logics of scarcity and the associated virtues of thrift. This valence underpins the continuum of approaches from vigorous retrenchment and austerian idealism, to austerian realism and socialist asceticism. A second prominent valence, often intersecting the first, was that public resources must be directed to enhancing attractiveness and supporting market-led growth. The significance of economic rationalism as an ideology-governmentality is illuminated by contrast with concepts accentuating relative abundance, like Galbraith's (1958) 'affluent society' or Giddens' (1996) diagnosis of 'post-scarcity', popularised during the neoliberal boom. Such framings were notable for their absence from counter-narratives during the age of austerity.

While neither city rejected economic rationalism outright, the uncoupling of scarcity and attractiveness formed part of the explanation for the distinctive governance arrangements in Barcelona and Nantes. Barcelona en Comú accentuated thrift and fiscal competence against the fecklessness of the right, while challenging the growth machine (Blanco et al, 2020): economic rationalism echoing principles of socialist asceticism. Nantes, conversely, was the only city in which scarcity was at least tacitly challenged by Keynesian ideas and modestly counter-cyclical budgeting. This approach was underwritten by confidence in the city as a developmental dynamo: economic rationalism in a boosterish, environmentalist guise (Griggs et al, 2020).

Table 8.1: Urban regime configurations in the age of austerity

	Consolidating austere neoliberal regimes				Fading regimes		Alternative regimes	
	Athens	Baltimore	Dublin	Leicester	Montréal	Nantes	Barcelona	Greater Dandenong
Governing regime	Emerging elite pluralist growth regime.	Elite-pluralist growth regime.	Revanchist national austerity regime.	Nationally mandated austerian realist regime.	Interregnum. Failed 'world city' project.	Corroding sustainable development regime.	Incipient new municipalist regime.	State-led intercultural revitalisation regime.
Political composition (2015–18)	Centre left coalition.	Democrat.	Centre-left coalition (Sinn Féin, Labour, Green).	Labour council and Labour Mayoralty.	Centrist (2015–17). Progressive (2017–).	Socialist Party.	Barcelona en Comú led coalition.	Labor council.
Prominent regime actors	Troika, national government, city mayor and municipality. Rising influence.	State of Maryland, City Mayor, Board of Estimates, anchor institutions, non-profits.	National austerity government, weak municipalities, property developers, pragmatic VCS.	Central government, City Mayor, municipality, LLEP, pragmatic elements in VCS.	Province, municipality. Ambivalent positioning of unions and VCS 'in and against'.	Metro-Mayor, city and Métropole, local economic elites. State-business-civil society networks.	City Mayor, municipality, anti-austerity movements, international municipalist milieu.	State, municipality, multicultural VCS and local business leaders.
Austerity construals	Austerity idealism, collective guilt.	De-signified amid permanent retrenchment.	Collective penance – we all partied.	Austerian realism: cut without fuss, mitigate.	Austerian idealism (Quebec), austerian realism (city).	We're Keynesian – modestly counter-cyclical.	Prudence vs fecklessness of the right.	Not significant – a European issue.

182

Resistance	Diminished. Trasformismo (Syriza), waning union struggles, fragmentary solidarity networks.	Re-invigoration of community organising since *The Uprising*.	Mass mobilisation, victory in water wars. Revitalisation of granular solidarities. Weak unions.	Generally low and contained. Some successful campaigns. Weak unions.	Maple Spring – high levels of struggle, moments of unity, fragmentation and co-optation.	Peripheral to city. Victory at Notre-Dame-des-Landes. Emerging 'slow growth' movement?	From 15-M to city hall. Historic 8-M mobilisations. Marginal unions.	Low and not evident in relation to revitalisation programme.
Regime powers	Delivering austerity. Radicalised state rescaling. Partnership with transnational organisations. Resistance contained. Degree of normalisation.	Delivering austerity. Enduring control of development resources, agendas and repressive apparatus.	Delivering austerity. Economic recovery, state domination of local politics.	Delivering austerity. Implementing multicultural growth agenda. Some co-optive power, resistance contained.	Delivering and mitigating *rigueur*. Some co-optive power and ability to contain resistance.	Established development coalition and Nantes Game. Tournament wins. Crisis-deflection.	International anti-austerity beacon. Inspiring leader, reform agenda, policy and culture change, shifts in economic priority.	Delivering revitalisation. Significant co-optive power across state, market and third sectors.
Regime liabilities	Grassroots alienation and resentment. Failure of new participatory institutions. Weak hegemony.	Mass alienation of black working class and activist VCS. More vocal and organised activist groups. Weakening hegemony.	Defeated in water wars. Weakening hegemony.	Jobless growth. Precarious and exploitative labour. Austerity eroding multicultural 'fix'? Weakening hegemony.	Regime failure: capital flight, retarded city-regionalism. Significant anti-austerity forces. Weakening hegemony.	Policy failure, sharpening contradictions, social ferment (across France). Weakening hegemony.	Electoral weakness, limited jurisdiction. Weak counter-hegemony.	Weakly institutionalised collaboration, dependence on higher tiers of government, threats on horizon.

With these partial exceptions, economic rationalism exercised a firm 'grip' (Griggs et al, 2020: 103) throughout the governmental apparatus and in spheres of civil society. As the legacy of previous economic crises and political struggles, it had major implications for urban governance and the continued dominance of austerity–growth imperatives. From a Gramscian vantagepoint, economic rationalism primarily served to anchor austere neoliberalism but could plausibly be coopted to a new politics to the left or the right. Waves of agitation around the climate emergency are one indication that tropes of scarcity and (democratic) rationing could resonate more in socialist counter-hegemonies of the future than the Communist pursuit of universal public luxury (Trainer, 2019). However, Davis makes an impassioned defence of luxury, arguing that the climate disaster is driven by the deformed and warped urbanity of capitalism, rather than development as such. The capitalist city 'represses' environmental efficiencies 'inherent in human settlement density' (2018: 218). Instead, public affluence signified by 'great urban parks, free museums, libraries, and infinite possibilities for human interaction—represents an alternative route to a rich standard of life based on Earth-friendly sociality' (2018: 218). From Davis's perspective, economic rationalism, even if it is turned against capital, conceals revolutionary possibilities and cedes unnecessary ground to presentism.

Weakening hegemony

Though economic rationalism provided ballast for austere neoliberalism, it does not in itself signify hegemony in Gramsci's strong sense of a power bloc exercising intellectual and moral leadership throughout society and constituting the ethico-political moment of a bourgeois state (Gramsci, 1971: 208; Q 10II, §15). Multiple symptoms of weak or weakening hegemony were evident in the (re)ordering of urban regime politics. In the years before the GEC, Arrighi (2005) argued, borrowing from Guha's (1998) analysis of colonialism, that the international order was entering a phase of 'dominance without hegemony'. The pre-eminent power, the United States, was increasingly unable to maintain its sphere of influence through consent and cooperation among allies and subordinates, illustrated by international divisions over the 2003 war on Iraq.

In a schematic interregnum, the power of ruling groups is exercised less through resonant leadership and, as popular resentments multiply, more through domination and bureaucratic fiat. Old institutions and rule regimes continue and may still be able to mobilise considerable governing resources (Kouvelakis, 2019: 79) but with diminished efficacy in managing contradictions and diminishing credibility with publics (Stahl, 2019). Central to diagnoses of the interregnum amid mounting contradictions of late capitalism (Streeck, 2016), weak hegemony is also widely recognised in social theory far beyond the Marxist tradition. Talcott Parsons coined the term 'power deflation' for a leadership deficit where states have to rely on threat or coercion (cited in Arrighi, 2005: 32). Perri Six's neo-Durkheimian conception of 'isolate ordering' similarly captures a mode of social organisation characterised by strong constraints on government action coupled with weak social integration. Governing occurs, he argues (2016: 221), 'without status, role, incentive or shared principle, collective action is difficult; access to resources and power is by force, fraud, guileful temporary evasion of particular constraints, or coping'.

Six sees isolate ordering as a generic characteristic of governing rather than the symptom of a fading hegemony. But his depiction captures prominent features of urban regime hollowing. Chapters 4 and 5 suggest that weak and weakening hegemony had several dimensions: the erosion of co-optive apparatuses and attendant socio-spatial distancing processes including the dis-embedding of local voluntary and community sectors (Clayton et al, 2016); the uprooting of neo-corporatist arrangements; the subjective intensification of political alienation, estrangement or anomie; economic duress; loss of trust, time and headspace for citizens and officials alike; and scalar re-orderings that further diminish urban democracy. It derives in part from the abandonment or repurposing of co-optive mechanisms by the state through austerity and in part from mounting contradictions and strategic weaknesses of the kind witnessed in the abortive mega-city project in Montréal (Hamel and Keil, 2020). It also derives from the politicisations discussed in Chapter 6, and their contagious characteristics discussed later.

Whither the 'collaborative moment'?

The introductory chapter explained that an initial purpose of the study was to consider the fate of collaborative governance in the age of austerity, in particular the promise of the 'collaborative moment' for ushering in an era of inclusionary and consensual governance based on trust: a putative 'post-hegemony', sustained through affect and warranted by epochalist declarations about the age of affluence, the emancipatory potential in the knowledge economy, the salutary effects of universal education in producing clever citizens, the erosion of structural cleavages and the rise of the autotelic personality.

Davies (2011b, 2012a) re-interpreted this current as the flawed regulatory ideal of a confident roll-out neoliberalism, which had failed to live up to its promise even in the comparatively benign circumstances of the neoliberal boom and the zenith of centre-left politics in the late 1990s.

What happened to this 'collaborative moment'? Greater Dandenong, with Australia experiencing a historically remarkable period of uninterrupted economic growth, sought with some success to construct a politics echoing its key values of community, inclusivity, trust and affect, but without much of the attendant institutional and ideological baggage. Nantes, distancing itself from austerity, re-embraced the spirit of the collaborative moment in revitalising its participatory apparatus, in response to the crisis Mayor Rolland saw threatening the legitimacy of the French state (Chapter 5). However, the revitalised apparatus internalised emerging contradictions, rather than resolving them (Griggs et al, 2020), also exhibiting limitations familiar in earlier critical accounts of the collaborative turn (for example, Cooke and Kothari, 2001; Davies, 2007). As a laggard in developing 'good governance', and under the influence of the Troika, Athens too sought to roll out participatory mechanisms after the GEC but with negligible impact on the austerity governance landscape. Its 'collaborative moment' never penetrated far into local civil society, and a very different 'elite pluralist' model prospered in the form of alliances between local political and transnational elites in their philanthropic guise (Chorianopoulos and Tselepi, 2019, 2020). In neither Nantes nor Athens did reinvigorating participatory governance from the top-down reinforce the co-optive powers, or hegemonic grip, of the governing regime let alone enhance the democratic culture.

Beyond these cities, the collaborative moment did not survive the age of austerity as a significant governing ethos or praxis. In Barcelona (prior to 2015), Dublin and Leicester, cities where it resonated strongly in the politics of the preceding period, participatory governance was marginalised, rolled back or eliminated. Voluntary and community sectors were hollowed out, community-facing municipal offices cut or restructured, as citizens became further disillusioned and aggrieved. In Montréal, the Québec Model was similarly undermined principally by the actions of the provincial government (Hamel and Autin, 2017), though institutions like Neighbourhood Tables retained their vitality where they were anchored in grass-roots organisation. In these cities, multi-stakeholder participatory institutions diminished in appeal, for governing elites and subalterns alike.

Once at its heart, new municipalist Barcelona had an ambivalent relationship with the spirit of the 'collaborative moment'. An earlier piece of research during the conservative Mayoralty of Xavier Trias (Blanco, 2015a; Davies and Blanco, 2017) found that the city's elaborate participatory governance apparatus was marginalised through institutional layering and because activists resisting austerity were becoming detached. With the election of Barcelona en Comú, the city began attempting a new and radicalised form of co-production rooted in democratic and egalitarian principles. These initiatives sought to reinforce the municipalist governing regime through partnerships between governmental and non-governmental actors prominent in anti-austerity struggles and in building the commons. However, they were not imbued with the benign perspective on markets envisioned by the third way, but rather as part of the struggle to de-neoliberalise the city (Blanco et al, 2020). The city sought, with many limitations and compromises, to radicalise the 'collaborative moment' for a democratic and egalitarian politics echoing radical traditions and older expressions of the Barcelona and Québec models.

The answer to the initial research question, then, is that ideas, institutions and practices associated with the collaborative moment survived the 'age of austerity' in some circumstances, but not the more aggressive, centralising and authoritarian practices of austere neoliberalism. Where it survived, it did so either in the 'abridged' form characterised by Griggs, Howarth and Feandeiro (2020: 105–6) as a shift from praxis to ideology, or in radicalised and re-politicised form (new municipalism). Abridgements, failures and rollback were further symptoms of diminishing co-optive capacity, especially in the heartlands of austere neoliberalism. The counter-experience of Greater Dandenong further reinforced the notion, as Davies and Blanco (2017: 1532) put it, that participatory governance is 'more likely to flourish in "good times", when investment is high, public services robust, and political commitment strong'. Otherwise, it had lost much of its grip, credibility and utility since the end of the neoliberal boom. This is no less true of the neo-corporatist plank of the 'social partnership' agenda, which went a considerable way towards neutralising the unions as austerity rolled out but is now increasingly defunct. It appeared significant as a governing tradition only in Montréal.

The unknitting of the shortlived attempt to embed collaboration as a hegemonic principle of roll-out neoliberalism can be read alongside other characteristics of the age of austerity: the renewal of brute poverty and outright crises of subsistence, and the degeneration of what Brown (2018) called the quality of 'intellection' amid the nihilistic despair channelled by the far right. These tendencies challenge the sociology of relative affluence, from which the idea of the collaborative moment germinated. If it was part of an attempt to rebuild society on the ruins of official communism and Keynesian welfarism by surfing the neoliberal boom, its degeneration in the age of austerity is a harbinger of rebalancing towards dominance on the one hand and re-politicisation on the other (Davies and Blanco, 2017). From the high point of its hegemonic endeavour, the multitude of 'authoritarianisms' and 'alienations' materialising through the age of austerity signified an end to the brief phase of social neoliberal optimism, to which revisionist social democratic currents aligned themselves. The political consequences of this tendency liquidating itself into austere neoliberalism are discussed later.

Retreat to dominance

Retreat to dominance is at once a symptom of weakening hegemony, a stabilising dimension of austere neoliberalism and a re-ordering factor in the urban sphere, marking the drift towards politically disempowered local government. Stahl (2019: 355) argued that 'the history of the 20th century shows that turbulence and instability are as natural a state for the capitalist world economy as stable hegemony'. To take the point a step further, the materialisation of an interregnum in no way necessitates that it will be resolved by rupture with the old, or the establishment of a new hegemony. Marx and Engels might have been right to warn in the Communist Manifesto that ultimately, 'the common ruin of the contending classes' will ensue if a fading order is not superseded.[1] However, Stahl's point was that an interregnum can endure for an extended period, as a relatively 'stable disequilibrium' (Thomas, 2009: 215). Chapters 3 and 4 highlight governance mechanisms through which relatively stable disequilibria were maintained. They show that amid weakening hegemony, agents of austere neoliberalism retained what Stone (1988: 83) called powers of pre-emption; the 'capacity to occupy, hold and make use of a strategic position' through state apparatuses, albeit without dominion in the realms of ideas, affects or biopolitics.

Chapter 3 discussed mechanisms of administrative dominance, the means by which the effective political autonomy of city government was undermined in the age of austerity through a raft of centralising and de-centralising measures to facilitate top-down control, bottom-up responsibilisation and market vulnerabalisation. Upward and downward state rescaling constituted a disempowering pincer enacted through cuts, downloading, ring-fencing, tax reforms, curtailment of spending powers, debt-discipline, law-making, planning controls, re-territorialisation, and regressive charges. Together with overtly coercive and authoritarian practices (Chapters 4 and 5), exercises in pre-emption further reinforced administrative dominance (Davies, 2012a), consolidated and aligned governing agendas vertically and cultivated market dependencies by imposing economic vulnerabilities.

Theodore (2020) explains how austerity operates as an economic vehicle for downward crisis-displacement. The re-orderings discussed in Chapters 3–5 highlight parallel political displacement mechanisms, reinforcing neoliberal path dependencies while narrowing the range of political choices available to local governments and limiting the powers and resources available to any putative anti-austerity administration. It is important to note that these mechanisms were conflict-prone and vulnerable to failure, exemplified for example by difficulties in consolidating city-regional governance along neoliberal lines (Chapter 3). Nevertheless, they further limited the potential for alternative currents to capture the local state, even as hegemony weakened. From the standpoint of Barcelona's new municipalists, or Preston's community wealth builders in the UK (Guinan and O'Neill, 2020), they made it harder to re-constitute hegemony through expansively radical urban regime transitions, at least while operating within non-insurgent, constitutional and legal parameters.

Whither the entrepreneurial city?

The convergences of economic rationalism, weakening hegemony and retreat to dominance played out through the conduct of entrepreneurial governance in four primary ways. The cities of Athens, Greater Dandenong and Leicester showed potential for radicalising governance based on entrepreneurial principles. Baltimore and Dublin pointed to ambiguities, as strong post-crisis growth in both cities intersected with rising protest and weakening hegemony. Montréal and Nantes highlighted political and economic constraints on entrepreneurialism as a policy regime, while Barcelona pointed to the potential for regime transformation.

As a laggard before the GEC, the governance of Athens was transforming more radically than in any other city in this study, with the implementation of its austerity programme, array of public–private partnerships, exposure to international capital, growing authoritarianism and openness to influence by transnational elites. Leicester was a relative latecomer; not to entrepreneurship as such, but to entrepreneurialism as a governing ethos premised on the recovery of the city's self-confidence and attractiveness (Davies et al, 2020: 63). It had experienced draconian retrenchment and restructuring measures, leaving one of Britain's poorest cities increasingly vulnerable to market whim, and playing the attractiveness game to compensate. The strategy of treating the city centre as its 'shop window' was executed with tangible success in revitalising the central retail economy and commercialised public realm, but with negligible impact in offsetting neighbourhood deprivation, austerity or earlier waves of neoliberalisation.

These cities were suggestive of avenues for radicalising entrepreneurial governance through the exercise of pre-emptive powers, in the context of weakening hegemony. Greater Dandenong provided an instructive contrast. Here, pre-emptive and co-optive powers accrued in tandem, cultivating a plausible vision for the city without proximate contradictions and conflicts. The entrepreneurial strategy for business-led city centre revitalisation fostered creative energy and conjured a resonant intercultural vison of the inclusive city (Sullivan et al, 2019: 36).

Dublin and Baltimore contrasted strong growth dynamics with rising political contention and disaffection. In Dublin, the revanchist national austerity regime executed its agenda successfully, revived the growth machine and confected a new property boom. Gains to capital from the renewal of its aggressively neoliberal strategy were once again tangible (Dublin City Council, 2019). Yet, resistance is now embedded in the political culture of the city, eroding the former grounds of regime hegemony. The housing boom signifying economic 'recovery' became simultaneously a social and political crisis (Gaynor, 2020). In Baltimore, the development regime remained dominant after an extended period of growth uninterrupted by the GEC. However, *The Uprising* weakened its hegemony and re-politicised structural inequalities, a pattern recurring in US cities ever since. Here, moreover, there were echoes of Peck's (2017b) account of Atlantic City in that for decades, Baltimore had seen endless rounds of disciplinary neoliberalism – more and more of the same thing year-on-year – without ever getting close to resolving its fiscal and social predicaments. Unlike the Barcelona, Nantes and Québec models in their heydays, Baltimore seemed unable to generate solutions or mitigate the crises in which it had long been mired. There was no inherent reason this combination of weakened hegemony and fiscal perma-crisis could not continue, but the regime appeared short of both legitimacy and problem-solving capabilities.

Montréal, and to a lesser extent Nantes, pointed to growing deficits in both co-optive and pre-emptive powers. Montréal posed the question of 'what comes next' in a sharper form, partly because of long-term failure in its development model and partly because of weak hegemony, articulated through attrition in the Québec Model and its unruly civil society. It was here that the idea of an 'interregnum' resonated most strongly in a specific city-region. It was unclear if long-term regime weakness might now be resolved through the combination of Valérie Plante's green progressivism and signs of a boom driven by creative and knowledge economies (Moser et al, 2019). Nantes was newer to the experience of governance failure, and the sharpening tensions in its model, amid national economic stagnation and fierce political ructions pitting the Caesarist figure of President Emmanuel Macron against the heterodox, innovative and durable assemblies of the Gilets Jaunes (Kouvelakis, 2019), and waves of mass strike from late 2019 into early 2020. As the study concluded, the once-productive synthesis of entrepreneurial, environmental and participatory politics was fraying in Nantes, while a potentially subversive 'slow city' narrative was gaining traction (Griggs and Howarth, 2020). Despite its enduring global reputation as an investment and tourism magnet, Barcelona pointed to a different set of constraints on entrepreneurialism, both as a development dynamic and hegemonic logic. These constraints are discussed later in the context of weak counter-hegemony and re-politicisation.

If late entrepreneurialism is understood as one facet of the interregnum, these examples are suggestive of four plausible trajectories. One is that entrepreneurialism can be radicalised through dominance, subsisting alongside weak hegemony (authoritarian neoliberal regime governance). Gramsci's analysis of the formation of the Italian state revealed that, despite feeble nation-building and developmental dynamics, a political order can well survive weak hegemony and turbulence, if subaltern classes fail to 'elaborate their own hegemonic apparatuses capable of resisting the absorptive logic of the passive revolution' (Thomas, 2009: 157). Given the ubiquity of weak hegemony in the passive revolutionary histories of capitalism, and the continuing absence of concerted political challenge, it is conceivable that relatively stable disequilibria could survive for a prolonged period. The need for continuous competitive 'innovation' is fundamental to capitalism, but especially to neoliberalism (Carroll, 2006). This characteristic itself mitigates against stable and durable hegemonies. Late, fast capitalism demands the constant uprooting of tradition, expectation and practice (Žižek, 2009: 18), which is one reason why harsh austerity regimes see little value in co-optive mechanisms, and neo-reactionaries look to leverage disorientation as a governing strategy. Equally, as Jessop put it (Jessop et al, 2014: 86), it is possible that some variant of neoliberalism could recover its hegemonic power. He warned that '[w]ithout further challenges to the macrostructures of domination, piecemeal changes risk absorption or neutralization'.

A second plausible scenario is that due to internal contradictions, conspicuous failures or incremental exhaustion, urban regimes become dysfunctional and lose the ability either to pre-empt or to co-opt. Such a dynamic portends increasingly 'unstable disequilibria' of the kind seen particularly in France and the USA since this study concluded, potentially sharpening the conflict between contending social forces and intensifying crisis dynamics. As an outlier, Greater Dandenong suggested a third plausible trajectory: the potential for politically generative expressions of entrepreneurialism, in this case supported by Australia's proximity to the Chinese boom, sustained growth in the national economy and the economic vitality of metropolitan Melbourne. A fourth possibility, heralded by Barcelona, is that radical political alternatives can generate the necessary pre-emptive and co-optive powers to (iteratively) constitute new regime formations, provided they bridge to the intra-urban and supra-urban scales. The contagious character of urban struggles discussed later is one feature of weak hegemony, emerging in parallel with the retreat to dominance.

A tentative answer to the 'how late' of 'late entrepreneurialism' question posed at the end of Chapter 2 is that a sharpening interregnum in the hegemony of neoliberal globalism need not necessarily translate into *specific* or localised crises of governability. It is true that entrepreneurial regimes face internal contradictions, failures and crises. However, they might be sustained through weak hegemony and diminishing co-optive power by a variety of means, particularly where robust pre-emptive (political) powers coincide with a strong (financialised) growth dynamic and limited resistance. Whether such regimes are sufficiently durable to survive the colossal, perhaps unprecedented recessionary onslaught of COVID-19, or renewed political eruptions, is another matter. Nevertheless, as Peck (2017a) also recognises, it would be premature to suggest that the entrepreneurial city is on any fast-track to obsolescence. Though strong hegemony confers obvious advantages on a governing bloc, the theory of passive revolution emphasises that it is not a necessary prerequisite of regime politics or of capitalist development as such. Sustained entrepreneurial governance, without hegemony, is a feasible pathway provided political eruptions can be contained and neutralised. Table 8.2 summarises these conclusions, with respect to the collaborative moment and entrepreneurial cities.

Table 8.2: Collaborative and entrepreneurial governance

	The collaborative moment	The entrepreneurial city
Athens	Laggard – stunted and underdeveloped	Radicalised
Baltimore	Did not resonate	Dominant but inertial?
Barcelona	Retrenchment through austerity, radicalisation through municipalism	Post-entrepreneurial municipalism?
Greater Dandenong	Strong intercultural collaborative ethos	Radicalised – 'inclusionary' variant
Dublin	Rollback and retrenchment	Radicalised but contested
Leicester	Rollback and retrenchment	Radicalised
Montréal	Rollback of participatory governance	Interregnum – development regime inertia. Potential for reinvigoration?
Nantes	Revitalised, but abridged and crisis prone	Decelerating, new contradictions

Contours of resistance: weak counter-hegemony

Weak counter-hegemony captures the variety of factors inhibiting and disrupting the forces opposing austere neoliberalism, discussed mainly in Chapter 7. This characteristic is also anticipated in the Gramscian framing of an interregnum, where adversaries of fading hegemons remain in the 'economic-corporate' phase, and are unable or unwilling, themselves, to constitute a new order. As Chapter 1 explained, the question of counter-hegemony is controversial. The idea of a counter-hegemonic struggle contrasts with anarchist and constructivist theories of change, articulated by scholars like Gibson Graham (2006), Day (2005) or Holloway (2005), who see transformative resistance occurring in the multiplication of practical, pre-figurative acts of affinity in the interstices of power, and also reject periodisation as a form of reification that feeds 'capitalocentrism' by glossing over fissures and cracks (discussed in Söderberg and Netzén, 2010).

One transparent advantage of the Gramsci-inspired approach, however, is that it calls for synchronic and diachronic analyses, weighing the balance of forces at a given moment and patterns of struggle over time including peaks, troughs and legacies. This approach tempers the tendency to dismiss historical subjects prematurely (the working class) or announce the primacy of new ones (like Multitude) over-hastily. Barker et al (2013: 2) argue that the Marxist approach to movement studies analyses not only events but also waves and 'cycles of contention'. Inspired by earlier revolts in Latin America, including Venezuela, Ecuador and the Zapatista uprising of 1994 (Gonzalez, 2018), the Battle of Seattle in 1999 is recalled as a watershed in the reconstitution of the radical left in the northern hemisphere; a turning point after defeats inflicted by neoliberal insurgents in the 1980s and early 1990s, the cooption of the centre-left and the collapse of Stalinism. Themes that converged in Seattle, anti-capitalism, feminism, environmentalism and anti-racism, have continued to set the tone for the past 20 years, influencing anti-austerity struggles and new municipalisms in which anarchist and libertarian socialist traditions coexist uneasily with Marxist, institutionalist and state-friendly variants of democratic or revolutionary socialism (Taylor, 2013; Barcelona en Comú, 2019).

May (2017) argued that within the current cycle of contention, political time is speeding up, with diminishing intervals between waves of disruption. Choonara (2020) identified three such waves in the post-Seattle period: the anti-globalisation, social forum and Latin American 'pink tide' movements of the late 1990s and early 2000s, the outbreak of anti-austerity struggles and the occupied squares movement peaking in 2011, and the explosions of the period since 2018, rolling across much of the globe until the outbreak of COVID-19 (see Afterword). Do the waves have higher peaks, shallower troughs, or merge together in a rising tide of durably transformative struggles? The research did not engage this question directly but offers some clues about direction of travel. In reviewing the legacies of Seattle, one obvious factor has been the repeated tendencies to defeat, recuperation, dissipation and attrition characterising the problem of weak counter-hegemony. The other, discussed in the following section, is the increasingly combustible, politicised and contagious character of equalibertarian struggles in parallel with the retreat to dominance.

In the first instance, it is impossible to give serious consideration to the balance of forces, without recognising the advances made by authoritarian, nationalist and neo-fascist expressions of the right and the enabling environment created by the (often self-inflicted) defeats of their antagonists (Taylor, 2013). We have yet to see a durable countermovement to match the international forces led by Bolsonaro, Duterte, Johnson, Orban, Putin and Trump, or surging reactionary currents like Germany's AfD and Le Pen's Front National. At the same time, anti-neoliberal forces in Latin America – from Argentina to Bolivia, Brazil, Ecuador and Venezuela – have faced major setbacks and defeats, just as they have in Greece. Recent events mark what dos Santos (2019) calls the exhaustion of the 'pink tide', with its attempts to divert revolutionary energy and deliver 'inclusion' through extraction and consumption, while avoiding confrontation with the USA. From a Gramscian perspective, the return of the extreme right is in no way surprising. It is a tried-and-tested passive revolutionary vehicle for reinforcing the rule of a divided, crisis-ridden capitalist class. If neoliberal globalism falls into disrepute, and emancipatory forces are unable to fill the vacuum, then the far right will have every opportunity to step into the breach.

With the pink tide receding in Latin America, much has also been written about the secular decline of traditional social democratic parties in Europe (for example, Streeck, 2016; Manwaring and Kennedy, 2018), their long-term complicity in driving neoliberalisation and delivering austerity. Little attention has been paid to the role of the municipal centre-left in this process. Throughout this study (2015–18), all eight cities were governed by parties or coalitions occupying ground from the centre to the left of the political spectrum. In the most aggressive cases of austere neoliberalism, Athens, Baltimore, Dublin and Leicester (including Barcelona in the pre-2015 period), organisations of the centre-left played a central role in consolidating austerity: through de-politicising it, disenfranchising or recuperating critics, rolling back or neutralising participatory governance, delivering market 'solutions', and implementing public service retrenchment, albeit with gradations of enthusiasm and regret. When explaining how austerity was made governable in these cities, the municipal centre-left is a key player. Its subordination to austere neoliberalism also contributes to explaining the political characteristics of the interregnum: mass disaffection with mainstream parties and institutions of the (local) state and socio-spatial distancing, aggravated by public service retrenchment. Long mired in neoliberal groupthink, it could conceive of no alternative to austerity once the crisis hit and, at a time when many were looking for political alternatives and moving into struggle, it was closing down debate.

The municipal centre-left has not always paid the electoral price extracted by the right nationally in many parts of the world. Yet, as a distinct political current with origins in egalitarian, democratic and solidarity norms, it has gone a long way to liquidating itself while vacating the field to reactionary forces. The crisis of neoliberal globalism is in part a crisis of social democracy, through which the wider left is also tainted by association. The anti-austerity left, still recuperating from earlier decades of defeat, faces a seemingly perpetual battle to disassociate itself from new, self-inflicted calamities perpetrated in its name by entities like Syriza, renew itself and rebuild its credibility. In this light, it is little surprise that authoritarian neoliberal and neo-reactionary forces have so far been major beneficiaries of the crisis. As Berman (2018: 4) put it commenting on the prospects for the centre-left, 'you can't beat something with nothing'.

Faced with repeated defeat and reaction, activist currents on the international anti-austerity left also appear fragile. Taylor (2013) pointed to system recuperation as an explanation for social movement decline, as corporations mirror demands for a greener, more ethical world. Bornstein (2009) defined Seattle as the early expression of a 'global civil society', eroded in the following decade by elite co-option and violent repression. Ultimately, affinity-based politics appear no less vulnerable to defeat and absorption than wage-bargaining trade unions mired in corporatism. Arguably, one of the greatest successes for the hard right has been its appropriation of anti-globalisation politics, initially popularised by the anti-capitalist left in the years after Seattle.

If crises of accumulation, hegemony, health and ecology are tending towards 'unstable disequilibria', the means of resolving them on democratic, egalitarian and solidary terms remain uncertain. Diversity in organisational form and philosophy can certainly be a strength from the point of view of experimentation and learning (Purcell, 2012), yet the inability to sustain unity of purpose-in-action, remains as much an impediment to circulating pre-figurative practices and nurturing logics of affinity as it is to organised insurgency and counter-hegemony. Fragmentation continues to impede anti-austerity forces, both in terms of competing ideas, goals and traditions and practical difficulties in bringing spheres of struggle together in meaningful conversation. These difficulties do not always arise from deep political differences. Chapter 7 suggested that asymmetries between the everyday concerns and practices of different mobilisations are also important. Hill's (1977) 'bucket of crabs' analogy, and 'ships passing in the night' both capture difficulties in building unity of purpose among disparate struggles.

Even if they espouse the same broad principles, struggles often face in different directions, illustrated by spatial and cognitive disconnections between battles over the environment and place-based race–class injustices, such as in Nantes (Chapter 7). Unity-in-struggle does emerge but is difficult to sustain and ever-vulnerable to disruption. Among anti-austerity activists in Dublin, suspicion towards badly weakened and compromised trade unions, political institutions and electoral setbacks to radical left parties left no plausible vehicle for translating new solidarities into a conscious and durable 'movement of movements' (Mertes, 2004). In Montréal, promising mechanisms to bring striking workers, militant community groups, students and social movements together emerged from the Maple Spring but could not prevent sectional traditions re-asserting themselves. In Leicester, public officials – themselves critics of austerity – disrupted resistance through the spatial and temporal segmentation of neighbourhood service restructuring. If, as Kipfer (n.d.) put it, 'class politics needs to be analysed with respect to its capacity, or, failure, to appropriate space across the social segmentations and spatial divides between workplace and neighbourhood', there is still a long way to go.

Cooptions and legacies of defeat create further barriers to unified struggle, exemplified by the fate of the left in Athens, cautionary memories of Thatcherism in Leicester, trade union conservatism in Dublin and Montréal and union peripherality in anti-austerity actions after 15-M in Barcelona. Nor is austerity urbanism confronted directly by militant municipal revolt of the kind witnessed in the UK during the 1920s and 1980s. Anti-austerity forces have engaged in fierce confrontation with upper tiers of the state on the streets, but local state apparatuses have not. The 'constitutionalist' orientation derives partly from the educative effects of defeat and state repression and partly from the constructivist disposition prevalent in new municipalist politics and scepticism towards direct confrontation (Newman, 2014a). Assuming control over governmental apparatuses creates other difficulties. As actors in an incipient new municipalist regime, respondents in Barcelona were very aware of their limited (counter) hegemony, played out in vertical and horizontal struggles between overlapping and competing political traditions, as well as in city hall. The structural-cultural dissonance between conservative municipal apparatuses and new municipalist governing priorities was a notable barrier to transformation, as Marxist state theory anticipates and Ada Colau highlighted in observing that 'the nature of the institution is not associated with the possibility of rupture' (cited in Blanco et al, 2020: 29).

Olin Wright (2019: 148) encapsulated the problem of weak counter-hegemony, buckets of crabs and ships passing in the night, writing that 'it is not the case the 99 percent share a common lived experience', and 'there is a pervasive fragmentation of lived experience that makes a common class identity difficult to forge'. From the system perspective, in contrast, Stone (1993) argued that capitalism does not require strong ideological affiliation or legitimacy to sustain itself, merely the perception that it is easier to muddle on or that the costs and risks of attempted rupture are invariably too high (also Olin

Wright, 2019: 67–9). Pro-market regimes are much easier to build than egalitarian ones, said Stone (1993: 12): 'the ready availability of means rather than the will of dominant actors may explain what is pursued and why. Hence, hegemony in a capitalist order may be more a matter of ease of cooperation around profit-oriented activities than the unchallenged ascendancy of core ideas'. In other words, the systemic 'incumbency' of capitalism makes weak counter-hegemony a much bigger problem for those seeking to transform a political order than weak hegemony is for those trying to sustain it, and able to fall back on the repertoires of dominance and pre-emption.

Politicisations: combustibility, generativity and contagion

Early in the age of austerity Peck (2012: 651) argued that 'just as austerity is, by its very nature, a form of redistributive politics—in spatial, scalar and social terms— so must its progressive alternatives reach beyond the local, to the realms of the cross-scalar and the interurban'. The research identifies a striking tendency for urban struggles to do this, generalising from both issue-based and spatial particularities. This element has considerable 'disordering' potential with respect to austere neoliberalism, and re-ordering potential with respect to transformative politics. Generative and contagious politicisations have been significant enough and frequent enough to suggest that this dangerous conjuncture remains open to radical and emancipatory transformations, if they can be channelled into hegemonic forms and apparatuses. This suggestion was reinforced by the dawn of a third wave of contention in 2018, engulfing much of the world in renewed struggles for democracy and economic justice. Choonara (2020) records uprisings leading to regime change in Algeria and Sudan, huge mobilisations for democracy in Hong Kong and, even as the pink tide reached its ebb, renewed uprisings in Latin America including Puerto Rico, Argentina, Chile, Colombia and Ecuador. Northern European revolt centred on France during this third wave, while uprisings and mass protests also occurred in Haiti, Guinea, Kazakhstan, Iran and Iraq. They were often uncoordinated internally or with each other, and politically nebulous. However, they support May's (2017) contention that political time is speeding up. The new European-American cycle of contention that erupted with Seattle has evolved in tandem with the weakening of neoliberal hegemony and the retreat to dominance. As hegemony weakens, the space for contagious and generative struggles also grows. Developments in the cycle of contention further erode hegemony, even if they have yet to produce counter-hegemonic politics. In the urban sphere, signs of the re-politicising effects of increasingly frequent struggles were evident in strategic internationalism, feminisation, the reconstitution of rebellious civil societies and occasional possibilities for counter institution building.

In the ebb and flow of global struggle, one portent of a globalised emancipatory politics with urban roots and capable of inspiring emulation, was the rousing feminist, environmentalist and anti-racist internationalism of Barcelona en Comú encapsulated by Mayor Ada Colau. Actions like 8-M 2018 and the mass demonstration for refugees and against tourism in 2017 (Chapter 6) address inherently international and global issues in a way that holds out the potential for trans-urban movements against neoliberal globalist and conservative nationalist currents, and for the radicalisation of democracy as the lifeblood of municipalism. Perhaps because of the preponderance of libertarian socialist thinking, the figure of Gramsci's organic intellectual, a collective body or persons capable of channelling and amplifying political struggle (Humphreys, 2013), is missing from accounts of urban struggles against austerity. However, despite political weaknesses and damaging compromises, Colau continued to embody some of these characteristics: a central figure from within the movements capable of shaping, knitting together and extrapolating public needs and demands. With less well known colleagues, she exercised mobilising power through the electoral platform, and mechanisms like the international network of self-proclaimed Fearless Cities (Barcelona en Comú, 2019). Fearless Cities, as a global imaginary, encompasses peri-urban and rural struggles. Far from falling into 'methodological cityism' it recognises no typological boundaries and instead seeks to propagate municipalist philosophy-in-action beyond narrow categorisations (Blanco and Gomà, 2020).

Vehicles for geographical diffusion are complemented by ideational generalisations, where issue-based campaigns, or single-issue movements come to recognise the deep, inter-connected roots and origins of different struggles. In addition to Barcelona's globalist-localism, activists in Baltimore's struggles for racial justice, Dublin's water wars, the campaign against the airport at Notre-Dame-des-Landes and Montréal's Maple Spring all saw activists grasping connections between the specificity of an immediate struggle and broader themes, including the critique of neoliberalism and capitalism itself. The eruptions of the post-Seattle period maybe typically short-lived, and always vulnerable to co-option and attrition, but the ease and frequency with which they recur, and translate across space into generalised claims on democracy, equality and solidarity, was very striking (Dikeç and Swyngedouw, 2017; Olin Wright, 2019: 149–50). The global urbanism of Fearless Cities (not without its own limitations, vulnerabilities and losses of momentum) was one notable translation mechanism for these tendencies (Russell, 2019); not a counter-hegemonic apparatus, but an example of something that could plausibly fulfil elements of this role.

If the figure of the organic intellectual is missing from the analysis of anti-austerity struggles, so too is a concrete sense of what apparatuses are adequate to the task of enacting durable transformations at any scale. Chapter 1 argued that the potential of a class or alliance of subalterns to exercise political power 'depends upon its ability to find the institutional forms adequate to the *differentia specifica* of its own particular hegemonic project' (Thomas, 2009: 227). The 'municipal assembly' in both localised and globalised forms could be one such form (Bookchin, 2019: 16). The best example of a nascent council or assembly-like institution in this study was Montréal's *Coalition Main Rouge*, with its ability to synthesise class, racial, environmental and gender demands and pose them in unity. It was only in Montréal that the potential for a full-blown 'social strike' against austerity was ever tangible and where an organising committee existed that was capable, tenuously and temporarily, of unifying the 'bucket of crabs' (Savard, 2016). The Coalition Main Rouge did not emerge from factory occupations, but perhaps prefigures the potential in periods of intense struggle for 'infrastructures of dissent' to become 'infrastructures of counter-hegemony'. Reflecting the politics of the post-Seattle cycle of contention, the question is whether such mechanisms, if and when they recur, evolve into multi-scalar 'councils of the subaltern' capable of synthesising and amplifying myriad 21st-century claims on equality, 'while avoiding becoming re-inscribed into the state apparatus and neutralised via means of passive revolutionary activity' (Hesketh, 2017: 184). The grand old question of political organisation, not least the future role of parties and platforms, remains open.

Conclusion

Writing at the end of a tumultuous 2011, Barker et al (2013: 30) concluded that austerity was a 'shallow hegemony indeed'. In the ebb-tide of 15-M and the 'Arab Spring', this seemed to be wishful thinking and the following period could be described as a 'brief moderation', in which parts of the geo-political landscape were re-normalised, while austerity was implemented and the great movements and reactions of the post-2016 period had yet to materialise. Today, the tide does seem to be going out on the hegemony of austere neoliberalism and neoliberal globalism more generally. Socialist ideas are becoming popular in many parts of the world, some even with professed conservatives (Meadway, 2019). A multitude of measures associated with austere neoliberalism continue in cities, but as a political imaginary it is much weakened, in discursive and ideological retreat and sustained increasingly by domination. The continued weakening of neoliberal hegemony, including growing uncertainty, division and vacillation among national and supra-national elites, arises partly from the imperative for perpetual 'innovation', partly from internal contradictions and failures, and partly from increasingly stentorian struggles mounted against it. To some extent, weakening hegemony is an achievement, attributable to recurrent waves within the 21st-century cycle of contention, which then create space for further politicisations in a positive feedback loop.[2] Equally, it is clear from the huge neo-reactionary backlash that weak hegemony does not automatically make austerity ungovernable or produce strong counter-hegemonies. Such is the character of an interregnum. Whether or not it is still embraced in elite discourse, urbanised expressions of austere neoliberalism are likely to continue in aggressive, defensive, variegated, hybridised, reactionary and zombified forms unless, until and wherever it encounters political organisation adequate to the task of terminating it.

Peck and Theodore (2019: 260) argued that the political nemesis of austere neoliberalism will not be found in a 'single event, or globally synchronized threshold moment, but rather an extended and geographically uneven interregnum, marked by atrophying consensus, regulatory ruptures, crisis-assisted transformations, social conflicts, squalid compromises, reactionary opportunism, and the unruly emergence of actually existing alternatives from across the political spectrum'. Their analysis echoes Stahl's (2019), and there is little in this study to contradict it. The contribution here is to specify variegated and multi-valent mechanisms through which urban dynamics of governability and ungovernability, continuity and change, normalisation and upheaval evolved through the age of austerity. These, in turn, contribute to a more refined understanding of the character and temporalities of the interregnum in concrete urban forms.

In summary, economic rationalism was predominantly, but not only, a stabilising factor in the reproduction of austere neoliberalism. Different aspects of the retreat to dominance constituted an ordering factor insofar as they facilitated the implementation of austerities, and a re-ordering factor marking the drift to authoritarianism in conditions of weak hegemony. Weakening hegemony was a prominent, but by no means universal disordering factor with overlapping explanations in the character of neoliberalism itself, the rollback of co-optive mechanisms, strategic contradictions and the impact of struggles, all of which have undermined the confidence of elites and subalterns in the old neoliberal globalist project. Where hegemony weakens, pre-emptive regime powers may or may not reinforce governability, depending on whether they are strengthened or undermined by resources including economic rationalism, domination and pre-emptive power. Weak counter-hegemony points to the variety of factors inhibiting and disrupting the forces opposing austere neoliberalism, thus contributing to regime continuity or – in the case of Barcelona – limiting the radical and expansionary potential in regime change. Weak counter-hegemony prolongs the interregnum and creates space in which vicious passive-revolutionary forces gain strength. Politicisation is defined by the notable tendency for urban struggles to generalise from ideational and spatial particularities, intersecting with recurrent waves of global struggle for political democracy and economic justice. This is a significant disordering factor in neoliberal governance and has considerable, if unrealised potential with respect to the constitution of counter-hegemonies. The potential grounds of a hegemonic apparatus are nevertheless evident in tacit and exemplary expressions of organic intellectualism, the rise of urban internationalism and the fleeting constitution of a subaltern structure in Montréal. The increasingly contagious character of political struggles is a positive symptom of weak hegemony and they are pregnant with possibilities for alternative ways of living and governing.

Table 8.3 summarises five dimensions of (un)governability in the crises of neoliberal globalism. Framed this way, they unsettle the characteristic depiction of the interregnum as a three-way struggle between neoliberal globalism (now largely indistinguishable from 'the centre'), insurgent conservative nationalism and counter-hegemonic 'left populism'. The three positions are by no means exhaustive, exclusive, or politically equidistant. Nor do they have equal coherence and weight. If the second is a passive revolutionary vehicle to secure the class relations constituting the first, the feral sibling, the third has great vitality, but remains fragmentary and faces major barriers. The more important distinction is between passive-reactionary and active-emancipatory politics. In an interregnum, where austere neoliberalism is likely to endure in some, perhaps resignified form for as long as the overwhelming mass of the world's population accepts the costs, 'late neoliberalism' (Enright and Rossi, 2018) is perhaps best construed as a political claim, a demand or a summoning to political action and as a warning about the increasing severity and urgency of the multiple crises

Table 8.3: Dimensions of (un)governability in the crises of neoliberal globalism

	Athens	Baltimore	Barcelona	Greater Dandenong	Dublin	Leicester	Montréal	Nantes
Economic rationalism	Mix of austerian idealism and realism.	Deeply embedded neoliberal governing rationalities.	Project fiscal prudence, vs fecklessness of the right.	Fiscal conservatism, prudence.	Austerity as penance. New bubble economy.	Austerian realism: cut without fuss, develop the city-centre.	Mix of austerity idealism and austerity realism.	Re-signified: 'we're Keynesian': underwritten by boosterish confidence.
Weakening hegemony	Bifurcating civil society, mass alienation. Failed participatory governance initiatives.	Undermined by the politics of *The Uprising*. Remote, inaccessible governing regime.	Neoliberal globalism undermined by anti-austerity struggles and new municipalism.	Counter-factual case. Enhanced through intercultural revitalisation regime.	Hegemony of austere neoliberalism undermined in struggle. Hollowing out of participatory apparatus.	Alienation, distancing, dismantling institutions. Hollowing out of participatory apparatus.	Vibrant struggles. Québec Model undermined. Possible revival under Plante?	Intensifying contradictions, also manifesting in participatory apparatus.
Retreat to dominance	Repression, downloading, transnational organisation influence in local state.	State violence and territory effects.	Fiscal centralisation, downloading, repression.	Municipal powers curtailed.	Revanchism, authoritarianism, repression. Very weak and pliable municipality.	Fiscal restructuring, municipal Stockholm syndrome.	Provincial authoritarianism and centralisation. Downloading.	Fiscal reform – downloading. Caesarism (Macron).

(continued)

Table 8.3: Dimensions of (un)governability in the crises of neoliberal globalism (Continued)

	Athens	Baltimore	Barcelona	Greater Dandenong	Dublin	Leicester	Montréal	Nantes
Weak counter-hegemony	Strategic defeat and fragmentation. Electoral defeat of the left.	Reconstitution of community activism at an early stage.	Limited local state capacity, multiple hegemony projects in play. Coopted unions. Weakened electorally.	No organised forces contesting city-centre revitalisation.	Fragmentation of anti-austerity forces, ebb and flow of struggle. Coopted unions. Electoral setbacks.	Low levels of episodic and fragmentary struggle.	Bucket of crabs – coopted unions, competing pressures on VCS.	Opposition to Nantes model weak and disorganised. 'Parallel tracks'. Emerging 'slow city' discourse?
Politicisations	Anti-systemic politics in diffuse 'solidarity networks'.	'Parallel tracks' against city of neighbourhoods.	Internationalisation – #FearlessCities. Colau as organic intellectual.	Intercultural solidarity through entre-preneurialism.	Generalisation through struggle, molecular solidarities in water wars.	Sporadic, mostly contained and fragmented.	Generalisation articulated through the Maple Spring and Coalition Main Rouge.	Generalisation inaugurated in campaign against airport. Revolt across France.

facing the world, and constantly erupting anew. The recent history of capitalism is, with the benefit of hindsight, full of conjunctural tipping points. Overcoming weak counter-hegemony and constructing durable collectivities and unities across the spheres of economic production and social reproduction is a prerequisite for re-defining and owning the organic crisis of neoliberal globalism and ensuring that future tipping points fall to the left. Channelling energies from contagious political struggles into new apparatuses of democracy and equality will be crucial as the fight goes on to break the interregnum, defeat the forces of reaction and bring the age of austerity to a decisive end.

Afterword: Into the Pandemic

It is difficult to write with confidence about the political implications of COVID-19, only a few months into the Anglo-European phase of what could be a very prolonged and multi-faceted crisis, even if the immediate public health crises are resolved relatively quickly. As the preface explains, I decided against retrofitting the text, and for this reason terms populating the pre-COVID manuscript such as 'socio-spatial distancing' and 'contagious' have been left as they were, despite taking on very different and potentially upsetting meanings in the pandemic.

To echo the conclusions reached in Chapter 8, it does seem that for the time being the overtly austere and globalist faces of neoliberalism are in abeyance; now even more so (Standring and Davies, 2020). Corporate bailouts, crony contracts and other forms of 'socialism for the rich' show that powerful neoliberal forces persist, but as of Autumn 2020 austerity has given way to massive state spending and subsidies to workers that would not long ago have been deemed irresponsible, generative of moral turpitude, or even impossible. The ideologies of capitalist 'globalisation' are in tatters, while the virus poses no less of a challenge to left internationalism and the defence of global mobility rights. The signs, moreover, are that COVID-19 is unleashing economic and social crises that could dwarf those of the GEC. Struggles over the narration, management and resolution of those crises have the potential to be immense, prolonged and brutal, but also transformative. Those who see recession/depression as an opportunity to radicalise austere neoliberalism, particularly in its neo-reactionary and passive-revolutionary forms, remain well-positioned within the Euro-American states system. However, with the case for state spending, borrowing, tax rises and worker subsidies now disinterred and many governments openly, if expediently, repudiating austerity, they could struggle to dominate ideas and common-sense to the extent they did after the GEC. The age of austerity and the struggles over governability captured in this volume can therefore be read as a great rehearsal. The book is likely to be a prequel to what lies ahead for cities, in an even more intense form than before: the possibility of further draconian austerity albeit within a different discursive frame, harsher state authoritarianism and possible urban dereliction, but also more intense, urgent and inventive struggles to ensure that things turn out differently this time.

The book concluded that in the period preceding COVID-19, five cross-cutting characteristics were prominent in shaping urban political (dis)orders: economic rationalism, weakening hegemony, the retreat to dominance, weak counter-hegemony and acute politicisations. Economic rationalism, administrative dominance and weak counter-hegemony tended to reinforce austere neoliberalism, while weakening hegemony and diminishing co-optive power created space for politicisations. How these pre-existing characteristics evolve will be important determinants of (un)governability as the pandemic, and struggles over its construals, evolve. The remaining paragraphs reconsider these themes to highlight issues that could reproduce, amplify or disturb the urban political (dis)orderings discussed in the book.

Economic rationalism: The virtues of prudence and the primacy of market-led urban development have not so much disappeared in the heat of the pandemic, with its lockdowns, cratering economies and spiralling public spending, as become temporarily irrelevant. Perhaps aware of weakening hegemony, and the rising threat of ungovernability, elites and intellectuals had already begun conceding the need for a more prominent role for government, and the mitigation of gross inequalities created by austere neoliberalism (for example, Summers, 2019). Echoing the United Nations, the British *Financial Times*, a journal of choice for economic and political elites, went so far as to articulate this sentiment as a programmatic demand for a new 'social contract', 'to forge a society that will work for all' (The Editorial Board, 2020). For these commentators, the interventionist, redistributive state is back, and it needs to stay while advancing a plausible hegemony project.

It could also be very difficult for governments and employers to restore austere neoliberalism while suppressing the demands of newly valued 'key workers'. Unions have been gaining members and winning concessions, in some cases for the first time in decades. A pre COVID-19 poll conducted by the Bertelsmann Foundation found that 84 per cent of Europeans supported a minimum wage, and 71 per cent universal basic income.[1] These are potentially significant disruptions to neoliberal groupthink, but in the face of unprecedented economic contractions there will be fierce pressures to revert to orthodoxy, particularly as many proponents of orthodoxy remain in power. It is hard to say how difficult this might be in structural terms. Some predict a global depression of unprecedented depth and duration, while it is also conceivable that at least some countries and sectors will emerge from the crisis into a renewed accumulation cycle.

Beyond basic accumulation drivers, however, the question of what might be construed as 'economically rational', and by whom, is far from certain. Everyone now knows that market-fundamentalist doctrines can be set aside if and when elites choose, which only makes the craven capitulation of social democratic parties in the age of austerity seem more tragic and futile. Equally, in a post-viral depression, former 'magnet' cities might repel. Agglomerations and supply chains could unravel. Highstreets could be wiped out by the viral boom in online shopping, coffee shops and pubs by entrenched distancing norms, the normalisation of working from home and – in the worst-case scenario if vaccines fail, are not taken up or are denied to the global masses – recurrent waves of disease. Networked cities could be isolated, with new centrifugal tendencies within individual city-regions. Urban flight could erode city-centres and gentrified neighbourhoods, wrecking commercialised 'public realms' and depopulating them, invoking anew the spectre of ghost towns. Even gung-ho city Mayors might be forced to give up on 'attractiveness', now not only ineffective but palpably ludicrous. This scenario opens up the question of whether the great urban boom and planetary urbanisation dynamics will continue. Could a COVID depression bring the age of the entrepreneurial city to a more decisive and perhaps unpleasant end than anticipated, either in Chapter 8 or in Peck's (2017b) cautious diagnosis of 'late entrepreneurialism'? Whether or not such drastic restructurings occur, and they are considered highly unlikely by many leading urbanists, the virus and its governance creates space to challenge orthodoxies and think anew about economy, governance, society, space, environment and infrastructure. New economic rationalities will emerge in, against and beyond austere neoliberalism but the window of opportunity for alternative forces to define and claim ownership of a crisis could be short-lived (Bayırbağ et al, 2017).

Weak hegemony: On the face of it, precipitous economic decline unleashed in the first wave of the pandemic, seems likely to further weaken hegemony and diminish the co-optive powers of urban regimes built around austere and boosterish variants of neoliberalism. An interregnum is, by definition, a crisis of governability (Streeck,

2016). However, the governance of COVID-19 suggests that other hegemonic strategies could gain traction. One notable feature in the first lockdown phase of the European crisis was the widespread (by no means universal) public tolerance and approval for directions and rules deemed obsolete by those who view the world as increasingly constituted by individualisation, trust-dependent networks and flows. People in Britain mostly followed the rules, often at considerable personal cost to health and wellbeing. Are these attitudes and behaviours confined to the emergency, are they transient, or do they reveal a suppressed appetite for modernist governing principles among citizens who have had enough of both neoliberal anomie and neo-reactionary chaos-mongering, but equally have no enthusiasm for the radical left? A recent household survey on attitudes to COVID-19 conducted by De Montfort University found that although trust in politicians and media is low, an overwhelming majority said they had complied, to the letter, with government directions. To lack trust in political elites is not necessarily to repudiate the idea of trust, or modes of governing founded on rules and the socialisation of risk.[2]

Retreat to dominance: Chapter 3 discussed state rescaling mechanisms through which the effective political autonomy of municipalities was curtailed through the age of austerity. In the pandemic, there have been signs of outright municipal defiance that we did not previously encounter. Faced with a COVID deficit of some €300 million, Ada Colau led a 'municipal rebellion', refusing to hand over Barcelona's 2019 budget surplus of €161 million to the Spanish government (Shea-Baird, 2020). Even in Britain, there were tentative signs that local governments will not necessarily be so compliant as in the past. Councils in Greater Manchester refused to reopen primary schools on the designated date, as UK lockdown conditions were first eased in May and June 2020. Manchester's Metro-Mayor Andy Burnham then attempted to resist the unilateral imposition of new restrictions by central government. These minor rebellions might not signify the end of municipal Stockholm syndrome (Copus et al, 2017: 180), but they do create ripples in the dependency culture of recent decades and confer new prestige on city leaders. So too might the 'build back better' campaign, promoted internationally by the UN and launched in the UK by Burnham, borrowing from a popular international approach to post-disaster recovery (Barwick, 2020).

At the same time, COVID-19 and lockdown endowed states with unprecedented opportunities to enhance repressive apparatuses, take 'emergency' powers and intensify surveillance as test, trace and track systems were rolled out. These are supposed to be temporary measures, but it is obvious how lockdowns could be treated as a rehearsal for curfews. The authoritarianism of austere neoliberalism, the influence of the neo-reactionary right, and the potential for mounting public resentment, instability and conflict in months and years ahead do not augur well for the rollback of 'emergency' powers. The transition of the Orban regime in Hungary into a fully-fledged 'temporary' dictatorship is the most overt and extreme instance, together with Trump's attempts to sabotage the November 2020 Presidential election, and his collusion with far-right paramilitary groups in US cities that have also been singled out for attack by federal police.

Politicisation: weak counter-hegemony, contagious, generative struggles: The 20 years preceding COVID-19 were marked by increasingly combustible and infective global political events and movements, which have tended to fizzle out, become recuperated, or remain in the 'corporate' phase, without overtly transformative agendas emerging. Lefebvrian urbanity is the means through which difference is reasserted and centrality claimed through mastery of physical and social space. The concept of 'propinquity' synthesises the relationship between proximity on the one hand, and affinity or solidarity on the other. COVID-19 initially halted the wave of struggles that rolled across the world in 2018–19. If the virus was to undermine proximity longer term, what could this do to propinquity, and the anti-austerity struggles discussed in Chapters 6 and 7? Even if 'normality' quickly resumes, there could be a longer-term behavioural hangover in terms of reticence about work, socialisation, crowds and mass gatherings.

Whichever re-sorting of urban populations and economies occurs longer term, however, the signs are that viral interruptions to the third wave in the post-Seattle cycle of contestation were brief. Revolts have recurred, and the streets have been reclaimed. Police atrocities against African Americans, brought to public attention once more by the murder of George Floyd in May 2020, triggered another huge outburst of urban rage, with vast street gatherings constituting a second wave of the #BlackLivesMatter movement, this time extending far beyond the USA to a global scale. In a different form, #BlackLivesMatter echoes the planetary potential in transnational urbanism represented by #FearlessCities. This struggle is understood and narrated by Trump and his fascist supporters as a conflict over the right to the city, and it can be countered on the same terms. In Beirut, the fight for survival has been such that it de-centred COVID-19, with crowds spilling back onto the streets in the heat of the crisis (Bar'el, 2020). The pathogen is of secondary importance for those who can no longer abide repression, cannot isolate, distance, quarantine or shield, and are compelled to live and work in precarity and proximity with disease. The sudden revaluing of low paid and precarious workers has, at once, exposed the dependence of capital on mundane labour, challenged neoliberal stereotypes about the relationship between pay, ability and talent, and presented new opportunities to organise and extract concessions from governments and employers.

If a tentative judgement is made as to the emerging balance of forces, it is that the idea of the interregnum remains valid, that it is potentially more intense, widespread and combustible, and that there are possibly more players in the game. The austere neoliberal globalist camp is on the defensive, jostling with surging neo-reactionary currents and heterodox movements for equality and justice. Both of the latter currents seek to claim the 'anti-austerity' mantle. Another vector is the international elite movement for a new 'social contract', replete with nostalgic references to the foundations of the UN, universalism and welfarism and couched terms of green, resilient and inclusive recoveries. This sentiment is capable of being cherry-picked by left or right. Highlighting the potential to splice the idea of a social contract to a right-wing agenda, UK Prime Minister Boris Johnson summoned the spirit of Roosevelt by promising a post-COVID 'New Deal' (greeted with much incredulity) (Parker and Giles, 2020). If austere neoliberalism continues to afflict British cities in some form, as seems very likely, it is to be governed through a very different discursive framework than it was under David Cameron.

Finally, it is important to reiterate that COVID-19 erupted into an already unstable, iniquitous and conflictual conjuncture. As Lebanon highlighted, the disease is not always and everywhere the worst or most important thing happening. If it is today, it might not be in six months or a year. English soccer player Raheem Sterling memorably wrote, when #BlackLivesMatter was erupting in the UK, that 'the only disease right now is the racism that we are fighting'.[3] Without trivialising the death toll, grief and chronic suffering that arises directly and indirectly from the virus, which will surely have to be borne far into the future, it is important to beware excessively COVID-centred optics on urban governance and resistance. This is why the text of the book has largely been left, as it was, to speak to questions about governance, resistance and transformation in the age of austerity. In whichever ways we construe, navigate and ultimately memorialise the pandemic, these dynamics are likely to recombine, remain operative and continue shaping urban futures. There remains much to be learned about possibilities for a better future after COVID-19, from the bitter and hopeful experiences of that period.

Notes

Preface

1   Six case study reports available at https://transgob.wordpress.com.

Introduction

2   A full record of Cameron's speech on 26 April 2009 can be read at https://conservative-speeches.sayit.mysociety.org/speech/601367.

3   Then Chancellor Sajid Javid declared an end to austerity in the UK in September 2019.

4   Citations from Gramsci are drawn from anthologies and referenced to the original Prison Notebooks through the International Gramsci Society's Concordance Tables at www.internationalgramscisociety.org/resources/concordance_table/.

5   Available at https://juablog.com/2020/01/28/special-issue-worlds-of-austerity-governance-and-resistance-in-eight-cities/.

6   https://cura.our.dmu.ac.uk/category/austerity-governance/.

Chapter 1

1   See https://salvage.zone.

2   Speech to the Labour Party Conference, 2 October 2001. Full text available at www.independent.co.uk/news/uk/politics/tony-blairs-speech-full-text-9269196.html.

3   Lenin's report to the Second Congress of the Communist International, *On the International Situation and the Fundamental Tasks of the Communist International* republished at www.marxists.org/archive/lenin/works/1920/jul/x03.htm.

Chapter 2

1   See www.budget.finances.gouv.qc.ca/statistiques-budgetaires/en/table-25.html.

2   Original Greek quotation at www.aftodioikisi.gr/ota/dimoi/athina-proipologismos-meion-21-emfasi-stis-efpatheis-omades/.

3   Citation from http://postindustrialmontreal.ca/post-industrial-montreal, where it is incorrectly attributed to Michael Savage.

4   See www.development.vic.gov.au/projects/revitalising-central-dandenong?page=overview.

5   Data from Trading Economics, at www.tradingeconomics.com.

6   Author's calculation taking account of compound inflation rates. The raw figure should be treated with considerable caution, as it takes no account of changes in tax base or levels of demand that might arise from population change, or administrative restructuring and downloading.

7   2016 data from OECD.Stat, at https://stats.oecd.org, at 2010 prices. Data for Baltimore from US Bureau of Economic Analysis (BEA), at www.bea.gov/data/gdp/gdp-metropolitan-area – 2009 prices, 2017 figures.

8   2015 was the most recent data for Metropolitan Athens, where GDP decline had yet to reach its trough.

Chapter 3

1   The Regions and Cities section of OECD.Stat, at https://stats.oecd.org.

2   The Regions and Cities section of Eurostat, at https://ec.europa.eu/eurostat/web/regions-and-cities

3   See https://legislativereference.baltimorecity.gov/city-codes#charter.

Chapter 4

1   The term 'elite pluralism' is here used to describe the form and appearance of regime politics – a plural coalition of governmental and non-governmental elites – not as an explanatory framework.

2   See https://strikeatimperial.net.

Chapter 5

1   From interview with José Arribas by Jacques Étienne, *Football Magazine* no 80, September 1966, pp. 8–10.

2   Explanation provided by the EU, at https://ec.europa.eu/environment/europeangreencapital/nantesvisit/

3   Source cited at https://cura.our.dmu.ac.uk/2017/04/26/nantes-and-collaborative-governance-participation-its-in-our-dna/.

4   See document at http://media.viablecities.com/2019/06/DialogueCitoyen_EN-web.pdf.

5   http://nantesnecropole.noblogs.org.

6   The page on the Victoria government's webpage from which this quote was taken in July 2019 is no longer available. It is duplicated at www.miragenews.com/next-step-for-new-central-dandenong/. See also information at www.development.vic.gov.au/projects/revitalising-central-dandenong?page=overview#.

7   Translated by Ismael Blanco from source at www.naciodigital.cat on 10 April 2017.

Chapter 6

1   Ada Colau speech on 16 July 2018, archived at https://ajuntament.barcelona.cat/alcaldessa/en/speeches.

2   Ada Colau speech on 16 May 2016, archived at https://ajuntament.barcelona.cat/alcaldessa/en/speeches.

3   Letter and signatories at https://medium.com/@BComuGlobal/bill-de-blasio-dilma-rousseff-noam-chomsky-naomi-klein-judith-butler-susan-george-david-15e8ca01a486.

4   As reported on 4 October 2018 in this anonymously authored article in *The Journal*, www.thejournal.ie/government-housing-motion-4268576-Oct2018/.

5   For example, https://stay-grounded.org.

6   From blogpost by Griggs, Howarth and Feandeiro, at https://cura.our.dmu.ac.uk/2016/07/26/follow-the-protest-exploring-the-limits-and-torsions-of-collaborative-governance-in-nantes/.

Chapter 7

1   Cited in the local newspaper, the Leicester Mercury. Link broken.

2   This quotation was included in a presentation to the project team by Ioannis Chorianopoulos in April 2016.

Chapter 8

1   Online at www.marxists.org/archive/marx/works/1848/communist-manifesto/ch01.htm.

2   I am grateful to an anonymous reviewer for suggesting that I should recognise weak hegemony as an accomplishment, and not only the outcome of structural contradictions and crises.

Afterword: Into the Pandemic

1   https://europeanmoments.com/opinions/eupinions.

2   https://iaesv.our.dmu.ac.uk/2020/05/26/coronavirus-survey/.

3   Unauthored story published 8 June 2020, at www.bbc.co.uk/sport/football/52959292.

References

Ali, T. (2018) *The Extreme Centre: A Second Warning*, London: Verso, 2nd edition.

Anderson, P. (2000) 'Renewals', *New Left Review*, 1: 1–20.

Angelo, H. and Wachsmuth, D. (2015) 'Urbanizing urban political ecology: a critique of methodological cityism', *International Journal of Urban and Regional Research*, 39(1): 16–27.

Anguita-Gonzalez, J. (2008) 'La Austeridad como palanca revolucionaria', *Mundo Obrero*, [online], 29 February, Available at: www.mundoobrero.es/pl.php?id=849.

Arapoglou, V. and Gounis, K. (2015) 'Poverty and homelessness in Athens: governance and the rise of an emergency model of social crisis management', *GreeSE Paper 90: Hellenic Observatory Papers on Greece and Southeast Europe*. London: Hellenic Observatory, London School of Economics and Political Science.

Armingeon, K. (2012) 'The politics of fiscal responses to the crisis of 2008–2009', *Governance: An International Journal of Policy, Administration, and Institutions*, 25(4): 543–565.

Arrighi, G. (2005) 'Hegemony unravelling – 1', *New Left Review*, 33(2): 23–80.

Association for Public Service Excellence (2016) *Sustainable Local Government Finance and Liveable Local Areas: Can we Survive to 2020?* Manchester: Association for Public Service Excellence.

Athens Partnership (2018) *Athens Partnership: 2018 Annual Report*, Athens: Athens Partnership, Available at: https://athenspartnership. org/news/2018-annual-report.

Atzeni, M. and Ghigliani, P. (2007) 'Labour process and decision-making in factories under workers' self-management: empirical evidence from Argentina', *Work, Employment and Society*, 21(4): 653–671.

Bailey, D.J., Clua-Losada, M., Huke, N. and Ribera-Almandoz, O. (2017) *Beyond Defeat and Austerity: Disrupting the Critical Political Economy of Neoliberal Europe*, Abingdon: Routledge.

Balbona, D.L. and Begega, S.G. (2015) 'Austerity and welfare reform in south-western Europe: a farewell to corporatism in Italy, Spain and Portugal?', *European Journal of Social Security*, 17(2): 271–291.

Barcelona en Comú., with Bookchin, D. and Colau, A. (eds) (2019) *Fearless Cities: A Guide to the Global Municipalist Movement*, Oxford: New Internationalist.

Bar'el, Z. (2020) 'Coronavirus stalled Lebanon protests: now the country is in flames', *Haaretz*, [online], 16 June, Available at: www.haaretz.com/middle-east-news/.premium-coronavirus-spring-threatens-lebanon-s-stability-as-economy-struggles-1.8919886.

Barker, C., Cox, L., Krinsky, J. and Nilson G. (2013) 'Marxism and social movements: an introduction' in C. Barker, L. Cox, J. Krinsky and G. Nilson (eds), *Marxism and Social Movements*, Leiden: Brill, pp. 1–37.

Barwick, S. (2020) 'The build back better campaign aims to shape COVID-19 recovery policy, *Municipal Journal*, [online], 28 April, Available at: www.themj.co.uk/The-Build-Back-Better-campaign-aims-to-shape-COVID-19-recovery-policy/217417.

Bayırbağ, M.K., Davies, J.S. and Münch, S. (2017) 'Interrogating urban crisis: the governance and contestation of austerity in cities', *Urban Studies*, 59(4): 2023–2038.

Béal, V. and Pinson, G. (2015) 'From the governance of sustainability to the management of climate change: reshaping urban policies and central–local relations in France', *Journal of Environmental Policy and Planning*, 17(3): 402–419.

Beatley, M. (2017) 'Inside the Catalan feminist plan to upend Spanish patriarchal rule', Radio *IQ, WVTF, Virginia's Public Radio*, [online], 6 October, Available at: www.wvtf.org/post/inside-catalan-feminist-plan-upend-spanish-patriarchal-rule#stream/0.

Bell, D.M. (2017) *Rethinking Utopia: Place, Power, Affect*, Abingdon: Routledge.

Berman, S. (2018) 'Foreword', in R. Manwaring and P. Kennedy (eds), *Why the Left Loses: The Decline of the Centre-Left in Comparative Perspective*, Bristol: Policy Press, pp. 1–4.

Berry, C. and Giovannini, A. (eds) (2018) *Developing England's North: The Political Economy of the Northern Powerhouse*, London: Palgrave-Macmillan.

Bertrana, X. and Heinelt, H. (2013) 'The second tier of local government in the context of European multi-level government systems: institutional settings and prospects for reform', *Revista Catalana de Dret Públic*, 46: 73–89.

Biesta, G. (2008) 'Toward a new "logic" of emancipation: Foucault and Rancière', in R. Glass (ed), *Philosophy of Education 2008*, Urbana Champaign, IL: Philosophy of Education Society, pp. 169–177.

Blair, T. (1998) *Leading the Way: A New Vision for Local Government*, London: Institute for Public Policy Research.

Blanco, I. (2015a) 'Between democratic network governance and neoliberalism: a regime-theoretical analysis of collaboration in Barcelona', *Cities: The International Journal of Urban Policy and Planning*, 44: 123–130.

Blanco, I. (2015b) *Working Paper 4: Collaborative Governance in Barcelona*, Unpublished.

Blanco, I. (2016) *Working Paper 12: Austerity Governance and Contestation in Barcelona*, Unpublished.

Blanco, I. (2017) *Working Paper 21: Barcelona Final Case Study Report*, Unpublished.

Blanco, I. and Gomà, R. (2020) 'New municipalism', in A. Kobayashi (ed), *International Encyclopedia of Human Geography*, London: Elsevier, vol. 9, pp. 393–398, 2nd edition.

Blanco, I., Salazar Y. and Bianchi, I. (2020) 'Urban governance and political change under a radical left government: The case of Barcelona', *Journal of Urban Affairs*, 42(2): 18–38.

Bliss, D. (2018) *Economic Development and Governance in Small Town America: Paths to Growth*, New York: Routledge.

Bonefeld, W. (2016) Science, hegemony and action: on the elements of governmentality, *Journal of Social Sciences*, 12(2): 19–41.

Bonessi, D.M. (2018) 'Pugh unveils 2019 city budget', *WYPR*, [online], 28 March, Available at: www.wypr.org/post/pugh-unveils-2019-city-budget.

Bookchin, D. (2019) 'The future we deserve', in Barcelona en Comú. with D. Bookchin and A. Colau (eds), *Fearless Cities: A Guide to the Global Municipalist Movement*, Oxford: New Internationalist, pp. 12–16.

Bornstein, A. (2009) 'N30 + 10: global civil society, a decade after the battle of Seattle', *Dialectical Anthropology*, 33(2): 97–108.

Boudreau, J.A. and Hamel, P. (2017) 'Social agency and collective action in the structurally transformed metropolis: past and future research agendas', in R. Keil, P. Hamel, J.A. Boudreau and S. Kipfer (eds), *Governing Cities Through Regions: Canadian and European Perspectives*, Waterloo, Canada: Wilfrid Laurier University Press, pp. 27–40.

Boudreau, J.A., Hamel, P., Jouve, B. and Keil, R. (2007) 'New state spaces in Canada: metropolitanization in Montreal and Toronto compared', *Urban Geography*, 28(1): 30–53.

Brandes, S. (2019) 'From neoliberal globalism to neoliberal nationalism: an interview with Quinn Slobodian', *Ephemera*, 19(3): 641–649.

Brenner, N. (2018) 'Debating planetary urbanization: for an engaged pluralism', *Environment and Planning D: Society and Space*, 36(3): 570–590.

Brenner, N. and Elden, S. (2009) 'Henri Lefebvre on state, space, territory', *International Political Sociology*, 3(4): 353–377.

Brenner, N. and Schmid, C. (2015) 'Towards a new epistemology of the urban?', *City*, 19(2–3): 151–182.

Bristow, G. (2019) 'Yellow fever: populist pangs in France. Reflections on the gilets jaunes movement and the nature of its populism', *Soundings: A Journal of Politics and Culture*, 72: 65–78.

Broomhill, R. (2001) 'Neoliberal globalism and the local state: a regulation approach', *Journal of Australian Political Economy*, 48: 115–140.

Broughton, K., Berkeley, N. and Jarvis D. (2013) 'Neighbourhood regeneration in an era of austerity? Transferable lessons from the case of Braunstone, Leicester', *Journal of Urban Regeneration and Renewal*, 6(4): 381–393.

Brown, W. (1999) Resisting Left melancholy, *Boundary*, 26(3): 19–27.

Brown, W. (2018) 'Neoliberalism's Frankenstein: authoritarian freedom in twenty-first century "democracies"', *Critical Times,* 1(1): 60–79.

Bruff, I. (2014) 'The rise of authoritarian neoliberalism', *Rethinking Marxism*, 26(1): 113–129.

Bua, A. and Bussu, S. (2020) 'Between governance-driven democratisation and democracy-driven governance: explaining changes in participatory governance in the case of Barcelona, *European Journal of Political Research*. https://doi.org/10.1111/1475-6765.12421.

Bua, A., Davies, J.S., Blanco I., Chorianopoulos I., Cortina-Oriol M., Feandeiro A., Gaynor, N., Griggs, S. Howarth, D. and Salazar, Y. (2018) 'The urban governance of austerity in Europe', in R. Kerley, J. Liddle and P. Dunning (eds), *The Routledge Handbook of International Local Government*, Abingdon: Routledge, pp. 280–296.

Burawoy, M. (2011) 'On uncompromising pessimism: response to my critics', *Global Labour Journal*, 2(1): 73–77.

Callinicos, A.T. (2001) *Against the Third Way*, Cambridge: Polity Press.

Callinicos, A.T. (2006) *The Resources of Critique*, Cambridge: Polity Press.

Callinicos, A.T. (2010) 'The limits of passive revolution', *Capital and Class*, 34(3): 491–507.

Callinicos, A.T. (2012) 'Contradictions of austerity', *Cambridge Journal of Economics*, 36(1): 65–77.

Cameron, S. and McAllister, I. (2019) *The 2019 Australian Federal Election Results from the Australian Election Study*, Canberra: Australian National University, https://australianelectionstudy.org/wp-content/uploads/The-2019-Australian-Federal-Election-Results-from-the-Australian-Election-Study.pdf.

Cannon, B. and Murphy, M.P. (2015) 'Where are the pots and pans? Collective responses in Ireland to neoliberalisation in a time of crisis: Learning from Latin America', *Irish Political Studies*, 30(1): 1–19.

Cappuccini, M. (2017) *Austerity and Democracy in Athens: Crisis and Community in Exarchia*, Basingstoke: Palgrave Macmillan.

Carroll, W.K. (2006) 'Hegemony, counter-hegemony, anti-hegemony', *Socialist Studies*, 2(2): 9–43.

Cerny, P.G. (2008) 'Embedding neoliberalism: the evolution of a hegemonic paradigm', *The Journal of International Trade and Diplomacy*, 2(1): 1–46

Choonara, J. (2020) 'A new cycle of revolt', *International Socialism*, 165: 21–36.

Chorianopoulos, I. (2012) 'State spatial restructuring in Greece: forced rescaling, unresponsive localities', *European Urban and Regional Studies*, 19(4): 331–348

Chorianopoulos, I. (2015) *Working Paper 2: Austerity and Rescaling: The Emergence of Collaborative Governance Structures in Athens*, Unpublished.

Chorianopoulos, I. (2016) *Working Paper 10: Austerity and Collaborative Governance in Athens*, Unpublished.

Chorianopoulos, I. (2017) *Working Paper 19: Athens Final Case Study Report*, Unpublished.

Chorianopoulos, I. and Tselepi, N. (2019) 'Austerity urbanism: rescaling and collaborative governance policies in Athens', *European Urban and Regional Studies*, 26(1): 80–96.

Chorianopoulos, I. and Tselepi, N. (2020) 'Austerity governance and bifurcated civil society: the changing matrices of urban politics in Athens', *Journal of Urban Affairs*, 42(1): 39–55.

City of Baltimore, Maryland (2018) *Comprehensive Annual Financial Report: Year Ended June 30*.

City of Greater Dandenong (2018) *Budget 2018–19: Proposed*.

Clark, T.J. (2012) 'For a left with no future', *New Left Review*, 74(2): 53–75.

Clarke, J. (2010) 'Of crises and conjunctures: the problem of the present', *Journal of Communication Inquiry*, 34(4): 337–354.

Clarke, S.E. (1995) 'Institutional logics and local economic development: a comparative analysis of eight American cities', *International Journal of Urban and Regional Research*, 19(4): 513–533.

Clayton, J., Donovan, C. and Merchant, J. (2016) 'Distancing and limited resourcefulness: third sector service provision under austerity localism in the north east of England', *Urban Studies*, 53(4): 723–740.

Cleaver, H. (1979) *Reading Capital Politically*, Brighton: Harvester Press.

Coates, T. (2014) 'The case for reparations', *The Atlantic*, [online], June, Available at: www.theatlantic.com/magazine/archive/2014/06/the-case-for-reparations/361631/.

Cobbina, J.E. (2019) *Hands Up, Don't Shoot: Why the Protests in Ferguson and Baltimore Matter, and How they Changed America*, New York: New York University Press.

Collombat, T. (2014) 'Labor and austerity in Québec: lessons from the Maple Spring', *Labor Studies Journal*, 39(2): 140–159.

Cooke, B. and Kothari, U. (2001) *Participation: The New Tyranny?*, London: Zed Books.

Copus, C., Roberts, M. and Wall, R. (2017) *Local Government in England: Centralisation, Autonomy and Control*, London: Palgrave Macmillan.

Cox, K. and Mair, A. (1988) 'Locality and community in the politics of local economic development', *Annals of the Association of American Geographers*, 78(2): 307–325.

Crabapple, M. (2020) 'The attack on Exarchia, an anarchist refuge in Athens' *The New Yorker*, [online], 20 January, Available at: www.newyorker.com/news/dispatch/the-attack-on-exarchia-an-anarchist-refuge-in-athens.

Crewe, T. (2016) 'The strange death of municipal England', *London Review of Books*, 38(24): 6–10.

Cromarty, H. (2019) *Adult Social Care Funding (England)*, House of Commons Library Briefing Paper, CBP07903, 3 October.

Crouch, C. (2004) *Post-Democracy*, Cambridge: Polity Press.

Crouch, C. (2009) 'Privatized Keynesianism: an unacknowledged policy regime', *British Journal of Politics and International Relations*, 11(3): 382–399.

Crouch, C. (2011) *The Strange Non-Death of Neoliberalism*, Cambridge: Polity Press.

Cucca, R. and Ranci, C. (2017) *Unequal Cities: The Challenge of Post-Industrial Transition in Times of Austerity*, Abingdon: Routledge.

Curry, R. (2020) 'Councils still face numerous barriers to building homes despite lifting of HRA cap, new research finds', *Inside Housing*, [online], 8 January, Available at: www.insidehousing.co.uk/news/news/councils-still-face-numerous-barriers-to-building-homes-despite-lifting-of-hra-cap-new-research-finds-64650.

Dahlum, S., Knutsen, C.H. and Wig T. (2019) 'Who revolts? Empirically revisiting the social origins of democracy', *The Journal of Politics*, 81(4): 1494–1499.

Davies, J.S. (2002) 'The governance of urban regeneration: a critique of the "governing without government" thesis', *Public Administration*, 80(2): 301–322.

Davies, J.S. (2007) 'The limits of partnership: an exit-action strategy for local democratic inclusion', *Political Studies*, 55(4): 779–800.

Davies, J.S. (2009) 'The limits of joined-up government: towards a political analysis', *Public Administration*, 87(1): 80–96.

Davies, J.S. (2010) 'Localism', in A. Gamble, C. Hay, M. Flinders and M. Kenny (eds), *The Oxford Handbook of British Politics*, Oxford: Oxford University Press, pp. 404–422.

Davies, J.S. (2011a) 'The limits of post-traditional public administration: towards a Gramscian perspective', *Critical Policy Studies*, 5(1): 47–62.

Davies, J.S. (2011b) *Challenging Governance Theory: From Networks to Hegemony*, Bristol: Policy Press.

Davies, J.S. (2012a) 'Network governance theory: a Gramscian critique', *Environment and Planning A: Economy and Space*, 44(11): 2687–2704.

Davies, J.S. (2012b) 'Active citizenship: navigating the conservative heartlands of the New Labour project', *Policy and Politics*, 40(1): 3–19.

Davies, J.S. (2015) *Working Paper 6: Collaborative Governance in Leicester*, Unpublished.

Davies, J.S. (2017a) 'Urban regime theory', in B.S. Turner (ed), *The Wiley-Blackwell Encyclopedia of Social Theory*, Oxford: Blackwell, doi:10.1002/9781118430873.est0549

Davies, J.S. (2017b) *Governing In and Against Austerity: International Lessons from Eight Cities*, Leicester: De Montfort University, ISBN 978-1-85721-432-1.

Davies, J.S. and Blanco, I. (2017) 'Austerity urbanism: patterns of neoliberalisation and resistance in six cities of Spain and the UK', *Environment and Planning A: Economy and Space*, 49(7): 1517–1536.

Davies, J.S. and Bua, A. (2016) *Working Paper 14: Austerity Governance and Welfare in Leicester*, Unpublished.

Davies, J.S. and Msengana-Ndlela, L.G. (2015) 'Urban power and political agency: reflections on a study of local economic development in Johannesburg and Leeds', *Cities: The International Journal of Urban Policy and Planning*, 44: 131–138.

Davies, J.S. and Pill, M.C. (2012) 'Hollowing out neighbourhood governance? Rescaling revitalization in Baltimore and Bristol, *Urban Studies*, 49(10): 2199–2217.

Davies, J.S. and Thompson, E. (2016) 'Austerity realism and the governance of Leicester', in M. Bevir and R.A.W. Rhodes (eds), *Rethinking Governance: Ruling, Rationalities and Resistance*, Abingdon: Routledge, pp. 144–161.

Davies, J.S., Bua, A. and Cortina-Oriol, M. (2017) *Working Paper 23: Final Report of the Leicester Case Study*, Unpublished.

Davies, J.S., Bua, A., Cortina-Oriol, M. and Thompson E. (2020) 'Why is austerity governable? A Gramscian urban regime analysis of Leicester, UK', *Journal of Urban Affairs*, 42(1): 56–74.

Davies, J.S., Blanco, I., Bua, A., Chorianopoulos, I., Cortina-Oriol, M., Gaynor, N., Griggs, S., Hamel, P., Henderson H., Howarth, D., Keil, R., Pill, M.C., Salazar, Y. and Sullivan, H. (Forthcoming) *New Developments in Urban Governance: Reframing Collaboration in the Age of Austerity*, Bristol: Bristol University Press.

Davies, W. (2017) *The Limits of Neoliberalism: Authority, Sovereignty and the Logic of Competition*, London: Sage, 2nd edition.

Davis, M. (2018) *Old Gods, New Enigmas: Marx's Lost Theory*, London: Verso.

Day, R.J. (2005) *Gramsci is Dead: Anarchist Currents in the Newest Social Movements*, London: Pluto Press.

Day, R.J. (2012) 'Re-inscribing the hegemony of hegemony: a response to Mark Purcell', *ACME: An International E-Journal for Critical Geographies*, 11(3): 525–529.

Dean, M. (2014) 'Rethinking neoliberalism', *Journal of Sociology*, 50(2): 150–163.

Deaton, C. (2015) 'The revolution will not be occupied: theorizing urban revolutionary movements in Tehran, Prague, and Paris', *Territory, Politics, Governance*, 3(2): 205–226.

Degen, M. and Garcia, M. (2012) 'The transformation of the "Barcelona Model": an analysis of culture, urban regeneration and governance', *International Journal of Urban and Regional Research*, 36(5): 1022–1038.

Della Porta D., Fernandez, J., Kouki, H. and Mosca, L. (2017) *Movement Parties against Austerity*, Cambridge: Polity Press.

Department of Legislative Services (2016) *Fiscal Challenges of Local Governments in Maryland*, State of Maryland.

Department of Legislative Services (2017) *Measuring Local Fiscal Conditions in Maryland: Demographic and Fiscal Trends*, State of Maryland.

Derickson, K. (2018) 'Masters of the universe', *Environment and Planning D: Society and Space*, 36(3): 556–562.

Di Mascio, F. and Natalini, A. (2015) 'Fiscal retrenchment in Southern Europe: changing patterns of public management in Greece, Italy, Portugal and Spain', *Public Management Review*, 17()1): 129–148.

Dikeç, M. (2018) *Urban Rage: The Revolt of the Excluded*, New Haven, CT: Yale University Press.

Dikeç, M. and Swyngedouw, E. (2017) 'Theorizing the politicizing city', *International Journal of Urban and Regional Research*, 41(1): 1–18.

Dinerstein, A.C. (2015) *The Politics of Autonomy in Latin America: The Art of Organising Hope*, Basingstoke: Palgrave Macmillan.

dos Santos, F.L.B. (2019) *Power and Impotence: A History of South America under Progressivism (1998–2016)*, Leiden: Brill.

Dublin City Council (2019) *Dublin Economic Monitor: May 2019*, Issue 17.

Dvorak, P. (2015) 'Baltimore riots: it is time for America to acknowledge its desperate, forgotten neighbourhoods', *The Independent*, [online], 28 April, Available at: www.independent.co.uk/voices/baltimore-riots-it-is-time-for-america-to-acknowledge-its-desperate-forgotten-neighbourhoods-10211061.html.

Eaton, G. (2020) 'Yanis Varoufakis: Covid-19 has "turbocharged" the EU's failures', *New Statesman*, [online], 11 May, Available at: www.newstatesman.com/world/europe/2020/05/yanis-varoufakis-covid-19-has-turbocharged-eu-s-failures.

Edwards, M. (2009) *Civil Society*, Cambridge: Polity Press, 2nd edition.

Eisinger, P. (2014) 'Is Detroit dead?', *Journal of Urban Affairs*, 36(1): 1–12.

Elliott, L. (2010) 'Alistair Darling: we will cut deeper than Margaret Thatcher', *The Guardian*, [online], 25 March, Available at: www.theguardian.com/politics/2010/mar/25/alistair-darling-cut-deeper-margaret-thatcher.

Enright, T. and Rossi, U. (2018) (eds), *The Urban Political: Ambivalent Spaces of Late Neoliberalism*, Basingstoke: Palgrave Macmillan.

Erne, R. (2013) 'Let's accept a smaller slice of a shrinking cake: The Irish Congress of Trade Unions and Irish public sector unions in crisis', *Transfer: European Review of Labour and Research*, 19(3): 425–430.

Escorihuela, I and Domingo, G. (2018) 'Dotze veritats i mentides sobre la nova obligació de destinar el 30% a habitatge protegit a Barcelona', 24 June, Available at: www.elcritic.cat/blogs/observatoridesc/2018/06/24/dotze-veritats-i-mentides-sobre-la-nova-obligacio-de-destinar-el-30-a-habitatge-protegit-a-barcelona/.

Evans, B.M. and McBride, S. (2017) 'The austerity state: an introduction', in S. McBride and B.M. Evans (eds), *The Austerity State*, Toronto: University of Toronto Press, pp. 3–21.

Federici, S. (2012) *Revolution at Point Zero: Housework, Reproduction, and Feminist Struggle*, San Francisco: PM Press.

Felski, R. (1989) *Beyond Feminist Aesthetics: Feminist Literature and Social Change*, Cambridge MA: Harvard University Press.

Fenna, A. (2013) 'The economic policy agenda in Australia, 1962–2012', *Australian Journal of Public Administration*, 72(2): 89–102.

Ferguson, J. (2010) 'The uses of neoliberalism', *Antipode,* 46(S1): 166–184.

Financial Times (2020) 'Virus lays bare the frailty of the social contract', *Financial Times*, [online], 3 April, Available at: www.ft.com/content/7eff769a-74dd-11ea-95fe-fcd274e920ca.

Fishwick, A. and Connolly, H. (2018) (eds), *Austerity and Working-Class Resistance: Survival, Disruption and Creation in Hard Times*, London: Rowman and Littlefield International.

Florida, R. (2003) 'Cities and the creative class', *City and Community*, 2(1): 3–19.

Foley, C. (ed) (2019) *In Spite of You: Bolsonaro and the New Brazilian Resistance*, New York: OR Books.

Fraser, N. (2012) 'On justice: lessons from Plato, Rawls and Ishiguro', *New Left Review*, 74(March/April): 53–75.

Fung, A. and Olin-Wright, E. (2001), 'Deepening democracy: innovations in empowered participatory governance', *Politics and Society*, 29(1): 5–41.

Galbraith, J.K. (1958) *The Affluent Society*, Boston, MA: Houghton Mifflin.

Gamble, A. (1994) *The Free Economy and the Strong State*, Basingstoke: Macmillan, 2nd edition.

Gaynor, N. (2011) 'Associations, deliberation, and democracy: the case of Ireland's social partnership', *Politics and Society*, 39(4): 497–519.

Gaynor, N. (2015) *Working Paper 5: Collaborative governance in Dublin: Centralisation and Protest*, Unpublished.

Gaynor, N. (2016) *Working Paper 13: Governing Austerity in Dublin*, Unpublished.

Gaynor, N. (2017) *Working Paper 22: Dublin Final Case Study Report*, Unpublished.

Gaynor, N. (2019) 'Neoliberalism, deliberation and dissent: critical reflections on the "community activation" turn in Ireland's community development programme' *Community Development Journal*, [online], 23 October, Available at: https://doi.org/10.1093/cdj/bsz019.

Gaynor, N. (2020) 'Governing austerity in Dublin: rationalization, resilience, and resistance', *Journal of Urban Affairs*, 42(1): 75–90.

George, S. (2004) *Another World is Possible If...*, London: Verso.

Gibson-Graham, J.K. (2006) [1996] *The End of Capitalism (as we knew it): A Feminist Critique of Political Economy*, Minneapolis, MN: University of Minnesota Press, 2nd edition.

Giddens, A. (1996) 'Affluence, poverty and the idea of a post-scarcity society', *Development and Change*, 27(2): 365–377.

Giddens, A. (2010) 'The rise and fall of New Labour', *New Perspectives Quarterly*, 27(3): 32–37.

Gleeson, B., Henderson, H. and Sullivan H. (2015) *Working Paper 7: ESRC Austerity Governance Project. Melbourne Case Literature Review*, Unpublished.

Gonzalez, M. (2018) *The Ebb of the Pink Tide: The Decline of the Left in Latin-America*, London: Pluto Press.

Government of Ireland (2000) *White Paper on a Framework for Supporting Voluntary Activity and for Developing a Relationship between the State and the Community and Voluntary Sector*, Dublin: Government Publications.

Graefe, P. and Rioux Ouimet, X.H. (2018) 'From the bailiffs at our doors to the Greek Peril: twenty years of "fiscal urgency" and Quebec politics', in B. Evans and C. Fanelli (eds), *The Public Sector in an Age of Austerity: Perspectives from Canada's Provinces and Territories*, Montreal: McGill-Queen's University Press, pp. 161–188.

Graham, S. and Marvin, S. (2001) *Splintering Urbanism: Networked Infrastructures, Technological Mobilities and Urban Condition*, London: Routledge.

Gramsci, A. (1971) *Selections from Prison Notebooks*, London: Lawrence and Wishart, Translated by Quintin Hoare and Geoffrey Nowell-Smith.

Gramsci, A. (1994) 'Letter from prison, 19th December, 1929', in *Letters from Prison (Vol. 1)*, New York: Columbia University Press. Edited by Frank Rosengarten, translated by Raymond Rosenthal.

Griggs, S. and Howarth, D. (2015) *Working Paper 9: Nantes Case Study Literature Review*, Unpublished.

Griggs, S. and Howarth, D. (2016) *Working Paper 17: Collaborative Governance Under Austerity*, Unpublished.

Griggs, S. and Howarth, D. (2020) 'Two images of Nantes as a "green model" of urban planning and governance: the "collaborative city" versus the "slow city"', *Town Planning Review*, 94(4): 415–436.

Griggs, S., Howarth, D. and Feandeiro A. (2018) *Working Paper 26: Collaborative Governance Under Austerity, Final Report: City of Nantes*, Unpublished.

Griggs, S., Howarth, D. and Feandeiro A. (2020) 'The logics and limits of "collaborative governance" in Nantes: myth, ideology, and the politics of new urban regimes', *Journal of Urban Affairs*, 42(1): 91–108.

Guarneros-Meza, V., Tellería, I., Blas, A. and Pill, M.C. (2018) 'The jewel in the crown: co-optive capacity and participation during austerity in Cardiff and San Sebastián-Donostia', *International Journal of Urban and Regional Research*, 42(6): 1096–1113.

Guha, R. (1998) *Domination without Hegemony: History and Power in Colonial India*, Oxford: Oxford University Press.

Guinan, J. and O'Neill, M. (2020) *The Case for Community Wealth Building*, Cambridge: Polity Press.

Gunn, S. and Hyde, C. (2013) 'Post-industrial place, multicultural space: the transformation of Leicester, c. 1970–1990', *International Journal of Regional and Local History*, 8(2): 94–111.

Hall, S. (1979) 'The great moving right show', *Marxism Today*, January, pp. 14–20.

Hall, S., Critcher, C., Jefferson, T., Clarke, J. and Roberts, J. (1978) *Policing the Crisis: Mugging, the State and Law'n'Order*, London: Macmillan.

Hamel, P. (1991) *Action Collective et Démocratie Locale, Montréal*, Montreal: Presses de l'Université de Montréal.

Hamel, P and Autin, G. (2017) 'Austerity governance and the welfare crisis in Montreal', *Alternate Routes*, 28(1): 165–188.

Hamel, P. and Jouve, B. (2008) 'In search of a stable urban regime for Montreal: issues and challenges in metropolitan development', *Urban Research and Practice*, 1 (1): 18–35.

Hamel, P. and Keil, R. (2015) *Working Paper 8: Facing Austerity while Undergoing Industrial and Post-Industrial Restructuring: the Montreal Case*, Unpublished.

Hamel, P. and Keil, R. (2016) *Working Paper 16: Austerity Governance and Welfare in Montreal*, Unpublished.

Hamel, P. and Keil, R. (2018) *Working Paper 25: Montreal Case Study Final Report*, Unpublished.

Hamel, P. and Keil, R. (2020) '"La coopération, c'est clé": Montreal's urban governance in times of austerity', *Journal of Urban Affairs*, 42(1): 109–124.

Hammer, N., Plugor, R., Nolan, P. and Clark, I. (2015) New industry on a skewed playing field: supply chain relations and working conditions in UK garment manufacturing, www2.le.ac.uk/offices/press/for-journalists/media-resources/Leicester%20Report%20-%20Final%20-to%20publish.pdf/.

Hardt, M. and Negri, A. (2004) *Multitude*, London: Penguin Books.

Harman, C. (2007) 'The rate of profit and the world today', *International Socialism*, 115, www.isj.org.uk/?id=340.

Harman, C. (2009) *Zombie Capitalism*, London: Bookmarks.

Harvey, D. (1989) 'From managerialism to entrepreneurialism: the transformation in urban governance in late capitalism', *Geografiska Annaler: Series B, Human Geography*, 71(1): 3–17.

Harvey, D. (2005) *A Brief History of Neoliberalism*, New York, NY: Oxford University Press.

Hassen, I. and Giovanardi, M. (2018) 'The difference of "being diverse": city branding and multiculturalism in the "Leicester Model"', *Cities: The International Journal of Urban Policy and Planning*, 80: 45–52.

Hastings, A., Bailey, N., Bramley, G. and Gannon, M. (2017) 'Austerity urbanism in England: the "regressive redistribution" of local government services and the impact on the poor and marginalised', *Environment and Planning A: Economy and Space*, 49(9): 2007–2024

Hatherley, O. (2017) 'Comparing capitals', *New Left Review*, 105: 107–132.

Haus, M. and Kuhlmann, S. (2013) 'Lokale Politik und Verwaltung im Zeichen der Krise'?, in M. Haus and S. Kuhlmann (eds), *Lokale Politik und Verwaltung im Zeichen der Krise?*, Wiesbaden: Springer VS, pp. 7–24.

Hay, C. (1999) 'Crisis and the structural transformation of the state: interrogating the process of change', *British Journal of Politics an International Relations*, 1(3): 317–344.

Hearne, R., Boyle, M. and Kobayashi, A. (2020) 'Taking liberties with democracy? On the origins, meaning and implications of the Irish water wars', *Geoforum*, 110: 232–241.

Helle, I. (2015) 'A new proletariat in the making? Reflections on the 14 November 2012 strike and the movements of 1968 and 1995', *Transfer: European Review of Labour and Research*, 21(2): 229–242.

Henderson, H., Gleeson, B. and Sullivan, H. (2016) *Working Paper 15: Melbourne Exploratory Research Paper*, Unpublished.

Henderson, H., Gleeson, B. and Sullivan, H. (2017) *Working Paper 24: Final report of the Melbourne Case Study: Revitalisation in Central Dandenong, Melbourne*, Unpublished.

Henderson, H., Sullivan, H. and Gleeson, B. (2020) 'Variations on a collaborative theme: conservatism, pluralism, and place-based urban policy in Central Dandenong, Melbourne', *Journal of Urban Affairs*, 42(1): 125–142.

Hesketh, C. (2017) *Spaces of Capital/Spaces of Resistance: Mexico and the Global Political Economy*, Athens, GE: Georgia University Press.

Hill, M. (2015) 'Conventional wisdom on government austerity: UK policy since the 1920s', in K. Farnsworth and Zoe Irving (eds), *Social Policy in Times of Austerity*, Bristol: Policy Press, pp. 43–66.

Hill, R.C. (1977) 'State capitalism and the urban fiscal crisis in the United States', *International Journal of Urban and Regional Research*, 1(1–3): 76–100.

Hobsbawm, E. (1984) 'The "new unionism" in perspective', in E. Hobsbawm, *Workers: Worlds of Labour*, New York, Pantheon, pp. 152–175.

Holland, E.W. (2011) *Nomad Citizenship: Free-Market Communism and the Slow-Motion General Strike*, Minneapolis, MN: University of Minnesota Press.

Holloway, J. (2005) *Change the World Without Taking Power*, London: Pluto Press, 2nd edition.

Hope, K. (2015) 'Greece's future hangs on 72 words', *Financial Times*, [online], 29 June, Available at: www.ft.com/content/9cc85638-1e75-11e5-ab0f-6bb9974f25d0.

Humphreys, E. (2013) 'Organic intellectuals in the Australian global justice movement: the weight of 9/11', in C. Barker, L. Cox, J. Krinsky and G. Nilson (eds), *Marxism and Social Movements*, Leiden: Brill, pp. 357–375.

Hutchens, G. and Jericho, G. (2018) 'Who is to blame for Australia's stalled wages', *The Guardian*, [online], 1 March, Available at: www.theguardian.com/australia-news/2018/mar/02/who-is-to-blame-for-australias-stalled-wages.

Imbroscio, D.L. (2003) 'Overcoming the neglect of economics in urban regime theory', *Journal of Urban Affairs*, 25(3): 271–284.

Jameson, F. (1991) *Postmodernism: The Cultural Logic of Late Capitalism*, Durham, NC: Duke University Press.

Jessop, B. (1997) 'A neo-Gramscian approach to the regulation of urban regimes: accumulation strategies, hegemonic projects and governance', in M. Lauria (ed), *Reconstructing Urban Regime Theory: Regulating Urban Politics in a Global Economy*, London: Sage, pp. 51–73.

Jessop, B. (1999) 'The changing governance of welfare: recent trends in its primary functions, scale, and modes of coordination', *Social Policy and Administration*, 33(4): 348–359.

Jessop, B. (2007) *State Power*, Cambridge: Polity Press.

Jessop, B. (2015) 'Crisis construal in the North Atlantic financial crisis and the Eurozone crisis', *Competition and Change*, 19(2): 95–112.

Jessop, B. (2016) 'The organic crisis of the British state: putting Brexit in its place', *Globalizations*, 14(1): 133–141.

Jessop, B., Mudge, S., Derbyshire, J. and Davies, W. (2014) 'The limits of neoliberalism', *Renewal: A Journal of Social Democracy*, 22(3–4): 81–100.

John, P. (2009) Why study urban politics, in J. Davies and D. Imbroscio (eds), *Theories of Urban Politics*, London: Sage, pp. 17–23, 2nd edition.

Jonas, A.E.G. and Moisio, S. (2018) 'City regionalism as geopolitical processes: a new framework for analysis', *Progress in Human Geography*, 42(3): 350–370.

Jones, S. (2018) 'More than 5m join Spain's "feminist strike", unions say', *The Guardian*, [online], 8 March, Available at: www.theguardian.com/world/2018/mar/08/spanish-women-give-up-work-for-a-day-in-first-feminist-strike.

Jordan, D. (2019) 'Chancellor Sajid Javid declares end of austerity', *BBC News*, [online], 4 September, Available at: www.bbc.co.uk/news/business-49577250.

Kavoulakos, K.I. and Gritzas G. (2015) 'Movements and alternative space in crisis stricken Greece: a new civil society', in N. Georgakis and N. Demertzis (eds), *The Political Portrait of Greece: Crisis and Deconstruction of Politics*, Athens: Gutenberg, pp. 337–355.

Keil, R. (2017) *Suburban Planet: Making the World Urban from the Outside In*, Cambridge: Polity Press.

Kelly, O. (2016) 'An Bord Pleanála overturns 28% of council decisions', *The Irish Times*, [online], 10 August, Available at: www.irishtimes.com/news/environment/an-bord-pleanála-overturns-28-of-council-decisions-1.2750588.

Kennedy, G. (2016) 'Embedding neoliberalism in Greece: the transformation of collective bargaining and labour market policy in Greece during the Eurozone crisis', *Studies in Political Economy: A Socialist Review*, 97(3): 253–269.

Kipfer, S. (2002) 'Urbanization, everyday life and the survival of capitalism: Lefebvre, Gramsci and the problematic of hegemony', *Capitalism, Nature, Socialism*, 13(2): 117–149.

Kipfer, S. (2012) 'City, country, hegemony: Antonio Gramsci's spatial historicism', in M. Ekers, G. Hart, S. Kipfer and A. Loftus (eds), *Gramsci: Space, Nature, Politics*, Chichester: Wiley, pp. 83–103.

Kipfer, S. (n.d.) 'Marxism, space and a few urban questions: a rough guide to the English language literature', *Historical Materialism* [Blog], Available at: www.historicalmaterialism.org/reading-guides/marxism-space-and-few-urban-questions-rough-guide-to-english-language-literature.

Kipfer, S., Parastou, S. and Thorben, W. (2012) 'Henri Lefebvre: debates and controversies', *Progress in Human Geography*, 37(1): 115–134.

Klepper, D. (2013) 'Political, popular obstacles block pension changes', *AP News*, [online], 7 October, Available at: https://apnews.com/894799daf3ba45eaa6d1c79154fc806a.

Koivisto, J. and Lahtenen, M. (2012) 'Historical-critical dictionary of Marxism: conjuncture, politico-historical', *Historical Materialism*, 20(1): 267–277.

Konvitz, J. (2016) *Cities and the Crisis*, Manchester: Manchester University Press.

Konzelmann, S.J. (2014) 'The political economics of austerity', *Cambridge Journal of Economics*, 38(4): 701–741.

Koutrolikou, P. (2016) 'Governmentalities of urban crises in inner-city Athens, Greece', *Antipode*, 48(1): 172–192.

Koutroukis, T. (2017) 'Social dialogue in post-crisis Greece: a sisyphus syndrome for Greek social partners' expectations', in J. Marangos (ed), *The Internal Impact and External Influence of the Greek Financial Crisis*, London: Palgrave Macmillan, pp. 71–83.

Kouvelakis, S. (2016) 'Syriza's rise and fall', *New Left Review*, 97: 45–70.

Kouvelakis, S. (2019) 'The French insurgency: political economy of the Gilets Jaunes', *New Left Review*, 116/117, 75–98.

Kraemer, S. (2012) *Urban governance and participatory revitalization in Montreal: two case studies of the Integrated Urban Revitalization (RUI) policy*, unpublished paper at https://escholarship.mcgill.ca/concern/papers/2v23vt62p?locale=en.

Kynaston, D. (2007) *Austerity Britain 1945–51*, London: Bloomsbury.

Lachance, É., Bernier J. and Herjean, P. (2004) *Étude exploratoire sur les tables de quartier. Montréal: Chaire Approches communautaires et inégalités de santé*, Montréal: Université de Montréal.

Ladi, S. (2014) 'Austerity politics and administrative reform: the Eurozone crisis and its impact upon Greek public administration', *Comparative European Politics*, 12(2): 184–208.

Las Heras, J. (2019) 'International political economy of labour and Gramsci's methodology of the subaltern', *The British Journal of Politics and International Relations*, 21(1): 226–244.

Las Heras, J. and Ribera-Almandoz, O. (2017) 'When corporatism fails: trade union strategies and grassroots resistance to the Spanish economic crisis', *Journal of Labour and Society*, 20(4): 449–466.

Lauria, M. (ed) (1997) *Reconstructing Urban Regime Theory: Regulating Urban Politics in a Global Economy*. Thousand Oaks, CA: Sage.

Le Gales, P. (2016) 'Neoliberalism and urban change: stretching a good idea too far?', *Territory, Politics, Governance*, 4(2): 154–172.

LeBaron, G. (2020) *Combating Modern Slavery: Why Labour Governance is Failing and What We Can Do About It*, Cambridge: Polity Press.

Leduc, G. (2014) 'Montréal, boulet ou locomotive?', *Le soleil*, [online], 15 November, Available at: www.lesoleil.com/affaires/montreal-boulet-ou-locomotive-03d63d674ff78b03943b53b4a4f79698.

Lefebvre, H. (2003) [1970] *The Urban Revolution*, Minneapolis, MN: University of Minnesota Press.

Lightbody, J. (2006) *City Politics, Canada*, Peterborough: Broadview Press.

Lipietz, A. (1982) 'Towards global Fordism?', *New Left Review*, 1/132: 33–47.

Loopmans, M. (2008) 'Relevance, gentrification and the development of a new hegemony on urban policies in Antwerp, Belgium', *Urban Studies*, 45(1): 2499–2519.

Lowndes, V. and McCaughie, K. (2013) 'Weathering the perfect storm? Austerity and institutional resilience in English local governance', *Policy and Politics*, 41(4): 533–549.

Luxemburg, R. (1900) *Social Reform or Revolution*, [online], www.marxists.org/archive/luxemburg/1900/reform-revolution/index.htm.

Machin, D. and Mayr, A. (2007) 'Antiracism in the British government's model regional newspaper: the "talking cure"', *Discourse and Society*, 18(4): 453–477.

Madden, D. (2012) 'City becoming world: Nancy, Lefebvre, and the global–urban imagination', *Environment and Planning D: Society and Space*, 30(5): 772–787.

Magnusson, W. (1985) 'Urban politics and the local state', *Studies in Political Economy: A Socialist Review*, 16(1): 111–142.

Manwaring, R. and Kennedy, P. (eds) (2018) *Why the Left Loses: The Decline of the Centre-Left in Comparative Perspective*, Bristol: Policy Press.

March, H., Grau-Satorras, M., Saurí, D. and Swyngedouw, E. (2019) The deadlock of metropolitan remunicipalisation of water services management in Barcelona, *Water Alternatives*, 12(2): 360–379.

Marcuse, P. (2015) 'Depoliticizing urban discourse: how "we" write', *Cities: The International Journal of Urban Policy and Planning*, 44: 152–156.

Marier, P. and Béland, D. (2018) 'Austerity, dismantling of the welfare state, and restructuring: what are we talking about?', *Pluralages*, 18(1): 10–12.

Marinetto, M. (2003) 'Governing beyond the centre: a critique of the Anglo-governance school', *Political Studies*, 51(3): 592–608.

Marquand, D. (2004) *The Decline of the Public*, Cambridge: Polity Press.

Mason, P. (2012) *Why it's Kicking Off Everywhere: The New Global Revolutions*, London: Verso.

May, T. (2017) 'Urban crisis: bonfire of vanities to find opportunities in the ashes', *Urban Studies*, 54(9): 2189–2198.

Mayer, M. (2016) 'Neoliberal urbanism and uprisings across Europe', in M. Mayer, C. Thörn and H. Thörn (eds), *Urban Uprisings*, London: Palgrave Macmillan, pp. 57–92.

Mazlish, B. (2017) [1976] *The Revolutionary Ascetic: Evolution of a Political Type*, London: Routledge.

McDaniel, S. (2017) 'French socialism in crisis: the undoing of Hollande's "anti-austerity" programme', *Renewal: A Journal of Social Democracy*, 25(1): 39–52.

McFarlane, C. (2010) 'The comparative city: knowledge, learning, urbanism', *International Journal of Urban and Regional Research*, 34(4): 725–742.

McLoughlin, S. (2013) 'Discrepant representations of multi-Asian Leicester: institutional discourse and everyday life in the "model" multicultural city'. Research Paper WBAC 012, *From Diasporas to Multi-Locality: Writing British Asian Cities*, Available at: www.leeds.ac.uk/writingbritishasiancities/.

McQuarrie, M. (2013) 'Community organizations in the foreclosure crisis: the failure of neoliberal civil society', *Politics and Society*, 41(1): 73–101.

Meadway, J. (2019) 'Winning the general election', *Tribune*, [online], 21 October, Available at: https://tribunemag.co.uk/2019/10/winning-the-general-election.

Medir, L., Magre J. and Tomàs, M. (2018) 'Mayors' perceptions on local government reforms and decentralisation in Spain', *Revista Española de Ciencia Política*, 46(1), 129–155.

Meegan, R., Kennett, P., Jones, G. and Croft J. (2014) 'Global economic crisis, austerity and neoliberal urban governance in England', *Cambridge Journal of Regions, Economy and Society*, 7(1): 137–153.

Merrifield, A. (2002) *Metromarxism: A Tale of the City*, London: Routledge.

Mertes, T. (ed) (2004) *A Movement of Movements: Is Another World Really Possible?*, London: Verso.

Miliband, R. (1961) *Parliamentary Socialism: A Study of the Politics of Labour*, London: Allen and Unwin.

Miró, J. (2019) 'Abolishing politics in the shadow of austerity? Assessing the (de)politicization of budgetary policy in crisis-ridden Spain (2008–2015)', *Policy Studies*, [online], 20 February, Available at: https://doi.org/10.1080/01442872.2019.1581162.

Molina, O. and Fausto, M. (2016) *Post-Crisis Social Dialogue in Spain: The Calm After the Storm*, Geneva: International Labour Organization, https://ddd.uab.cat/pub/worpap/2016/170995/wcms_536007-1.pdf.

Moody, K. (2017) *On New Terrain: How Capital is Reshaping the Battleground of Class War*, Chicago, IL: Haymarket Books.

Moore-Cherry, N. and Tomaney, J. (2019) 'Spatial planning, metropolitan governance and territorial politics in Europe: Dublin as a case of metro-phobia?', *European Urban and Regional Studies*, 26(4): 365–381.

Morton, A.D. (2011) *Revolution and State in Modern Mexico: The Political Economy of Uneven Development*, Plymouth, NJ: Rowman and Littlefield.

Moser, S., Fauveaud G. and Cutts, A. (2019) 'Montréal: towards a post-industrial reinvention', *Cities: The International Journal of Urban Policy and Planning*, 86: 125–135.

Mouffe, C. (2018) *For a Left Populism*, London: Verso.

Mufti, A. (2005) 'Global comparativism', *Critical Inquiry*, 31: 427–89.

Murphy, G. (2015) ' "Residents are fearful that their community will die around them": some thoughts from inside the 2013 Local Electoral Area Boundary Committee', *Irish Political Studies*, 30(4): 555–574.

Murphy, M.P. (2015) 'Gendering the narrative of the Irish crisis', *Irish Political Studies*, 30(2): 220–237.

Musgrave, R.A. (1959) *The Theory of Public Finance: A Study in Public Economy*, New York: McGraw-Hill.

Neill, C. (2017) 'Historic strike comes to an end', *Star Journal*, [online], 25 May, Available at: https://dandenong.starcommunity.com.au/news/2017-05-25/historic-strike-comes-to-an-end/.

Newman, J. (2014a) 'Governing the present: activism, neoliberalism, and the problem of power and consent, *Critical Policy Studies*, 8(2): 133–147.

Newman, J. (2014b) 'Landscapes of antagonism: local governance, neoliberalism and austerity', *Urban Studies*, 51(15): 3290–3305.

Nielsen, E.H. and Simonsen, K. (2003) 'Scaling from "below": practices, strategies and urban spaces', *European Planning Studies*, 11(8): 911–927.

ODPM (Office of the Deputy Prime Minister) (2005) *National of Local Strategic Partnerships – Issues Paper: Local Strategic Partnerships, Multi-Level Governance and Economic Development*, London: ODPM.

Ogman, R. (2020) '"Ethical capitalism" in the city: embedded economy or marketization? The case of social impact bonds', *Journal of Urban Affairs*, 42(6): 833–855.

Olin-Wright, E. (2019) *How to be an Anti-Capitalist in the 21st Century*, London: Verso.

Olusoga, D. (2019) 'The cult of optimism got us into this mess. It's time to embrace pessimism', *The Guardian*, [online], 14 July, Available at: www.theguardian.com/commentisfree/2019/jul/14/brexiters-blind-optimism-pitiful-dose-of-pessimism-realistic.

Painter, M. (1998) *Collaborative Federalism: Economic Reform in Australia in the 1990s*, Cambridge: Cambridge University Press.

Palmer, E. (2019) 'Popularity of socialism spiking in U.S., with 43 percent now saying it would be good for the country', *Newsweek*, [online], 25 May, Available at: www.newsweek.com/socialism-america-gallup-poll-1431266.

Papanastasiou, N. (2019) *The Politics of Scale in Policy: Scalecraft and Education Governance*, Bristol: Policy Press.

Parker, G. and Giles, C. (2020) 'Johnson seeks to channel FDR in push for UK revival', *Financial Times*, [online], 29 June, Available at: www.ft.com/content/f708ac9b-7efe-4b54-a119-ca898ad71bfa.

Parkinson, M. (2016) 'UK city regions: policies, performance and prospects', *The Town Planning Review*, 87(6): 629–653.

Peck, J. (2010) 'Zombie neoliberalism and the ambidextrous state', *Theoretical Criminology*, 14(1): 104–110.

Peck, J. (2012) 'Austerity urbanism', *City: Analysis of Urban Trends, Culture, Theory, Policy*, 16(1): 626–655.

Peck, J. (2017a) 'Transatlantic city, part 1: conjunctural urbanism', *Urban Studies*, 54(1): 4–30.

Peck, J. (2017b) 'Transatlantic city, part 2: late entrepreneurialism', *Urban Studies*, 54(2): 327–363.

Peck, J. and Theodore, N. (2019) 'Still neoliberalism? ', *South Atlantic Quarterly*, 118 (2): 245–265.

Peck, J. and Tickelll, A. (2002) 'Neoliberalizing space', *Antipode*, 34(3): 380–404.

Pill, M.C. (2015) *Working Paper 3: Baltimore Literature Review*, Unpublished.

Pill, M.C. (2016) *Working Paper 11: Baltimore Exploratory Research*, Unpublished.

Pill, M.C. (2017) *Working Paper 20: Baltimore Final Case Study Report*, Unpublished.

Pill, M.C. (2019) 'Embedding in the city? Locating civil society in the philanthropy of place', *Community Development Journal*, 54(2): 179–196.

Pill, M.C. (2020) 'The austerity governance of Baltimore's neighborhoods: "The conversation may have changed but the systems aren't changing"', *Journal of Urban Affairs*, 42(1): 143–158.

Pineault, E. (2012) 'Quebec's red spring: an essay on ideology and social conflict at the end of neoliberalism', *Studies in Political Economy: A Socialist Review*, 90(1): 29–56.

Pratt-Harris, N.C., Sinclair, M.M., Barbara Bragg, C., Williams, N.R., Ture, K.N., Davis Smith, B., Marshal, I. and Brown, L. (2016) 'Police-involved homicide of unarmed Black males: Observations by Black scholars in the midst of the April 2015 Baltimore uprising', *Journal of Human Behavior in the Social Environment*, 26(3–4): 377–389.

Pugalis, L. and Bentley, G. (2013) 'Storming or performing? Local Enterprise Partnerships two years on', *Local Economy*, 28(7–8): 863–874.

Purcell, M. (2012) 'Gramsci is not dead: for a "both/and" approach to radical geography', *ACME: An International E-Journal for Critical Geographies*, 11(3): 512–524.

Radio Canada (2017) 'Phillippe Couillard 2.0', *Radio Canada*, [online], 27 November, Available at: https://ici.radio-canada.ca/nouvelle/1069647/philippe-couillard-2-0-analyse-sebastien-bovet?depuisRecherche=true.

Renard, J. (2000) 'Nantes, metropole inachevee?', *L'information Geographique*, 64(2): pp. 117–133.

Roberts, M. (2016) *The Long Depression: How it Happened, Why it Happened and What Happens Next*, Chicago, IL: Haymarket Books.

Robinson, C.J. (1983) *Black Marxism: The Making of the Black Radical Tradition*, Chapel Hill, NC/London: The University of North Carolina Press.

Robinson, J. (2011) 'Cities in a world of cities: the comparative gesture', *International Journal of Urban and Regional Research*, 35(1): 1–23.

Robinson, J. (2016) 'Thinking cities through elsewhere: comparative tactics for a more global urban studies', *Progress in Human Geography*, 40(1): 3–29.

Robinson, J. (2018) 'New unitary council planned for Leicestershire', *Insider Media Limited*, [online], 29 June, Available at: www.insidermedia.com/news/midlands/New-unity-council-planned-for-Leicestershire.

Roitman, J. (2013) *Anti-Crisis*, Durham, NC: Duke University Press.

Rosenberg, J. (2005) 'Globalization theory: a post mortem', *International Politics*, 42: 2–74.

Roth, L. (2019) 'Which municipalism? Let's be choosy', *Open Democracy*, [online], 2 January, Available at: www.opendemocracy.net/en/can-europe-make-it/which-municipalism-lets-be-choosy/.

Rothstein, R. (2015) 'From Ferguson to Baltimore: the fruits of government-sponsored segregation', *Journal of Affordable Housing and Community Development Law*, 24(2): 205–210.

Russell, B. (2019) 'Beyond the local trap: new municipalism and the rise of the fearless cities', *Antipode*, 51(3): 989–1010.

Sait, E.M. (1913) 'Theocratic Quebec', *The Annals of the American Academy of Political and Social Science*, 45: 69–82.

Savage, K. (2003) 'Monuments of a lost cause: the postindustrial campaign to commemorate steel', in J. Cowie and J. Heathcote (eds), *Beyond the Ruins: The Meanings of Deindustrialization*, Ithaca, NY: Cornell University Press, pp. 237–256.

Savard, A. (2016) 'Quebec's wave of resistance: from the Maple Spring to the general strike', *International Socialist Review*, 101, [online], Available at: https://isreview.org/issue/101/quebecs-wave-resistance.

Savitch, H.V. and Kantor, P. (2002) *Cities in the International Marketplace: The Political Economy of Urban Development in North America and Western Europe*, Princeton, NJ: Princeton University Press.

Schindler, S. (2016) 'Detroit after bankruptcy: a case of degrowth machine politics', *Urban Studies*, 53(4): 818–836.

Scott, A.J. (2019) 'City-regions reconsidered', *Environment and Planning A: Economy and Space*, 51(3): 554–580.

Sears, A. (2014) *The Next New Left: A History of the Future*, Black Point, NS: Fernwood Publishing.

Shea-Baird, K. (2020) 'A municipalist response to COVID-19', *Trademark Belfast*, [online], 28 August, Available at: http://trademarkbelfast.com/a-municipalist-response-to-covid-19/.

Sissons, M. and French, P. (1963) *The Age of Austerity: 1945–1951*, London: Philip Hodder and Stoughton.

Six, P. (2016) 'Explaining styles of political judgement in British government: comparing isolation dynamics (1959–1974)', *Journal of Public Policy*, 36(2): 219–250.

Skelcher, C. (2005) 'Jurisdictional integrity, polycentrism, and the design of democratic governance', *Governance*, 18(1): 89–110.

Smart, A. and Lin, G.C. (2007) 'Local capitalisms, local citizenship and translocality: rescaling from below in the Pearl River Delta Region, China', *International Journal of Urban and Regional Research*, 31(2): 280–302.

Smith, A. (2015) 'The austerity backlash', *Jacobin*, [online], 21 November, Available at: www.jacobinmag.com/2015/11/quebec-couillard-public-sector-strikes-classe-asse-austerity/.

Söderberg, J. and Netzén, A. (2010) 'When all that is theory melts into (hot) air: contrasts and parallels between actor network theory, autonomist Marxism, and open Marxism', *Ephemera*, 10(2): 95–118.

Sørensen, E. and Torfing, J. (2018) 'Governance on a bumpy road from enfant terrible to mature paradigm', *Critical Policy Studies*, 12(3): 350–359.

Spotlight (2013) 'Localism in Irish politics and local government reform', *Spotlight*, No 2, February, https://data.oireachtas.ie/ie/oireachtas/libraryResearch/2013/2013-02-08_spotlight-localism-in-irish-politics-and-local-government-reform_en.pdf.

Stahl, R.M. (2019) 'Ruling the Interregnum: politics and ideology in nonhegemonic times', *Politics and Society*, 47(3): 333–360.

Standring, A. and Davies, J.S. (2020) 'From crisis to catastrophe: the death and viral legacies of austere neoliberalism in Europe?', *Dialogues in Human Geography*, 10(2): 146–149.

Stilwell, F. and Troy, P. (2000) 'Multilevel governance and urban development in Australia', *Urban Studies*, 37(5–6): 909–30.

Stone, C.N. (1980) 'Systemic power in community decision making: a restatement of stratification theory', *American Political Science Review*, 74(4): 978–990.

Stone, C.N. (1988) 'Pre-emptive power: Floyd Hunter's community power structure reconsidered', *American Journal of Political Science*, 32(1): 82–104.

Stone, C.N. (1989) *Regime Politics: Governing Atlanta 1946–1988*, Lawrence, KS: University of Kansas Press.

Stone, C.N. (1993) 'Urban regimes and the capacity to govern', *Journal of Urban Affairs*, 15(1): 1–28.

Stone, C.N. (2004) 'It's more than the economy after all: continuing the debate about urban regimes', *Journal of Urban Affairs*, 26(1): 1–19.

Stone, C.N. (2009) 'Who is governed? Local citizens and the political order of cities', in J.S. Davies and D.L. Imbroscio (eds), *Theories of Urban Politics*, London: Sage, pp. 257–273, 2nd edition.

Stone, C.N. (2015) 'Reflections on regime politics: from governing coalition to urban political order', *Urban Affairs Review*, 51(1): 101–137.

Stone, C.N., Henig, J.R., Jones, B.D. and Pierannunzi, C. (2001) *Building Civic Capacity: The Politics of Reforming Urban Schools*, Lawrence: KS: University Press of Kansas.

Storper, M. and Scott, A.J. (2016) 'Current debates in urban theory: a critical assessment', *Urban Studies*, 53(6): 1114–1136.

Streeck, W. (2016) *How will Capitalism End? Essays on a Failing System*, London: Verso.

Sullivan, H., Henderson, H. and Gleeson, B. (2019) *Central Dandenong: Australia's Comeback City? Lessons about Revitalisation for Diverse Places*, Melbourne: The University of Melbourne.

Sum, N.L, and Jessop, B. (2014) *Towards a Cultural Political Economy Putting Culture in Its Place in Political Economy*, Cheltenham: Edward Elgar Publishing.

Summers, L. (2019) 'Christine Lagarde enters the European central bank at a perilous moment', *Washington Post*, [online], 9 July, Available at: www.washingtonpost.com/gdpr-consent/?next_url=https%3a%2f%2fwww.washingtonpost.com%2fopinions%2fchristine-lagarde-enters-the-european-central-bank-at-a-perilous-moment%2f2019%2f07%2f08%2f7e9e47e4-a1b6-11e9-bd56-eac6bb02d01d_story.html.

Swyngedouw, E. (2005) 'Governance innovation and the citizen: the Janus face of governance-beyond-the-state', *Urban Studies*, 42(11):1991–2006, doi: 10.1080/00420980500279869.

Taylor, B. (2013) 'From alterglobalization to Occupy Wall Street: neoanarchism and the new spirit of the left', *City*, 17(6): 729–747.

Teague, P. and Donaghey, J. (2015) 'The life and death of Irish social partnership: lessons for social pacts', *Business History*, 57(3): 418–437.

Theodore, N. (2020) 'Governing through austerity: (il)logics of neoliberal urbanism after the global financial crisis', *Journal of Urban Affairs*, 42(1): 1–17.

Theodore, N., Peck, J. and Brenner, N. (2011) 'Neoliberal urbanism: cities and the rule of markets', in G. Bridge and S. Watson (eds), *The New Blackwell Companion to The City*, Oxford: Wiley-Blackwell, pp. 15–25.

Thomas, P. (2009) *The Gramscian Moment: Philosophy, Hegemony and Marxism*. Leiden: Brill.

Thomas, P. (2020) 'After post-hegemony', *Contemporary Political Theory*, First published 16 June, doi: 10.1057/s41296-020-00409-1.

Thompson, G.F. (2003) *Between Hierarchies and Markets: The Logic and Limits of Network forms of Organization*, Oxford: Oxford University Press.

Thompson, M. (2020) 'What's so new about New Municipalism?', *Progress in Human Geography*, First published 9 March, doi: 10.1177/0309132520909480.

Tilly, C. (1984) *Big Structures, Large Processes, Huge Comparisons*, New York: Russell Sage Foundation.

Tomaney, J. (2016) 'Limits of devolution: localism, economics and post-democracy, *The Political Quarterly*, 87(4): 546–552.

Tomàs, M. (2017) 'Explaining metropolitan governance: the case of Spain', *Spatial Research and Planning*, 75(3): 243–252.

Tomàs, M. (2019) 'Le gouvernement du changement? L'approche de Barcelona en Comú de la gouvernance métropolitaine', *Pôle Sud*, 51(2): 43–60.

Trainer, T. (2019) 'Entering the era of limits and scarcity: the radical implications for social theory', *Journal of Political Ecology*, 26(1): 1–18.

Tuckman, A. and Knudsen, H. (2016) 'The success and failings of UK work-ins and sit-ins in the 1970s: Briant colour printing and imperial typewriters', *Historical Studies in Industrial Relations*, 37: 113–139.

Vertovec, S. (2019) 'Talking around super-diversity', *Ethnic and Racial Studies*, 42(1): 125–139.

Walliser, A (2013). 'New urban activisms in Spain: reclaiming public space in the face of crises', *Policy and Politics*, 41(3): 329–350.

Ward, K. (2010) 'Towards a relational comparative approach to the study of cities', *Progress in Human Geography*, 34(4): 471–487.

Weaver, T. (2017) 'Urban crisis: the genealogy of a concept', *Urban Studies*, 54(9): 2039–2055.

Weiner, R.R. and Lopez, I. (2018) *Los Indignados: Tides of Social Insertion in Spain*, Alresford: Zero Books.

Wheatcroft, G. (2005) *The Strange Death of Tory England*, London: Allen Lane.

White, J. (2020) 'Where next for Britain's labour movement? Reflecting on issues arising from the 2019 election', *Theory and Struggle*, 121(1): 10–19.

Whitham, B. (2018) 'Post-crash neoliberalism in theory and practice', *Political Studies Review*, 16(4): 252–264.

Wigglesworth, R. (2019) 'US economic expansion becomes longest in history' *Financial Times*, [online], 2 July, Available at: www.ft.com/content/5c443804-9c41-11e9-b8ce-8b459ed04726.

Williams, R.Y. (2005) *The Politics of Public Housing: Black Women's Struggles against Urban Inequality*, New York: Oxford University Press.

Žižek, S. (2009) *First as Tragedy, Then as Farce*, London: Verso.

Zografos, C., Klause, K.A., Connolly, J.T. and Anguelovski, I. (2020) 'The everyday politics of urban transformational adaptation: struggles for authority and the Barcelona superblock project', *Cities: The International Journal of Urban Policy and Planning*, 99: 1–12.

Index

Page numbers ending in t refer to tables.